Food Culture in Germany

North Sea

Baltic

Königsberg
(Kaliningrad, Russia)

DENMARK

Eckernförde
Kiel

Rügenwalde

SCHLESWIG-
HOLSTEIN

Rostock

WEST
PRUSSIA

Lübeck

MECKLENBURG-
WESTERN POMERANIA

Ostfriesland

HAMBURG
Hamburg

Lüneburg

BREMEN
Oldenburg
Bremen

BRANDENBURG

POLAND

LOWER SAXONY

Elbe
Eberswalde

Oder

THE NETHERLANDS

Braunschweig

Brandenburg

BERLIN
Berlin
Teltow

Frankfurt/Oder

Münster

Magdeburg
Beelitz

Bielefeld

SAXONY-ANHALT

Wittenberg

Spree

Neisse

NORTH RHINE-
WESTPHALIA

WESTPHALIA

Harz

Saale

Elbe

SILESIA

Dortmund

Kassel

SAXONY

Rhine
Düsseldorf

Leipzig

Meissen

Cologne

Naumburg/Saale

Altenburg

Dresden

Bonn

HESSE

Erfurt
Weimar

Chemnitz

BELGIUM

RHINELAND-
PALATINATE

Rhön

THURINGIA

Eiffel

Frankfurt/Main

Coburg

BOHEMIA

Mosel
Hunsrück

Rheingau

Main

CZECH REPUBLIC

Bingen
Ingelheim

Mainz

Bamberg

LUXEMBOURG

Idar-Oberstein

Würzburg

Nürnberg

SAAR-
LAND

PALATINATE
Bad
Dürkheim

Mannheim
Schwetzingen

FRANCONIA

BAVARIA

Saar

BADEN-
WÜRTTEMBERG

Regensburg

Bayerischer Wald

Büchelstein

FRANCE

LORRAINE

Rhine

Stuttgart
Cannstatt

Neckar

Schwäbische Alb

Vosges

ALSACE

Rhine

Black Forest

Ulm

SWABIA

Augsburg

Munich

ALLGÄU

Reichenau
Tettnang

Basel

Lake
Constance

Lindau

Bad Reichenhall

AUSTRIA

SWITZERLAND
Alps

Alps

N

100 km

60 mi

Courtesy of Golden Section Graphics/Katharina Erfurth.

Food Culture in
Germany

URSULA HEINZELMANN

Food Culture around the World

Ken Albala, Series Editor

GREENWOOD PRESS
Westport, Connecticut • London

Library of Congress Cataloging-in-Publication Data

Heinzelmann, Ursula.
    Food culture in Germany / Ursula Heinzelmann.
        p. cm. — (Food culture around the world, ISSN 1545–2638)
    Includes bibliographical references and index.
    ISBN-13: 978–0–313–34494–7 (alk. paper)
    1. Cookery, German.   2. Food habits—Germany.   I. Title.
TX721.H453   2008
641.30943—dc22   2008007892

British Library Cataloguing in Publication Data is available.

Library of Congress Catalog Card Number: 2008007892
ISBN: 978–0–313–34494–7
ISSN: 1545–2638

First published in 2008

Greenwood Press, 88 Post Road West, Westport, CT 06881
An imprint of Greenwood Publishing Group, Inc.
www.greenwood.com

Printed in the United States of America

∞™

The paper used in this book complies with the
Permanent Paper Standard issued by the National
Information Standards Organization (Z39.48–1984).

10   9   8   7   6   5   4   3   2   1

Illustrations by Gottfried Müller

The publisher has done its best to make sure the instructions and/or recipes in this book
are correct. However, users should apply judgment and experience when preparing recipes, especially parents and teachers working with young people. The publisher accepts no
responsibility for the outcome of any recipe included in this volume.

Contents

Series Foreword

The appearance of the Food Culture around the World series marks a definitive stage in the maturation of Food Studies as a discipline to reach a wider audience of students, general readers, and foodies alike. In comprehensive interdisciplinary reference volumes, each on the food culture of a country or region for which information is most in demand, a remarkable team of experts from around the world offers a deeper understanding and appreciation of the role of food in shaping human culture for a whole new generation. I am honored to have been associated with this project as series editor.

Each volume follows a series format, with a chronology of food-related dates and narrative chapters entitled Introduction, Historical Overview, Major Foods and Ingredients, Cooking, Typical Meals, Eating Out, Special Occasions, and Diet and Health. (In special cases, these topics are covered by region.) Each also includes a glossary, bibliography, resource guide, and illustrations.

Finding or growing food has of course been the major preoccupation of our species throughout history, but how various peoples around the world learn to exploit their natural resources, come to esteem or shun specific foods and develop unique cuisines reveals much more about what it is to be human. There is perhaps no better way to understand a culture, its values, preoccupations and fears, than by examining its attitudes toward food. Food provides the daily sustenance around which families and communities bond. It provides the material basis for rituals through which people celebrate the passage of life stages and their connection to divinity. Food preferences also serve to separate individuals and groups from each other, and as one of the most powerful factors in the construction of identity, we physically, emotionally and spiritually become what we eat.

By studying the foodways of people different from ourselves we also grow to understand and tolerate the rich diversity of practices around the world. What seems strange or frightening among other people becomes perfectly rational when set in context. It is my hope that readers will gain from these volumes not only an aesthetic appreciation for the glories of the many culinary traditions described, but also ultimately a more profound respect for the peoples who devised them. Whether it is eating New Year's dumplings in China, folding tamales with friends in Mexico, or going out to a famous Michelin-starred restaurant in France, understanding these food traditions helps us to understand the people themselves.

As globalization proceeds apace in the twenty-first century it is also more important than ever to preserve unique local and regional traditions. In many cases these books describe ways of eating that have already begun to disappear or have been seriously transformed by modernity. To know how and why these losses occur today also enables us to decide what traditions, whether from our own heritage or that of others, we wish to keep alive. These books are thus not only about the food and culture of peoples around the world, but also about ourselves and who we hope to be.

Ken Albala
University of the Pacific

Preface

I have been cooking and baking since before I could read and write. I was born in Berlin in 1963 and absorbed a wide array of food influences from family and friends. Apprenticing as a chef, later taking on a restaurant on Lake Constance, then training as a sommelier in Heidelberg and establishing a French cheese shop back in Berlin all helped me develop a deep understanding of the foodways of Germany and finally resulted in my switch to food journalism, writing, and history. The familiar ways at home were put into perspective by trips abroad, first with my parents and brothers to France and Scandinavia, then on my own to the North American East Coast. More recently, I have continued my culinary explorations with trips to England as well as the North American West Coast, India, Thailand, Australia, and New Zealand. In every corner of the world, food has always been my link to people, to understand their ways and their lives. During that time, German food has changed markedly, and its perception abroad gradually followed suit.

ACKNOWLEDGMENTS

I am very grateful to Ken Albala, editor for the Greenwood Press Food Culture around the World Series, as well as Wendi Schnaufer, senior editor at Greenwood Press, for offering me this opportunity to paint a picture of contemporary German food culture. This book would not have been written without the background of the Oxford Symposium on Food and

Cookery, to which I was first introduced by Harlan Walker in 2003 and which I have been attending ever since. It has developed into my intellectual home of gastronomy. Here I met Barbara Ketcham Wheaton ("never confuse what is mentioned in cookbooks with what people cook and eat in reality!"), Darra Goldstein (who at our first meeting trusted me enough to commission articles for *Gastronomica* magazine), William Rubel (who has been the most inspiring food-friend ever since), Susan Rossi-Wilcox (a soulmate who sadly seems to have disappeared from my life), and many others whom I would like to thank for their friendship and assistance.

My friend Ebba Drolshagen has proved to be the perfect Internet scout, often coming up with exactly the right bit of information at the right time. Richard Hosking not only made me aware of the exceptional quality of Königsberg marzipan but also very patiently corrected my English text. In the last stage of writing, Sabrina Small came along like a foodwriter's deus ex machina and provided invaluable information. She helped to make the final manuscript more friendly to English speakers. I am deeply indebted to all of them, but all errors in the finished book are entirely mine.

Gottfried Müller obligingly rose to the challenge to illustrate, in his usual precise way, some less well-known aspects of German food culture. Jan Schwochow and Katharina Erfurth from Golden Section Graphics in Berlin expertly managed to put a seemingly impossible wealth of information onto the small map of Germany. I very much appreciate their help.

However, without three people in particular, I would have never been able to write this book: Birgit Biessmann not only taught me English and logical thinking at school but has become a dear friend and most inspiring critic. Stuart Pigott, my London-born husband, continues to open new doors I did not even know existed inside and around me. And finally my mother, first provider of food, love, and unwavering loyalty—*danke*.

Introduction

Food culture in Germany—where should one start? With the herrings, sausages, sauerkraut, and Black Forest cherry gâteau clichés? Or, at the other extreme, with the widely consumed fast food from countless chains, as ubiquitous in Germany as in the rest of the Western world? For this country east of France, west of Poland, north of Switzerland, and south of Denmark, the question of national culinary identity seems particularly difficult to answer.

Food culture has been described as the link between agriculture and nutrition. Once primarily defined by geography and climate, over the ages it has been shaped by language, religion, culture, and economics, thus revealing cultural and social differences. Since the onset of industrialization, with the introduction of modern food technology and transportation (often described by the somewhat vague term "globalization"), food can seem utterly detached from any particular country or region. However, the notion of home strongly links it to particular places, and this is particularly clear in the case of Germany.

After World War II, several generations of Germans (and others) were trying to look in only one direction: the future. Some tried to forget what seemed unbearable (the Holocaust and other Nazi crimes); others were simply tired of hearing the same stories about war, hunger, and hardships again and again. Even postwar generations became fed up with the two inevitable comments that came up as soon as one revealed one's nationality abroad: sauerkraut and Adolf Hitler. Why couldn't one be from a "normal" country with food everybody adored, like France?

But gradually, Germans have learned to live with and accept their history, even the most sour and unpalatable bits of it. Normality today—the normality Germans craved so much in postwar times—does not mean suppressing what is bitter or uncomfortable, quite the opposite. Germany as a nation has grown up, and Germans are now able to explore and acknowledge their cultural identity, the soil on which they live, the food that grows and is produced around them. For some years now, traditional dishes have been rediscovered and revived. Until recently they had seemed to be slowly transforming into exhibits in a food museum, produced for tourists, while everyday people in Hamburg and Berlin, Munich and Cologne ate mozzarella and pizza, *Döner Kebab,* and *poularde de Bresse.* A return to regionality has occurred, counteracting the effects of globalization and industrialization. Because of this and a host of new culinary traditions, writing about food culture in Germany today, including sauerkraut, is a very exciting task.

Germany—on a geohistorical level—is a land in the middle of the European continent, situated between Slavs and Romans, cold and heat, sea and mountains. In the course of history it has been enormously influenced from all sides—one could even say it is *composed* of those influences. Thus, to understand the past, which forms the background of all this meeting, joining, melting, is to understand the reasons for what and how people in Germany eat today.

Unlike, for instance, its neighbor France, Germany has no single national, overarching haute cuisine, not even a national dish like Brazil's *feijoada.* Although Germany is not a particularly large country (in terms of land area, it is slightly smaller than Montana, and its population is between a quarter and a third of that of the United States), its culture is complex. In addition to geographic, climatic, and religious reasons, this is mainly due to migrations throughout history, with new peoples bringing their foods and foodways with them, as well as the fact that until the declaration of the German empire in 1871, Germany was composed of countless small individual kingdoms, fiefdoms, and free cities. This made for a variety of regional cuisines.

When industrialization reached Germany around 1850 (compared with almost a century earlier in England), the effects were far-reaching. In the process, agrarian Germany was quickly and thoroughly urbanized and came to rely more and more on "modern" food industries. As nineteenth-century industrialization gave way to twentieth- and twenty-first-century globalization, German food culture shifted once more to contend with worldwide food trends. Despite heated debates about the rights and wrongs of fast food versus "real" food, world cuisine versus "home-style" regional cooking, food scares, and one of the highest standards of living worldwide, culinary Germany today seems to have returned to a more balanced normality. This is also reflected in the new turn its wine industry has taken, uplifted by the fresh energy of a young generation of winegrowers from previously overlooked regions.

Because this book is about food culture *in* Germany, German emigrants can only be briefly mentioned. Silesian Lutherans, for instance, brought poppy seed dishes to South Australia in the 1840s, just as North American beer brewing owes a lot to its German roots—think of Budweiser, brewed by the Anheuser family. Pennsylvania Dutch ("Dutch" is derived from *deutsch*, that is, German, not from the Netherlands) cuisine reflects the historic cooking styles of the regions along the Rhine. It has been said that the only marked non-British early influence on white American cuisine was German. More than 50 German-language cookbooks appeared in the United States between the middle of the nineteenth century and World War I, one of the most important undoubtedly being the *Practical Cookbook* by Henriette Davidis.[1]

Especially in New York City, where German immigrants had settled beginning in the early days when it was still called New Amsterdam, influxes of German migration have shaped American cuisine. The biggest wave of German immigrants arrived in the 1840s and 1850s. Some of them were Jews, and their food culture later mixed with that of the eastern European Jews who arrived in the 1880s. But the cultures had mixed before. Just as Yiddish, the Ashkenazi-Jewish lingua franca (note that Ashkenazi means "German" in Hebrew), originated as a thirteenth-century southern German dialect and took on its present form in eastern Europe, where many Jews from the Rhine and Elbe regions had fled, Ashkenazi-Jewish cuisine mixed German and eastern European elements and adapted them to the dietary laws of the kashruth.[2]

This particular mix of German, Jewish, and Yiddish cultures resulted in what today has come to be regarded as archetypical New York fare: pastrami, chopped liver and lox, hot dogs, pumpernickel, corned beef, and sour dill pickles. Although the *-essen* in *delicatessen* does not seem to derive from the German verb *essen* (to eat), as it etymologically originated in the French *délicat/délicatesse* (delicate, exquisite/delicacy), the New York shops under that name were originally German. Apart from fine groceries, they offered all kinds of take-out food and often included a restaurant. Delicatessen came to stand above all for beef-based products, in contrast to dairy- and fish-centered "appetizer" shops and restaurants. The importance of these roots for wider white American food culture can hardly be overstated.

For Germans born after World War II, to walk into any of these New York delis is to discover a food world that is at once familiar—the salted "Dutch" herring, pickles, smoked fish, rye bread, and challah—and unfamiliar—the matzo ball soup, knishes, gefilte fish, bialys, and rugaluch. It forms a facet of German food culture that today can almost exclusively be experienced on the North American continent, as it is nearly imperceptible in Germany itself. Some of it, like bagels with cream cheese and lox, has been "re-imported" to contemporary Germany as typical American food (although hardly anybody here knows the true salted lox, with which this combination makes real sense; instead, smoked salmon is used). A lot has survived on American ground precisely because it came to be seen as Jewish, as opposed to German.

Drawing on a wide range of sources as well as my 45 years of hands-on experience as a Berlin-born foodie, *Food Culture in Germany* attempts to present Germany's food culture in all its countless variations. It hopes to make sense of how German food is linked to New York delis, as well as incorporating French, Italian, Turkish, Russian, and many other influences. Despite this fracturing, I believe German food firmly stands its own ground. There is more than herring, sauerkraut, and fast food to modern German cuisine—*guten Appetit!*

NOTES

1. The following reprint of this cookbook going back to 1879 includes a very good introduction on the subject and offers a fascinating insight into the food habits of one of America's largest immigrant groups as well as an English-German list of kitchen-related vocabulary of the time: Henriette Davidis, *Pickled Herring and Pumpkin Pie: A Nineteenth-Century Cookbook for German Immigrants to America* (1904; rpt., Madison, WI: Max Kade Institute, 2003).

2. For an introduction to the subject as well as a wealth of recipes, see Claudia Roden, *The Book of Jewish Food: An Odyssey from Samarkand and Vilna to the Present Day* (London: Penguin, 1999).

Timeline

Prehistory (before 10,000 B.C.)	Skulls are used as communal drinking vessels in the earliest Paleolithic period.
	Fireplaces are used in caves or simple tents.
	The gathering of mushrooms, berries, nuts, roots, and plants is a common way of finding food.
	Hunting becomes a means of finding food.
Mesolithic period (c. 10,000– c. 5,000 B.C.)	Advances in fishing help to increase the variety of humans' diet.
	Boiling food becomes an alternative to roasting.
Neolithic period (c. 5,000– c. 3,000 B.C.)	The first settlements with permanent dwellings are established.
	The cultivation of plants is established in addition to gathering; two of the main crops are *Einkorn* and *Emmer*.
	Simple flat breads baked in subterranean dome-shaped ovens become an alternative to gruel.
	The domestication of pigs, cattle, goats, and sheep begins.
c. 3,000– c. 750 B.C.	Copper and bronze are worked into weapons and tools.
from c. 750 B.C.	The use of iron weapons and tools make for higher crop yields.
	Sourdough is first used for bread.

Smoking meat is a widespread method of preservation.

People begin keeping chicken, geese, and ducks.

Agriculture expands as people begin cultivating pears, plums, and sweet cherries.

Dairy farming is introduced.

A ruling class forms as they create separate settlements for themselves.

51 B.C. Roman troops under Julius Caesar advance up to the Rhine, bringing a monetary system, writing system, and state system to the southwest of modern Germany. The Romans also introduce viticulture.

c. 100 A.D. Roman writer Tacitus describes Germanic tribes in his *Germania* as wild barbarians surviving on unhung fresh game, a thin, ale-like fermented beverage, and curdled milk.

371 Roman poet Ausonius first describes viticulture in the Moselle Valley in his poem *Mosella*.

476 Germanic troops invade Rome; cultures mingle through complex migrations all across Europe following the collapse of the Roman Empire.

736 Benedictine missionary Boniface prohibits the eating of horsemeat.

787 Charlemagne issues the *Capitulare de Villis*, an inventory and set of rules for the management of his estates, emphasizing hunting, mostly a royal privilege, and agriculture, leading to a general diet based more on grains and vegetables.

9th century The three-field system slowly spreads in Germany; summer and winter grains are rotated with root crops and fallow, making for higher crop yields. This remains the norm until it is given up in the eighteenth and nineteenth centuries in favor of clover and potato cultivation.

817 The first record of viticulture in the Rheingau region for a hillside that today belongs to the Schloß Johannisberg estate.

843 Charlemagne's kingdom is split in three parts that correspond roughly to modern Germany, France, and, in the center, Alsace/Lorraine.

With the diminishing influence of the Holy Roman Emperor over the following centuries, a multitude of kingdoms, fiefdoms, and free cities become ever stronger.

Expansion and Christianization progress eastward.

956	Lüneburg is officially recognized for its saltworks (followed by Reichenhall in 1163 and Halle in 1177).
1040	The monastery of Weihenstephan near Munich receives brewing rights.
11th century	Hops begin to be used for beer production.
	Brewing slowly moves out of individual homes to become an industry organized in guilds.
1178	The word *Weihnachten*, in the form *wihe nacht* (Christmas), is first used.
1240	The first recorded trade fair in Frankfurt am Main takes place.
1272	The bakers' guild in Berlin is founded, which requires a baking test for potential members.
	Baked goods in Berlin begin selling at a fixed price.
1329	The first recorded mention of *Christstollen* (Christmas yeast cake) is found in Naumburg/Saale near Leipzig.
1341	The first recorded carnival parade in Cologne, which goes back to Saturnalia in connection with the worship of a late Roman goddess of shipping and fertility, takes place.
1348	The first German university is founded in Prague, beginning the emergence of educated classes as a third power besides church and state.
1348–49	The Plague (Black Death) reduces the European population by a third.
c. 1350	The oldest German cookbook, *Daz buch von guter spise* (The Book of Good Food) is thought to have originated during this time.
	There is a rising awareness of regional differences in food.
1356	Hanse trade organization founded by northern German cities as the counterpart to the southern German trade companies.
15th century	The patrician family Fugger of Augsburg builds elaborate trade systems with the South and Orient through Venetian and Arab traders.
	Fuggers becomes the most important European banker and imports spices from East India by sea.
1435	The Riesling grape is recorded for the first time at Rüsselsheim, near the eastern end of the Rheingau region.

1437	After devastating frosts, viticulture in Germany recedes south, which until then had been common as far north as East Prussia.
1485	The first printed German cookbook, the *Kuchen maysterey*, is published in Nuremberg.
1516	The German *Reinheitsgebot* (purity law) for beer originates in a Bavarian law only allowing *Hopfen* (hops), *Gerstenmalz* (barley malt), and *Wasser* (water) in beer production.
1517	Theologian Martin Luther's declaration of Protestant theses against the Catholic church provokes division of faiths and migrations across Europe, eventually leading to the Thirty Years' War (1618–48), furthering the separation of Austria from Germany, and accentuating food differences between north and south.
1539	As a result of a ban on brewing beer during the summer because of fire risk, beer gardens around Munich become popular as brewers start to sell a special beer brewed in March directly from their premises.
	The first Christmas tree in Strasbourg cathedral is recorded.
1573	The first German sugar refinery is established in Augsburg.
16th century	Lemons, cauliflower, savoy cabbage, and salad are introduced from Italy.
	Buckwheat is introduced from Russia, possibly linked to the important cattle imports coming from there.
	In aristocratic circles, influences from Polish, Bohemian, and Turkish cuisine join those from Italy and Spain.
1580	French philosopher and politician Michel de Montaigne passes through Lindau on Lake Constance and remarks favorably on the cooking.
	Dutch weavers settle in the Spreewald area southeast of Berlin and start cultivating cucumbers.
1581	Marx Rumpolt publishes what is probably the first German potato recipe in his *Ein New Kochbuch*, the first printed guide for professional cooks, but the new crop catches on very slowly.
1609	The first regular weekly newspapers appear in Augsburg and Strasbourg.
1679	The first German coffeehouse opens in Hamburg and although very expensive, coffee proves highly popular among all classes.

1685	Persecuted French Huguenots are welcomed in Prussian Berlin following the abolition of Edict of Nantes.
1688	The first monovarietal Riesling vineyard is recorded in Germany, the Löhrer Berg in the Nahe region, which belonged to the bishop of Mainz at the time.
1710	King August the Strong of Saxony sets up porcelain manufacture in Meißen.
1720	Prussian King Frederick William I introduces potato cultivation in Brandenburg. Later on his son Frederick II (the Great) heavily promotes the same.
1726	The first mention of the vineyard site on a German wine label (Marcobrunn of Erbach/Rheingau) is recorded.
1751	A huge wine barrel is built in Heidelberg, containing about 58,653 gallons.
1755	The last wild *Wisent* (local bison) is shot in East Prussia.
1770	The first coffee surrogate is produced from roasted chicory root.
1771–72	Famines caused by bad grain harvests make for the rapid spread of potato cultivation, first as poor person's food and animal feed, but soon also leading to the production of inexpensive spirits.
1775	At Schloß Johannisberg/Rheingau, final proof is procured that better-quality wine results from late picking, ending long disputes on this matter.
1797	Soup kitchens serving Rumford soup are set up in Munich for poor people. By 1800 there are also soup kitchens in Berlin.
from 1803 on	Under Napoleonic influence, the widespread secularization of church property begins. The property is split up among German rulers as compensation for the losses caused by the French annexations on left side of the Rhine. This, in tandem with the geographic reshuffling after Napoleon's defeat in Russia, leads to the end of extreme territorial fragmentation in Germany.
from 1804 on	Johann Wolfgang von Goethe regularly has his friend Carl Friedrich Zelter, the composer and founder of the Berlin Choral Academy, send him bushels of Teltow turnips in Weimar.
1806–13	The Continental System (Napoleon's trade embargo against England), indirectly leads to the invention of mock turtle

	soup in German Lower Saxony, where a rich peasant's cook is said to replace the embargoed turtle meat with a calf's head so as to serve her master's favorite dish.
1810	The first freedom of trade is decreed and a general trade tax is introduced in Prussia, allowing new structures and free exchange between cities and countryside.
	The first *Oktoberfest*, or *Wiesn*, takes place in Munich on the occasion of the Bavarian crown prince marrying Princess Therese. The celebration includes a horserace on the *Theresienwiese*.
1811	Almost all Rheingau vineyards are picked late; the wines of this *Jahrhundertjahrgang* (vintage of the century, also called *Kometenwein*) make for a quantum leap in German wines' international reputation.
1812	Jewish emancipation declared by Prussian decree.
1815	Congress of Vienna following defeat of Napoleon leads to a Germany composed more or less of the *Länder* (states) of today (although Silesia and East and West Prussia today are part of the Czech Republic and Poland, respectively, whereas the Saar region back then belonged to France).
1818	Berlin's first *Lese-Conditorei* (literally, reading pastry shop, where patrons could read newspapers while having coffee and cake) opens.
1822	Karl Friedrich von Rumohr's *Geist der Kochkunst* (The Essence of Cookery) is published.
1823	First *Rosenmontag* (literally, Rose Monday, the Monday before Ash Wednesday) parade takes place in Cologne.
1827	Karl Baedeker establishes a publishing house for travel books.
1833	Berlin café Kranzler offers the city's first smoking room.
1839	The first German long-distance railway (Dresden to Leipzig) opens; middle classes increasingly take to traveling by rail.
	First German chocolate factory opens in Cologne.
1843	First German jam factory opens in Dresden.
1845	First edition of Henriette Davidis's hugely popular *Praktisches Kochbuch* (Practical cookbook) is published; thereafter, numerous new editions appear until 1963.
1848	General social unrest leads to a revolution and the abolition of all feudal laws.

1851	First Christmas trees arrive by railway in Berlin.
1860	Gas for lighting and cooking arrives in German households (running water does not become widely available until the beginning of the twentieth century).
1862	Kempinski Weinstube opens on Friedrichstraße in Berlin.
1864	The founding of *Schrebergärten-Vereine* (association of allotments/community garden owners) in Leipzig.
	The first commercial production of Liebig's meat extract appears.
1871	Foundation of German Empire with the capital in Berlin and Prussian King William I as emperor follows victory in the Franco-German war.
	Germany has 41 million inhabitants (in 1841, 33 million, in 1933, 66 million).
	State decree allows free movement and settlement for all German citizens, making possible huge migrations following new industries, mainly toward the west and south.
1872	*Krebspest*, a crayfish disease, destroys all German freshwater crayfish.
1874	First refrigeration machine developed by Carl von Linde; combined with rapidly expanding railway system, this leads to wider food distribution.
1879	First state legislation and inspections introduced for milk, beer, and meat.
	First German market hall opens in Frankfurt am Main.
1887	The general pasteurization of milk is introduced.
1888	William II ("Kaiser Bill"), grandson of William I, becomes Kaiser, leading to a rise in nationalism and neobaroque pomp as well as aggressive global politics.
1889	*Kneipp-Kaffee*, a coffee surrogate made from roasted malted barley, is produced commercially for the first time.
1892	The last German cholera epidemic in Hamburg.
	The first German wine law seeks to combat *Kunstwein* (artificial wine), but instead achieves the opposite.
early 1890s	first canning factory for sausages in Frankfurt am Main opens.

1895–1915	German wines are highly esteemed internationally and frequently more expensive than those from top Bordeaux châteaus.
1898	*Deutscher LandFrauenverband* (German Countrywomen's Society) founded in East Prussia.
1901	The term *Naturwein* (natural wine) is introduced, referring to a monovarietal wine with natural alcohol content and from a single vineyard and vintage.
1902	State law for compulsory inspection of all slaughtered pork for trichinosis is introduced.
1907	German grocery stores form the shopping cooperative *Edeka* (today a supermarket chain).
1908	First Maggi soup stock cubes introduced to the public.
1909	*Sektsteuer* (sparkling wine tax) introduced to finance national fleet, which is still in place today.
	Legal protection of vineyard names is introduced, now tied to actual geographic locations.
1914	Sterile filtration is developed to supply soldiers with clean drinking water.
1916	During World War I, food rationing starts with meat, initially at 0.55 lb. weekly per person.
1916–17	*Rübenwinter:* very severe cold winter temperatures combined with insufficient food provisions (due to the failed potato crop and general unpreparedness for the long war) necessitate that rutabagas (swedes), until then considered cattle feed, are eaten as a last, scarce resort.
1918	The concept of equal rights is introduced, with women gaining the right to vote as well as eligibility for political office. However, household work remains their unpaid, legal duty, and husbands are still seen as providers who rule over any legal and financial decisions.
1919	Treaty of Versailles is imposed following German defeat in World War I; the victors demand very high reparation payments as well as the return of Alsace and Lorraine to France.
1922	*Gummibärchen* (gummy bears) invented in Bonn.
1923–24	With inflation, a large part of the middle class loses their savings or becomes impoverished.
1925	*Das Reformhaus*, a monthly newspaper promoting a healthy lifestyle, is first published as part of the *Lebensreform* movement

that began as a counterreaction to industrialization, advocating natural food and lifestyle since 1860s.

1926   *Frankfurter Küche* designed by Viennese architect Margarete Schütte-Litotzky, commissioned by Frankfurt city council for new apartments.

1927   First general German food law is enacted.

1928   *Die Ernährung* nutrition show is in Berlin.

1930   Electricity arrives in German households.

Official legislation accepts technological progress in the form of sterile filtration for wine, which leads to the production of *Süßreserve* (sterile, filtered grape juice used to sweeten wine) and stopped wine fermentation, resulting in sweet wines; both methods are legally accepted for *Naturwein*.

1932   Sterilization method for pickled cucumbers is introduced, enabling industrial-scale production of Spreewald pickles and shipments over longer distances.

Fifty-two percent of fat used in Germany is imported.

1933   Adolf Hitler is elected chancellor; six months later Germany becomes a one-party state.

Emigration numbers jump up; about half the Jewish population (about a half million in 1933) emigrate by 1939; including many leading artists, engineers, scientists, and politicians.

1935   Nazi Hermann Göring is made *Reichsjägermeister* (the Reich's hunting master).

1936   Germany revives whaling industry in search of self-sufficiency.

November 9,   On *Reichskristallnacht* (night of the broken glass), the per-
1938   secution of Jews by the Nazi dictatorship enters its savage phase. Jewish emigration accelerates. During the following six and a half years, Germany systematically eradicates almost all its Jewish population, and with it a vital facet of its culinary identity.

1939   The invasion of Poland by German troops leads to the beginning of World War II.

Until the German defeat in spring 1945 the civilian population is provided with food partly through the raiding of invaded countries.

Ration cards for food and clothing are introduced.

One thousand nine hundred five miles of *Autobahn* (highway) are finished, with 1,149 more under construction.

1945–46   A hunger winter; for the urban population of Germany the food supply remains erratic until 1949–50.

1946   American CARE parcels sent to Germany.

1947   Black market prices in Berlin: 20 American cigarettes, 150 Reichsmark (RM); 2.2 lb. coffee, 1,100 RM; 1 egg, 12 RM; 1 box of matches, 5 RM.

Seitz of Bad Kreuznach/Nahe launches the first affordable sterile filter, enabling the *Süße Welle*, a wave of sweet German wine which quickly grows in scale after 1960.

1948   Deutschmark (DM) introduced by Western Allied forces, 1 DM = 1 RM (in 1950 1 DM in West Germany corresponds to about 5 Mark in East Germany).

The first state-run HO-grocery stores open in East Berlin and East Germany (in 1950 private stores are down to 52%).

June 1948– Soviet blockade of West Berlin, with city surviving thanks to
May 1949   *Luftbrücke* (airlift). Food and coal is flown in by so-called *Rosinenbomber* (literally, raisin bombers), Western Allied planes land up to every 3 minutes. On the busiest day 896 planes fly in about 7,716 tons of goods; in total 274,718 flights cover almost 100 million miles and bring in over 2.2 million tons of supplies.

May 1949   *Bundesrepublik Deutschland* (Federal Republic of Germany, or West Germany) founded.

Onset of *Wirtschaftswunder* (economic miracle), which lasts until 1967, the first year of zero growth of the gross national product.

1949   *Deutscher Hausfrauen-Bund* (German Housewives' Alliance) founded.

September 4, This day is commonly believed to be the date of invention of
1949   the *Currywurst* (curried sausage) by a certain Herta Heuwer at her food stall on the Kantstrasse in Berlin. However, some claim Hamburg and an earlier date in 1947 as the starting point for this highly popular snack.

October 1949 Founding of the *Deutsche Demokratische Republik* (German Democratic Republic, or East Germany). In East Germany equal rights for women are part of the constitution from the start: "Through the Republic's rights the necessary institutions

	will be created which guarantee that a woman can reconcile her tasks as citizen and worker with her duties as woman and mother" (paragraph 18).
1950	Food rationing and price controls are abolished in West Germany, ending the black market.
1951	A West German worker needs to work 240 minutes to buy 2.2 lb. butter, an American needs to work only 68 minutes.
1952	There are now 200,000 tractors in Germany (in 1949, 75,000) and 1.36 million horses (in 1950, 1.57 million).
1953	Long-distance water pipes are built from Lake Constance to Stuttgart to satisfy increasing water needs.
1954	British chain *Wimpy* introduces West Germans to hamburgers.
1955	First *Wienerwald* opens in Munich, a fast-growing chain of take-out food outlets selling grilled chicken. It also doubles as a family restaurant.
	West Germany becomes a member of NATO.
	Consumers strike because of rising milk prices.
	Levels of unemployment in West Germany reach their lowest since the war (about 495,000 people are unemployed in West Germany and 115,900 in West Berlin).
1952	First German pizzeria, Sabbie di Capri, opens in Würzburg.
June 17, 1953	Workers' revolt in East Berlin is put down by Soviet tanks.
1955	The first Italian guest workers arrive in Germany.
1958	Food journalist Wolfram Siebeck writes his first articles in the magazine *Twen*.
	East Germany abolishes food rationing (although it is partly reintroduced in 1961).
	The restructuring of West German food law introduces bans and requires labeling of additives.
1959	The beginning of the European Common Market.
August 13, 1961	East Germany builds the Berlin Wall, sealing off West Berlin.
1963	Milk price increases in West Germany.
	Following the example of the United States, the first shopping centers and supermarkets open in West Germany.
1969	West German labor market reaches a record high with only 861,000 vacancies, more than 1.5 million foreign workers, and 0.5% unemployment.

early 1970s   First sighting of German-Turkish fast-food favorite *Döner Kebab* in Berlin-Kreuzberg.

1971   Austrian chef Eckart Witzigmann starts working at Munich restaurant Tantris.

Germany's first McDonald's opens in Munich.

The new German wine law, a so-called modernization, enables mass production and the marketing of wines under the famous vineyard names of neighboring villages (so-called *Großlagen*).

1972   First German food magazine for the general public, the monthly *essen & trinken* (eating and drinking), begins publication.

1973   Oil crisis shakes West Germans' belief in unlimited technology-based progress.

Because of the energy crisis, recruitment of foreign workers stops (then about 2.6 million in West Germany, of whom about 0.5 million are Turkish).

The legal blood alcohol limit for driving set to 0.8 per thousand.

Trimm Dich-Bewegung (official fitness campaign) increases the popularity of hiking.

mid-1970s   Oyster farming reintroduced to island of Sylt.

1975   Nonsmokers start to be respected in public gatherings and spaces.

1977   Through legal reforms in West Germany, male dominance is replaced by the principle of partnership, and a married woman no longer needs permission from her husband to take a paid job outside the household.

The end of the fishing treaty with Iceland leads to fish scarcity in West Germany.

West German sparkling wine consumption has quadrupled since 1957 to more than 7.4 pints per capita.

1978   Bonn restaurateur Karl Heinz Wolf starts his firm Rungis-Express, regularly importing French gourmet food products from the Paris wholesale market and distributing them among his colleagues in Germany.

West German narcotics law strictly limits poppy (*papaver somniferum L.*) cultivation to scientific purposes; any poppy seeds for culinary purposes are imported, mostly from Turkey, later also from Austria and Hungary.

1979	Eckart Witzigmann becomes the first chef in Germany with three Michelin stars.
1980	The political party *Die Grünen* (the Greens) founded.
	Record high of alcohol consumption in West Germany (almost 27 pints per capita per year); 1.5 million people are estimated to be alcoholics.
1981	Commercial use of *Waldmeister* (woodruff) officially banned because of risk of toxicity from its cumarin content.
	Food-related economy is the strongest industry in West Germany, with 140 billion DM (in 1970, 66 billion).
	West German potato production down to 8.37 million tons (from 27 million in 1953).
1984	West German parliament decides on "milk pension" to reduce milk production.
	The workweek in West Germany is reduced to 35 hours (1972, 40; 1918, 48; 1885, 65; 1882, 82).
	Forty-two percent of the West German population is employed in agriculture (in 1962, 48%; in the United States, it was 3% in 1984 and 7% in 1962).
1985	Meat consumption in West Germany stands at 221.6 lb. per capita per year (in 1960, 143.3 lb.).
	A wine scandal breaks out when diethylene glycol is found in Austrian (and subsequently German) wines.
1986	The cost of living in West Germany is lower than in previous year for the first time since 1949 (by 0.2%).
	Nuclear catastrophe in Chernobyl in the Ukraine provokes lasting anxiety among Germans; consumers are concerned about the safety of milk, wild mushrooms, and fruit as well as game meat.
1987	European law forces Germany to open its market to foreign beer not brewed according to *Reinheitsgebot*.
	In November the first reports about bovine spongiform encephalopathy (BSE) in the United Kingdom reach Germany.
1988	The use of growth hormones in meat production banned in Germany.
November 9, 1989	Following months of social unrest and demonstrations in East Germany (most importantly the *Montagsdemonstrationen* [Monday demonstrations] in Leipzig), the Berlin Wall falls, internal German border opens, and untold

	thousands of East Germans pour over the border for a taste of the West.
1990	A German health inspector discovers first indications of BSE in Germany but loses her job after she reports her findings to the public.
	On October 3, German reunification is declared, with Berlin as the capital.
1993	First good vintage for East German wine regions following reunification.
1996	*Dresdner Christstollen* (Christmas yeast cake from Dresden) recognized with a European Union Protected Geographical Indication (PGI) seal.
1997	Preemptive cullings of cattle for fear of BSE take place in Germany, with government officials insisting that Germany is BSE-free and at no risk.
1999	European PGI seal granted to pickled Spreewald cucumbers.
2000	Germany has to admit its first official BSE case, which is followed by a total ban on using meat and bone meal for animal feed, as well as nationwide tests of all animals slaughtered at under 24 months of age.
	First signs that a new generation of winegrowers is revolutionizing German wine, with whole regions coming out of the shadows (Rhenish Hessia, Franconia).
2001	Because of the BSE crisis and the irresponsible handling of it, several ministers have to leave office, and Renate Künast (of *Die Grünen*) takes over as Federal Minister for Nutrition, Agriculture, and Forestry, which was subsequently re-named the Ministry for Consumer Protection, Nutrition, and Agriculture; she helps organic products achieve wider acceptance, leading to the first organic supermarkets.
January 1, 2002	New European currency, the Euro, introduced in Germany.
2004	Stargarder Land north of Berlin is declared an officially recognized German wine region.
2005	First *Gammelfleisch* (literally, rotten meat) discovered at a German wholesaler, then nationwide.
2006	Angela Merkel elected chancellor; she is the first woman and the first East German to hold the job.
September 1, 2007	Smoking in public spaces banned by federal law.

1

Historical Overview

Modern Germans can be traced back to Germanic, Celtic, and Slavic origins. Situated in the center of the European continent, the region that is now Germany experienced migrations as early as in Roman times. These migrations brought endless contacts and cultural influences from all over Europe. They also led to a mixing of northern and southern, western and eastern European cultures and ethnicities within the region. With the decline of Charlemagne's kingdom in 843, only France and England retained strong centralized power. The remaining regions dissolved into small, individual kingdoms, fiefdoms, and free cities (a process that was not reversed until Napoleon's restructuring of the European map beginning in 1803). In terms of food, that meant Germany developed a variety of regional cuisines rather than one overarching haute cuisine. When industrialization finally reached Germany around 1850 (as compared to about a century earlier in England), the effects were far-reaching. In the process agrarian Germany was quickly and thoroughly urbanized and came to rely more and more on "modern" food industries.

ORIGINS

The further one goes back in time, the more difficult it is to separate specifically the area that is Germany today from the development of central Europe in general. In fact, not until the eleventh century did anyone eating and drinking between the Baltic, the North Sea, and the Alps refer to themselves as German at all.

Apart from some human skulls that have been found, which were prob-ably used as communal drinking vessels, very little is known from before the Paleolithic period about humans in this region. The vessels belonged to *Homo sapiens neanderthalensis* (Neanderthals), named after the loca-tion near Düsseldorf where archaeologists first found their traces. They apparently had fireplaces in their caves or simple tents, collected all kinds of mushrooms, berries, nuts, roots, and plants, and hunted reindeer, elk, bear, wild horse, bison, mammoth, rhinoceros, wild donkey, and deer.

Around 10,000 B.C. the method of boiling food became an alternative to roasting: smallish holes in the ground were sealed and filled with water, which was then heated by adding hot stones from the fire—the first soups might have been eaten using this technique. At around the same time advances were made in fishing.

During the Neolithic period Middle Europeans started to settle down, build permanent dwellings, and cultivate crops instead of merely collect-ing plants. The main crops were two primitive wheat varieties, *Einkorn* and *Emmer* (both of which are seeing a revival today within the organic movement). Grain was dried for better conservation, then ground and baked into simple flat breads in subterranean dome-shaped ovens. The ancient meal of *Grütze* (gruel), however, continued to play an important role—in certain rural areas it continued as a typical dish up until the twentieth century. Peas and lentils were cultivated, as were linseed and poppy seed for oil. Pigs, cattle, goats, and sheep were kept near the dwell-ings and regularly slaughtered. Around 4,000 B.C. naked barley and dwarf wheat yielded more reliable crops. New baking and roasting methods be-came possible during this period because of advances in pottery.

However, the most important changes of the Neolithic era came with the ability to work metal—first copper and bronze, then, beginning around 800 B.C., iron. This happened several thousand years after the same devel-opment in Mesopotamia between the Euphrates and Tigris rivers. With more effective weapons and tools made from metal, cultivation was easier and more efficient, enabling higher crop yields. Sourdough from finely ground, bran-free grain was used to make bread. Meat was preserved by smoking, and at the same time chicken, goose, and duck became part of the protein menu. In addition to apples, pears, plums, and sweet cher-ries were cultivated more easily. With improved animal husbandry, milk began to play a more important role as well. New trades and trading goods developed, which increased commerce and enabled the birth of a ruling class who did not cultivate their fields themselves. These elite members of society lived in separate settlements and might have enjoyed different foodways as well.

ROMANS AND GERMANS

The military advances of Julius Caesar and his Roman troops into Gallic territory and up to the Rhine (51 B.C.) brought a monetary system, writing system, and state system to what is now southwestern Germany. The Romans were unable to realize their plans to push the border of their empire all the way to the river Elbe due to their inability to conquer the people living there. The belligerent Nordic tribes continually tried to enter Gaul from across the Rhine. These tribes, which included the Angles, Saxons, Vandals, Goths, Franks, Teutons, and Swabians, to name only a few, were known as "Germans," a word the Romans adopted from the Gauls (the "French" Celts). Julius Caesar correspondingly called the area beyond the Rhine and the Danube *Germania*—but these Germans were not aware of themselves as such.

The Roman historian Tacitus (c. A.D. 55–c. 115), in his work *Germania*, provides the only written evidence of the food habits of these "wild" German tribes. He was mostly interested in showing his effeminate, degenerate compatriots an unspoiled, naturally strong people. According to Tacitus the Germans survived on wild fruits, game meat that was fresh and had not been hung (a serious sign of lack of civilization from a Roman point of view), and *lac concretum* (curdled milk or quark). Pigs fattened in the oak woods, as well as fish, certainly played an important role in the German diet but were not discussed in *Germania*. However, Tacitus does mention the cultivation of fields and a wine-like beverage made from fermented barley.

Clean, fresh water was a precious commodity at that time, especially in larger cities. The Romans built long and costly aqueducts. Cologne from the first century A.D. was supplied with water from the Eiffel Mountains about 56 miles away. Viticulture made significant progress in the Roman territories. In contrast with today's preferences, wine was often mixed with spices, honey, or resin. For the lower classes, vinegar was mixed with water, or *Lora* was made by soaking skins and seeds in water, producing a drink that was only slightly alcoholic but at least somewhat lower in germs. The latter was also true for beer, a kind of ale made from barley or *Emmer*.

During the complex migrations all over Europe from the end of the fourth century on, various Germanic tribes were pushed west by the Huns, who were followed by Slavs. The more rustic culinary habits of the east met the gourmet world of sophisticated Romans like Decimus Magnus Ausonius (c. 310–c. 394), a Roman patrician from Aquitaine living in Trier who described the wealth in fish and wine along the Moselle River in his poem *Mosella* (written in 371).

The immoderate consumption of their simple alcoholic brew, according to Tacitus, ought to have made it easy for the Roman troops to conquer the uncivilized Germans. Actually the opposite happened. Some of the belligerent "Barbars" who constantly pushed over the Limes, the border wall the Romans had built to protect their empire, had been allowed to serve as border troops, as well as being granted Roman citizenship. Eventually, they deposed the ever-weaker emperor (A.D. 476) and took over. Traditional ways of trading, food culture, commerce practices, and related social rules perished with the fall of the Roman Empire. In addition, climatic conditions worsened.

AGRICULTURE AND HUNTING UNDER CHARLEMAGNE DURING THE MIDDLE AGES

The Frankish Carolingian king Charlemagne (747–814) sought to reunify the vast Holy Roman Empire, which stretched from the Pyrenees south to Rome and north to Denmark, including all of France and almost all Germanic kingdoms and duchies. The territory reached the Elbe and Saale rivers in the east, as well as the borders of the "pagan" Slav kingdoms.

At the same time he sought to build up the economy. With the *Capitulare de Villis*, an inventory of his estates, Charlemagne issued precise rules on all aspects of agriculture for the running of the royal estates. A shared meal had strong symbolic meanings under his reign, often taking the place of today's written and signed treaties. The turbulent early Middle Ages, after the collapse of the Roman Empire, had led to a relapse toward hunting and gathering for common people. Hunting, however, was very important to Charlemagne. His primary aim was to protect game, the object of his passion. The *Capitulare Missorum* (802) elevated royal hunting rights over individual hunting rights. The high status venison enjoys in Germany today can be traced back to these hunting laws. Under Roman law hunting had not been regulated. But with Charlemagne the *Wald* (wood) became *Forst* (managed forest), and its use was determined by royal decree rather than by legal ownership. Even woods held communally could be reclaimed for the king's hunting enjoyment, and common folk were required to provide hunting services to the king, such as the maintenance of the royal hunting grounds and the keeping of hunting dogs for the king's use.

Social differentiation was clearly mirrored in food practices. Higher status was defined in terms of the quantity of meat one could consume. However, under Charlemagne grains and vegetables came to play a more important role. Especially in the north, new grains such as oats, millet, and rye (the latter formerly regarded as a weed) had joined the various kinds of wheat and barley. As for meat, beef gained in popularity over pork. Fish played a role as well, but the well-managed carp ponds of Roman times only lived on in monasteries. The same was true for the abundant use of herbs: sage, fennel, chervil, pennyroyal, lovage, mint, and celery are still familiar today, but monasteries also cultivated more exotic-sounding varieties such as horehound, rue, catnip, asafoetida, agrimony, betony, and wormwood. Walahfrid Strabo's poem (written in 827) on the cultivation of gardens at his abbey on the island of Reichenau is even more telling in terms of German food culture of that time than the often quoted plan of the St. Gall kitchen garden published in 820 (although Reichenau is admittedly on the southern edge of Germany and very much favored by the special climate of Lake Constance). Strabo mentions a wide variety of vegetables in his poem, among them red chard, radishes, broad beans, cucumbers, and gourds, which might have included marrows and watermelons.[1] Similarly, Roman viticulture survived thanks to monasteries endowed with vineyards that were tended by local peasants.[2]

The majority of the population lived in small rural settlements tied to a feudal system in which they were required to hand over a large percentage of their crop. They subsisted on what they cultivated themselves, mostly grain eaten in the form of gruel. Food shortages and famines induced by war, crop failures, or the lack of exchanges between regions were common. Hunger and subsequent epidemics were mostly regarded as divine punishment for human sins and often seen in connection with extraordinary natural phenomena such as solar and lunar eclipses, or the apparition of comets. The monasteries represented, at least for some, a kind of social welfare system in hard times and also often acted as hospitals and medical centers for those in need. Another form of medieval welfare was the practice of the *Almusfass*, still present in the word *Almosen* (alms): a barrel used to collect leftover food for distribution to the poor.

Medicine and food were inextricably linked during this time, mostly based on the ancient holistic system of the Greek physician Galen (probably 129–99) and later the Salerno school. The system centered around the four elements: fire, water, earth, and air (corresponding to heat, humidity, dryness, and cold), which had their equivalents in the human body with the four fluids, humors, or temperaments: choleric, phlegmatic, melancholic, and sanguine. The goal was to achieve balance between the elements and the humors. Thus, health was attainable through the consumption of the right foods. Each plant and food item itself had certain humoric qualities, that is, was hot or cold, dry or humid, depending on its provenance, color, and texture. Coloring a dish with saffron, for instance, was not simply done to please the eye but was thought to have a certain medical quality. Good food was therefore balanced or "tempered" food, and one's health depended on it. In that sense, food was the best doctor. Major advocates of this doctrine in Germany later on were the Benedictine abbess Hildegard von Bingen (1098–1179) and the Dominican scholar Albertus Magnus (c. 1200–80). Some seemingly obvious modern food combinations go back to that time. Hildegard, for instance, tempered the strong (harmful) coldness of green salad with vinegar, dill, or leek.

From the early Middle Ages on, fasting was a church-mandated part of virtuous Christian life, and it started to influence the greater food culture. Meat, milk, butter, cheese, and eggs were not permitted during Lent, the 40 days preceding Easter, as well as on numerous other days and periods throughout the year.[3]

EXPANSION TO THE EAST AND THE CRUSADES

Following Charlemagne's death in 814, his kingdom in 843 was divided into western and eastern parts, roughly coinciding with modern France and Germany. Originally there was a third part in the center of the kingdom, Lotharingia (present-day Alsace and Lorraine), which was soon annexed by the eastern part; since then, this territory has many times been the cause of aggressive encounters and has often changed sides. The Main Franks, Saxons, Frisians, Thuringians, Bavarians, and Swabians in the east formed a rather loose German Reich and as such were part of the Holy Roman Empire, with the emperor as the single focal point. Without any fixed capital, this empire slowly lost power over the centuries, in favor of regional rulers. Territorialization advanced with a multitude of kingdoms, fiefdoms, and free cities. The more efficient three-field system that rotated summer and winter grain with root crops and fallow, led to enhanced productivity and economic growth.

Expansion toward the east made lasting progress from the twelfth century on. Smaller western Slavic tribes living between the Baltic Sea and the eastern Alps beyond the river Elbe were assimilated through fighting, politics, and religion. The *Deutscher Orden* (Order of German Knights) as well as the Cistercian order played an important role in that process. The Cistercian order had developed at the beginning of the twelfth century out of the reforms and restraints St. Bernard de Clairvaux saw necessary for the wealthy Benedictines. Cistercians were permitted only two meals daily of coarse bread plus vegetables seasoned with oil. This meant that they were well prepared for mission life in the most unwelcoming areas. For instance, in 1180 the Margrave of Brandenburg called on the Cistercians to found a monastery in Lehnin just south of Berlin. During the following centuries rye, barley, buckwheat, linseed, millet, and hops were cultivated there; later crops included tobacco and potatoes along with sheep flocks for wool production. Linguistic and cultural assimilation of the Slavs was furthered by settlers from the Rhine, Flanders, and Thuringia. Very few cultural islands have persisted, like the Lausitz southeast of Berlin, where the Sorbs, a Slavic minority, have cultivated their original customs and language until today.

The Crusades (eleventh through thirteenth centuries) increased contact with the Islamic and Oriental world. Whoever was lucky enough to return safely brought back hitherto unknown sweets and spices that are still strongly reflected in the Christmas baking of today.

FIRST WAVE OF URBANIZATION

The population grew steadily, and most of the modern German cities were founded between the twelfth and fourteenth centuries. About one-fifth of the population lived in one of the 4,000 towns, which ranged in size from small *Ackerbürgerstädte* (towns whose inhabitants mostly subsisted on the food grown on their smallholdings) to larger cities specializing in some trades, for instance, the ever-important mining industry. Cologne was the largest city, with around 40,000 inhabitants, followed by Prague and Lübeck. All of them were small compared to Paris, which had about 100,000 inhabitants during this period, but in the German context, Cologne was a true hub and a center of innovation. Wares of all possible origins were on offer here.

As more people, especially in the cities, bought their food instead of producing it themselves, famines were now not only referred to (in Latin) as *fames* but often *caristia* (rise in prices). That did nothing to diminish their effects. When the plague arrived in 1348–49, the population was weakened from several years of hunger and one-third succumbed to the Black Death. Meat consumption rose sharply again, as many fields lay fallow and were used for grazing.

In 1348 the first university in the German countries[4] was founded in Prague (whereas France already had five universities by 1300). However, many students of the "German nations" attended the universities in Paris, Bologna, and Salamanca. Cultural influences left their mark on German culture—the land at the center absorbed culture from the south and west and passed it on to the east. A bourgeois class started to form in the cities, a third power besides church and state.

Regional food habits became more distinctive. As paper became more widely available and affordable, it was also used for writing down recipes. The oldest example of a German cookbook, *Daz buch von guter spise* (*The book of good food*, c. 1350) gives a glimpse of how the urban upper class in Würzburg saw themselves foodwise: getting "great meals from many small things," one of the book's tenets, points to thrift as a virtue. Time is measured by paternosters (Lord's Prayers), and recipes named after specific places indicate contact with the wider world. White bread and saffron demonstrate a certain degree of wealth, whereas local vegetables such as beets, beans, cabbage, peas, leeks, and turnips play only a minor role, as they were generally regarded as peasant food. The frequent mentioning of chicken for meat is evocative of the urban setting—they were the easiest to raise in crammed surroundings.[5] Together with an abundance of herbs many familiar ingredients are found in this ancient cookbook. Very few ingredients, such as heron, are considered inedible today.

TRANSNATIONAL TRADING AND FURTHER SOCIAL DIFFERENTIATION

Sugar slowly replaced honey in the fourteenth century, and the inclusion of spices,[6] rice, and almonds[7] in the diet was based on the elaborate trade system that had been formed with the south and Orient via Venetian and Arab merchants. Rich patrician families like the Fuggers in Augsburg ran vast and highly capitalized trading companies with offices in all the important European commercial centers. Their dealings later extended as far as the Americas and the West Indies. They also acted as house bankers for the emperor and the pope. Besides these families, numerous southern German cities created their own trading companies. Frankfurt am Main, Frankfurt an der Oder, and Leipzig in central Germany emerged as the most important fairs.

The Hansa trade organization was officially founded in 1356 by merchant trading groups in northern German cities on the Baltic and North seas, most prominently Lübeck, Bremen, and Hamburg, to create a counterpole in the north. The Hansa cities first concentrated on the exchange of local wares but gradually extended their trade as a privileged alliance of German merchants abroad, establishing *Kontore* (offices) in other important cities like London and Novgorod. Their ships traveled through the English Channel, along the French coast, down to Spain, and up to Norway, reaching as far as Moscow. Their wares included raw material from the east as well as refined products of the west, thus dealing in wool, fur, leather, grain, linen, herring, salt, wine, and beer, as well as tools and timber.[8]

With urban growth, clean water again became a problem, as garbage was commonly disposed of in the streets and next to wells. Monasteries, districts, and churches often had their own cisterns. Poisoning of wells was part of war strategies. As the connection between polluted water and epidemics became more obvious, accusations flew as to who was responsible. Misplaced accusations concerning the poisoning of wells were an early reason for the persecution of Jews.

As for beer, there now was a choice between *grutbier* (the cheaper, light ale-like drink of ancient style, which was made with herbs and spices, sometimes even resin) and the new stronger ones made with hops. These were also more stable and could be traded over longer distances, so that regional specialties became known. Vines were widely planted in the north, much farther than what is considered the limit for viticulture today.[9] But for the upper classes the preferred wines came from the Rhine, Moselle, and Alsace regions, as well as dessert wines from southern Europe.

Communal storage systems and early attempts at municipal provisioning for the poor meant that hard times were no longer a matter of sheer starvation. Food was divided into *gemein* (common) for the laborers and *gute spise* (good fare) for the higher classes and nobles. As for food preparation, smokefree rooms and fireplaces with brick chimneys became the norm. The amount of meat one could afford continued to be an indicator of social standing (bread and/or gruel, often *geschmaltzt* [enriched with lard], were more affordable alternatives). Fat meat was valued more highly than lean, and roasting more highly than boiling. Spoiled meat was a common problem, increasingly tackled with local legislation. In most cities it was forbidden to slaughter sick animals, and fresh meat could only be offered over a limited period of time. Although offenders were severely punished, as were all kinds of food adulterers, bad meat seemed to appear again and again, one reason certainly being the anonymity of urban living.

As in Charlemagne's times, meals and representations of status were closely linked in the sixteenth century. Food—often enormous quantities of it—was served to demonstrate economic and political power. In 1571, a Cologne councilman gave a dinner for seven officials on the occasion of being accepted among the city's standard-bearers. It began with baked ham surrounded by beef, mutton, tongue, chicken, boiled meat, Bingen sausage, sauerkraut, and lamb pie. The second course consisted of roast hare, leg of venison, and wild boar, accompanied by rabbit, capon, chicken, snipe, and quails. Pastries followed, together with crayfish, pike, carp, marzipan, and headcheese. The meal concluded with almonds, dates, pears, aniseed, cinnamon sticks, and other sweets. Wine from silver flagons was served throughout the meal.

In the sixteenth century lemons, cauliflower, and savoy cabbage increasingly found their way from Italy over the Alps, as did the idea of salad, that is eating cold raw leaves and vegetables dressed with oil and vinegar. Only the upper classes could afford to prepare it with olive or nut oil, whereas ordinary people used vinegar and meat broth. Another stream of culinary influence began to flow from the east. Buckwheat from Russia became an important crop in the northeast of Germany until it was replaced by the potato.[10] Cattle for slaughter were imported in large numbers from eastern Europe as well. Food words of Slavic origin appeared, such as *Bemme* (bread spread with butter), *Graupen* (pearl barley), *Gurke* (cucumber), and *Jause* (snack).[11] Many of these words are still used. In aristocratic circles, Polish, Bohemian, and Turkish cuisines seem to have had an important influence in addition to the already celebrated Italian and Spanish ones.

However, for the majority of the growing population, life was dominated by subsistence farming. Regardless of the region there were two main meals per day, around nine o'clock in the morning and five o'clock in the afternoon. They consisted of warm dishes, often from a communal bowl, with occasional bread-based meals in-between. Beer—mostly made from barley—was the most popular drink after water. Breweries started in the monasteries, often combined with bakeries, and monastic beer spread to the villages.

In the west and southwest of what is Germany today, inheritance laws divided property between all the successors. Therefore, families settled in the same area in order to receive their inheritance, and villages formed with families as the smallest social units. The families usually ate at home but celebrated as a village on special occasions. In the north, in Westphalia, and in the newly assimilated east, however, Saxon inheritance laws passed entire property holdings to one person. Large feudal estates became the dominant social structures in these areas. Workers shared their meals with the estate owner on workdays, just as in cities, craftsmen and apprentices (organized in trade guilds) shared homes and meals with their master and his wife.

Further regional differences emerged. In the north, buttered bread played an important role for ordinary people, so much so that it had already made its way into the common language. The first meal of the morning was called *morgenbrot* (morning bread). It was combined with herring, simple cheese, lard, or groat sausage. In central Germany, unbuttered bread accompanied the main meal or was eaten with cheese and/or a beverage as a snack. In the south, however, gruel and soup still dominated, and bread was seldom eaten.

Despite all the progress, the food supply in general was unstable, and times of scarcity alternated with times of abundant feasting for most regions. Meat was more abundant in the autumn and winter, after slaughtering. On fast days and meat-free Fridays, fish, either fresh or dried, was the most common meal. The highest-prized fish were fresh salmon and crayfish from local streams. In addition, numerous fishponds were installed in a wide belt reaching from Bohemia, Silesia, and Poland to Württemberg and Lorraine.

ENLIGHTENMENT AND REFORMATION

In spite of the first written imperial constitution in 1356, the small kingdoms, self-governing territories, and cities grew ever more independent. The unquestioning subservience expected by old structures was met with increasing rebellion, civil wars, and voices critical of the church, among them Martin Luther (1483–1546). Luther, a theologian from Wittenberg, challenged the pope's primacy and infallibility. In spite of threats and risks to his own person he developed a new, reformed, sober version of Christianity. Protestantism was devoid of all pomp, and the church no longer was the sole mediator between God and humankind. The Reformation also prompted regional changes in territories that did not convert to Protestantism. Subjects generally had to follow their ruler's religion but at least had the right to migrate to a territory where their chosen belief was practiced. This migration led to religious homogenization within regions. The division between faiths roughly divided north from south, within Germany as well as in the whole of Europe. The staunchly Catholic Hapsburg emperor gradually withdrew to his Austrian home territory during this period, which initiated the separation of Austrian from German history.

Food differences between the north and south became ever more accentuated. In the south, with the population numbers growing due to immigration, meat became scarcer. As food prices rose, in the sixteenth century a whole culture of dishes with a simple flour base developed. The famous *Mehlspeisen* (flour dishes) of southern Germany and Austria include dumplings, pancakes, and noodles in endless variety, savory and sweet. In the northwest, however, cattle breeding flourished and even replaced the imports from eastern Europe, so that there was no scarcity of meat but rather a certain affluence among the peasants and the meat dealers. There was a clear distinction between lordly and lowly meats, the latter comprising offal (variety) meats, sausage, or tough, old beef. Even today, offal meats are seen as less desirable in northern Germany and are seldom eaten.

BOOKS

Thanks to the development of a new printing technique by Johannes
Gutenberg (1400–1468), Martin Luther was able to print his translation of
the Bible from Latin (only understood by scholars) into the popular Saxon-
German. From the first edition in 1534 the new Bible became an absolute
best seller, and it was followed by a stream of other manuscripts and authors. The reading public grew rapidly, above all in Protestant areas. The
German language quickly gained ground, not the least with cookbooks.
Marx Rumpolt's *Ein New Kochbuch* (*A New Cookbook*, Frankfurt am Main,
1581) is one of the most prominent examples. Books on behavior likewise flourished. Until then there had not been much social differentiation
in table manners. Emperors as well as peasants used a personal knife and
bread to eat from a communal dish, and a personal spoon was dipped into
a communal bowl—only the material of the knives and spoons varied.
The use of personal forks, hitherto used primarily for serving and carv-
ing, spread slowly from Italy around the seventeenth century, eventually
trickling down to the lower classes. As changes took place in all levels of
society and areas of life, advice was needed, such as not to put one's hand
into the communal bowl first, not to put back what one had already had in
one's mouth, and not to blow one's nose with the tablecloth.[12]

THE THIRTY YEARS' WAR AND NEW INFLUENCES

Following the Reformation, the Huguenot wars in France and the Civil
War in England widened into the Thirty Years' War (1618–48) throughout Europe. War casualties, marauding soldiers, devastation, famine, and
epidemics reduced the population from 17 to 10 million. Many of the
common people were completely uprooted from their homes and origins.

World trade shifted from the Mediterranean to the Atlantic, with the
Netherlands and England as the two leading trading nations. Germany
had no access to the Atlantic world trade and, with the (unsuccessful) exception of Brandenburg, no colonies. On top of that capital was generally
lacking, so that the economy stagnated. The extreme territorial fragmentation also meant an abundance of customs barriers: a merchant taking
his wares down the Rhine from Basel to Cologne had to stop about every
10 kilometers (about 6 miles) at a customs house.

The German states and their nobility were a colorful mix of ecclesiasti-
cal and secular. They followed the examples of Versailles and Vienna in
all issues pertaining to taste. In the north and the west, they also began
to look toward French cuisine. Searching for more refinement in their

food and seeing food as a new class marker, they introduced dishes such as *ragoût, fricassée,* and *côtelettes.* Along the northern coast, above all in Hamburg, English cuisine was an important influence as well. The *bürgerliche Küche* (bourgeois cooking) began to emerge through the imitation and refinement of familiar regional styles of cooking according to the noble "French" cuisine, and later also adapting it to simpler dishes.

Politically, the German Reich as a whole was weak, a situation that France profited from by pushing eastward to its "natural" frontier on the Rhine, this river back then being still unregulated and therefore difficult to cross. French troops occupied and devastated the Palatinate area, following the orders of the French King Louis XIV. They were to burn the region down, *"brûler le Palatinat"* (1668–97). Without much opposition from the Holy Roman Emperor, they quickly succeeded in their task.

CULINARY INNOVATIONS: COFFEE, POTATOES, AND SCHNAPPS

When Christopher Columbus and Vasco da Gama went looking for alternative routes to Asia, the whole world was to change—not the least through a variety of new foods. However, it took a long time following the "discovery" of the American continent (in 1492) until potatoes, corn, tomatoes, or tobacco were available, and even longer until they were widely consumed in Germany. The scholars of the time mostly regarded them as suspicious—the tomato for instance, a member of the poisonous nightshade family, was welcomed to German garden plots and salad bowls only around the beginning of the twentieth century.

In the progressive teachings of the Swabian physician Paracelsus (1493–1541), food and medicine were still related, but the rules became more flexible. Menus began to sound more familiar to the standards of a modern palate. Melchior Sebizius, a physician from Strasburg (1578–1674), mentions, for instance, mustard and grated horseradish as condiments, pork prepared in all possible ways, sauerkraut, chestnuts, and strawberries with cream as elements of the German diet.

As the general economy recovered around the late eighteenth century, imports from overseas grew. Thanks to Columbus and the other explorers, spices were now more affordable and no longer seen as necessary for healthy nutrition, but rather were to serve taste and give pleasure. Three innovations in particular changed the culinary scene and gradually led to new meal patterns in Germany: coffee, potatoes, and schnapps (an inexpensive spirit most often made from potatoes). The trio widely replaced the gruel and related dishes, although the substitution was not linear due to complex territorial fragmentation and regional differences.

The first German coffeehouse opened in Hamburg in 1679 (one had opened in Paris in 1643). By around 1750, coffee had become so trendy in the northwest and center of Germany that officials sought severe measures to rein in the popularity of the expensive foreign drink. Consumed with the equally luxurious product sugar, coffee was seen as economically befitting only the uppermost classes. Much money was going abroad for imported luxury goods such as these, and cheaper surrogates for high-class products emerged. *Zichorienkaffee,* that is, imitation coffee made from roasted chicory root, emerged in Germany from 1770 and created a whole new industry with centers in Brunswick and Magdeburg.

In contrast to the hedonistic pleasures of coffee and sugar, the basic potato caught on much more slowly, as it required more adaptations to daily food habits in order to pervade the existing diet. In Germany the potato made its first appearance in the seventeenth century in the southwest, although an earlier potato recipe can be found in Marx Rumpolt's *New Kochbuch* of 1581 (an example of the discrepancy between what is in cookbooks and what is in the majority of pots and pans). Potato cultivation caught on more widely only after the famines of 1771–72, which were caused by bad grain crops. Initially the potato was considered a poor person's food and was used as animal feed in less profitable regions.

Soon, however, potato cultivation also led to an abundance of spirits. Previously made from grain, they were expensive to produce and mostly considered medicine. Potatoes were not only cheaper but also needed to be used in a shorter time span because they could not be stored as well as grain. Coffee (or its surrogates) and schnapps, along with potatoes, became a part of ordinary people's meals.

SHIFTING OF POWER TOWARD PRUSSIA

The Prussian King Frederick II (Frederick the Great, 1712–1786), was one of the most ardent advocates of the potato, which his father had introduced in Brandenburg around Berlin in 1720. Brandenburg was poor in natural resources and sparsely populated after the Thirty Years' War. Thus, when the Huguenots were persecuted in France after the abolition of the Edict of Nantes in 1685,[13] Frederick the Great promised them religious freedom in Brandenburg and welcomed them to the capital Berlin as highly skilled and sophisticated inhabitants.[14] In the city's jargon, many words with French roots bear witness to the Huguenot influence even today. The famous *Buletten* (small fried meat patties) are an example. Brandenburg, with its newly acquired Kingdom of Prussia, emerged as a new power, largely based on strong will, organizational talent, and military strength. Through several wars Prussia took the rich province of Silesia from Austria, thus reinforcing the division of Germany along the river Main into a Protestant, Prussian-influenced north and a Catholic south that was culturally close to the Hapsburg emperor. In accordance with the mercantile ideas of the time, Frederick the Great encouraged and actively promoted his state's productivity to increase the tax volume (with high import taxes for anything he considered unnecessarily luxurious). For instance, the mid-1770s saw a significant increase in livestock and dairies, so-called *Holländereien* ("dutcheries"/dairies) run by Dutch and East Frisian immigrants. For tobacco cultivation Walloon colonists were called in. Tobacco smoking had first started among Dutch and English troops during the Thirty Years' War, then spread to Germany and quickly become widely popular.

NEW STRUCTURES AND THE EMERGENCE OF THE FOOD INDUSTRY

All over Germany a new class of administrative functionaries formed from the academies and universities of the numerous small states. Part noble, part bourgeois, they no longer inherited their posts but acquired them on the basis of knowledge. Tacitus' *Germania* (which reemerged in 1455 among Italian scholars in Rome) furnished the central mythos of the strong, brave, and unspoiled ancient Germans, around which national consciousness started to form slowly. A German culture developed through intellectual exchange, unified in judgment and taste, transcending the numerous inner-German national frontiers.

At the end of the eighteenth century, not only in Prussia, but all over central Europe, *Manufakturen* (workshops) for porcelain, glass, silk, wool, cotton, and linen emerged as forerunners of modern factories. Similarly, the division between urban consumers and rural, self-reliant food producers deepened. The immediate surroundings were less and less capable of catering to the needs of the rapidly growing cities.[15] Food provision started to become an industry in itself, comprising many trades other than the long-established butchers, millers, bakers, brewers, and vintners. Gradually this led to ever less food made at home and came to break up the traditional guilds.

BEGINNINGS OF THE MODERN CENTRAL STATE

Church authorities, absolute monarchy, and scholastic teachings continued to be questioned. This bourgeois-driven Enlightenment (known as the Rational Critique) culminated with the writings of the German philosopher Immanuel Kant (1724–1804), who propagated a general awakening of self-determination. The tumultuous French revolution of 1789 was at first seen as positive among German intellectuals, who regarded it as an upheaval of the old regime in favor of reason. But the violent French revolutionary period known as the Reign of Terror seemed to Germans a catastrophic failure of reason and led to a withdrawal from politics, toward romanticism. This private reverie did not last long either. Napoleon (1769–1821) soon appeared with his highly motivated, patriotic troops and made it hard for Germans to ignore the world at large. The Rhine once again became the western border of France, and the whole of Europe was soon enveloped in a war for world dominance.

Napoleonic influence led to reforms in most German states and to the widespread secularization of church property. The latter was divided among German rulers as compensation for the losses caused by the French annexations on the left side of the Rhine. The extreme territorial fragmentation was reversed: Württemberg's land area thus suddenly doubled, Baden's even tripled. Another geographic reshuffling occurred when Napoleon's troops were finally defeated by the cold of the Russian winter. Following the Congress of Vienna in 1815, Germany became composed, more or less, of the *Länder* (states) of today, although Silesia and East and West Prussia today are part of the Czech Republic and Poland, respectively, while the Saar region then belonged to France.

REGIONAL DIFFERENCES BEFORE INDUSTRIALIZATION

Food prior to industrialization depended on social standing as much as on local, natural, and economic conditions. It was profoundly structured by the seasons. Austerity alternated with abundance on festive occasions. For ordinary people breakfast consisted of gruel, often from a communal bowl, although, for example, in Berlin, it was already largely replaced by bread, mostly from rye. In the north, meat with vegetables (including a lot of cabbage, turnips, and potatoes) was the main option for hot dishes. Bread and butter were eaten with coffee or tea. In central Germany, around the lower mountain ranges and throughout most of Saxony, meat was scarce and potatoes played a very important role in daily meals, with few variations. In the south and most of Silesia, flour-based dishes dominated, enhanced by fat and cheese for the harder-working laborers. Here, meat was very rare and strictly reserved for feast days. In the south, influences from Italy were noticeable in the cuisine. Vegetables were not cooked together with meat like in the north and were also eaten raw; potatoes and coffee played a lesser role. Gradually, imported spices were replaced by local herbs such as parsley, celeriac, chives, bay leaves, juniper, caraway, thyme, lovage, and savory. Of the more exotic spices, only nutmeg, lemons, pepper, and cinnamon survived in certain recipes.[16]

FOOD DISTRIBUTION AND FREEDOM OF TRADE

Traveling peddlers sold schnapps, coffee, sugar, tobacco, cheese, and rarer varieties of fruit and vegetables throughout Germany. Grain merchants supplied the armies, extending their wares to include livestock, hops, flax, wine, and fruit, thus developing into grocers. Peasants sold surplus food at the markets of nearby towns rather than handing it over to their masters as in earlier times. In general, strict local legislation, like the *Marktbann* (market ban), regulated who could sell where and when. For instance, foreign suppliers were only allowed at fairs that took place on religious holidays. On a larger scale, towns and cities traded grain to guarantee supplies. Prices were stabilized by storing emergency reserves in municipal granaries.

Freedom of trade was decreed for the first time in Prussia in 1810, providing the basis for new structures and free exchange between the rapidly growing cities and the countryside.

Similarly, a royal *Edikt* (decree) in 1812, declared Jewish emancipation in Prussia after centuries of discrimination and limited rights. Although there were still riots against them, for instance in Würzburg (1819), in Frankfurt and Hamburg (1830), and at the onset of the revolution (1848), the Jewish population grew. Jews gained more equality in 1871, and many assimilated easily into the bourgeoisie, ascending the social ladder quickly.

POVERTY AND THE REVOLUTION OF 1848: FREEDOM FOR PEASANTS

Peasants' rights were still limited by feudal systems (although in the south rents had replaced tithes). Cooperative village systems with shared commons and compulsory systems of cultivation may have appeared as an improvement for rural farmers, but they were a hindrance for new crops such as sugar beets. Agricultural production could not keep pace with population growth, and meat was generally scarce. Most impoverished people could afford only potatoes. Among the fast-growing population and with increasing urbanization, unrest and tensions arose.

Emigration had been the solution to overpopulation before.[17] From 1820 on, millions of people went to the United States (above all Michigan, North Dakota, Nebraska, Missouri, and Ohio), South America (Uruguay

and southern Brazil), and South Australia, as well as to Namibia in the
1840s. Thus German food culture spread to distant shores. But many
could not even afford to leave in search of distant promises. The establishment attempted to relieve hunger with communal soup kitchens, milk
distribution, and so-called *Volkshallen* (people's halls). Count Rumford
developed his *Armensuppe* (poor man's soup), made from water, potatoes,
pearl barley, peas, stale white bread, salt, and vinegar or sour beer with a
nominal addition of meat.

Conservative officials tended to suppress any rebellions by force. But
failed potato crops (because of rot) in the 1840s added to the pressure and
led to social protests by desperate peasants in the southwest. Many liber-
als of the time called for a national state and a constitutional monarchy.
Their feelings circulated in choral societies and gymnastics clubs, which
held huge national festivals in the 1840s, as well as in student fraternities,
one of which furnished the black, red, and gold flag of Germany today
(these colors belonged to the Lützow volunteer corps who fought against
Napoleon). In March 1848, a revolution spread all over Germany. It
combined with the nationalist movement, and a national assembly at the
Paulskirche in Frankfurt am Main was formed. But there were too many
problems to be solved and it quickly collapsed.[18] In the end, neither the
national state nor the constitutional assembly could be agreed upon, and
the old German Alliance was restored. However, in spite of this political
turmoil, all feudal laws were abolished, and peasants were now free.

THE ONSET OF INDUSTRIALIZATION

As political unrest was quelled for the moment, the onset of industrialization was furthered by the capital flowing in from Californian and Aus-
tralian gold mines. Loans were cheap and consumer demand rose. Labor
was inexpensive, and although working conditions in the new factories
were tough, they provided a regular income for the impoverished masses.
New food industries developed, partly replacing the home production of
pasta, for instance, as well as vinegar, dairy products like quark (a fresh
white cheese somewhat similar to cottage cheese), cheese, jam, salted
meat, and dried and pickled fruit and vegetables. New products developed based on the findings of modern nutritional sciences concerning the
chemical composition of food and its role in human nutrition.

In 1823, a patent for the production of artificial mineral water was
granted, following the fashion for drinking cures among the higher classes.
In 1826 the first German sparkling wine factories were founded in Silesia
and Württemberg, and others quickly followed. In 1839 the Stollwerck

factory in Cologne started to produce sweets and chocolate, and in 1843 the first German jam factory opened in Dresden—although it was very small and catered exclusively to the cake and pastry industry. Up until the turn of the twentieth century, jam was a luxury product mostly imported from England.[19]

In an endeavor to make Prussia less dependent on imports, a method was developed to make sugar from beets, replacing expensive cane sugar. The first (albeit small) operation began in 1802 in Silesia. The Continental System (the trade embargo imposed by Napoleon against England from 1806 to 1813) spurred the development of local sugar production. The initial sugar beet factories yielded spirits and vinegar as by-products and were founded by already-existing sugar enterprises that relied on colonial cane sugar. Napoleon had heavily promoted beet sugar through tax exemptions, in 1813 prohibiting any use of colonial cane sugar in France. Given that all the land left of the Rhine was then under French government, it should not be surprising that sugar beets have competed with viticulture until today in the region of Rhenish Hessia. Whereas the French sugar beet industry flourished, the factories founded in Germany vanished after the end of the Continental System, and the industry only resurged in the 1840s.

As for milk, from 1850 on, milk-producing estates in the proximity of cities guaranteed fresh supplies, later developing into large dairies and cooperatives (of which more than 2,900 existed in 1900). After 1887, full-cream milk was pasteurized and became a mass beverage that was promoted as a healthy alternative to coffee and alcohol through distribution of milk in schools and *Milchhäuschen* (specialized milk kiosks).

FOUNDATION OF THE GERMAN STATE IN 1871

In 1866, after a successful war against Austria, the North German alliance united all of Germany north of the river Main under Prussian leadership. A customs union with the southern German states anticipated the German state of 1871. France objected to the new power structure but indirectly furthered it by fostering German national sentiment. As a result of the war of 1870–71, which France lost, Alsace and Lorraine became German once more. King William I of Prussia was declared German Kaiser in the mirrored hall of Versailles on January 18, 1871. The new German state consisted of 22 territories as well as three city-states, with Prussia and Berlin at the helm.

Science and research were promoted through the unification of existing universities and academies as well as the founding of new ones, with a special focus on natural sciences. Around this time, Germany also made a gigantic leap in industrialization. In 1840 it had been lagging 50 years behind England,[20] yet in 1914 it was the leading industrial state in Europe.[21] This was mostly due to the chemical industry, including synthetic fertilizers,[22] electrical engineering, as well as the rapid development of mechanical engineering and heavy industry. Silesia, the Ruhr, and the Saar regions became new industrial regions as coke replaced charcoal for iron production. Following the American example of mass fabrication, new industrial centers also formed around many cities, such as Berlin, Hamburg, Bremen, the Rhine-Main and the Rhine-Neckar regions, Stuttgart, Magdeburg, Leipzig, and Chemnitz.

EFFECTS OF THE INDUSTRIAL REVOLUTION

The founding of the German state in 1871 also brought a decree allowing free movement and settlement for all throughout the state. The new industries subsequently led to massive migrations during the boom of the Gründerjahre (literally, founder years, the economic boom following the founding of the German state). Historians estimate that in 1907 about 50% of the population no longer lived in their birthplace. People tended to move from east to west, and from the countryside to the cities. The agrarian world of the east, beyond the river Elbe with its large estates, was a stark contrast to the industrial west. The food habits and influences of rural and urban peoples mixed as migrants tried to assimilate to life in the quickly rising tenement houses or, if they were lucky, the "suburbs" where one had small garden plots.[23] Silesian, East-Prussian, Bohemian, and Pomeranian dishes were adapted to use foods that were available in the new surroundings.

The ever-growing demand for food was met by rising agricultural productivity through chemical fertilizers, general rationalization processes, and mechanized agriculture, as well as (in some areas) a re-parcelling of land. New food preservation methods were developed, culminating in the invention of the first refrigeration machine by Carl von Linde in 1874, thus allowing distribution over larger distances and longer time spans. The construction of railways had started in 1835; by 1880, tracks extended more than 67,000 kilometers (about 41,875 miles). This made workers more flexible. Along with ocean shipping the railways also moved raw materials and processed goods easily and over great distances. Agricultural surplus and scarcity could now be equalized faster and more easily than before. Crop failures, natural disasters, and cattle epidemics were still influencing food supplies, but they no longer had such devastating effects as in the 1840s.

Telegraph communication and the rapidly growing banking system added to commercial flexibility. More food and a wider selection were available for a larger part of the population than ever before. But these new possibilities and the growing dependence on food imports also had their disadvantages. Low prices abroad, for instance for grain imported from the Midwest in the United States, threatened the interests of German producers. They forced the government to introduce protective duties in 1879. This resulted in a significant rise in food prices. An intense public debate began to rage between unhindered economic growth and industrialization on the one hand (depending on imports), and the call for a minimum level of agricultural self-reliance on the other.

In 1879 state regulations for basic food items such as milk, beer, and meat were introduced to maintain a minimum quality. These were the precursors of the modern food regulation system of the European Union. Communal slaughterhouses, the gradual prohibition of private slaughtering,[24] and decrees requiring meat inspection increased meat safety. Inspection for *trichinae* (trichinosis) in pork became obligatory by state law in 1902. Once again, health and nutrition became a general focus of attention, as they had been during the Renaissance. Now Galen's holistic system was replaced by modern science; instead of balancing humors and temperaments, one measured vitamins and calories. Special diets for infants, the infirm, and the elderly were based on new nutritional knowledge. Mass catering for the army, prisons, and large institutions also improved.

Urbanization and industrialization developed their own dynamics. Working times in the factories were dictated by machines and efficiency rather than sun cycles, and most women were now part of the labor force. City dwellings did not offer much in the way of food storage space and there was little time or space for a garden; therefore, new food products and distribution methods were developed. Many of those new products started as army or ship provisions. Canning was first used for luxury goods such as peaches or asparagus but gradually extended to pickles, basic fruit and vegetables, fish, and meat. Beginning with Justus Liebig's meat extract (which transformed the abundant cattle of the South American plains into an easily transportable concentrate), soups in powdered or cube form were developed for mass consumption. Eventually these bouillons were made from nonmeat ingredients as well. The *Erbswurst* (pea sausage) still available today was invented by the Berlin chef Grünberg as part of the soldiers' "iron ration" in the war against France in 1870–71. It consists of a mix of ground peas, bacon, and seasoning, which is dried and pressed into sausage shape and can then easily be diluted in boiling water to make a soup.

Workers demanded food that was quick to prepare, affordable, and easy to digest but that also offered a stimulating change from the monotony of work. *Maggiwürze* (liquid seasoning), baking powder, and *Haferflocken* (rolled oats) were developed to make cooking easier and faster. While away from home, they ate sandwiches, made with white bread and sold through street vendors and vending machines. According to the vision of August Bebel (1840–1913), cofounder of the Social Democratic Workers' Party, individual private kitchens were a waste of time and energy altogether and were to be replaced by large communal ones instead.

In cities, it became more and more normal to shop at grocers instead of the traditional markets. These grocery stores often specialized in milk, coffee, or tobacco and sometimes formed franchises throughout the city. Certain branches created their own retail businesses, especially dairies and coffee roasters, whereas others diversified. All these stores are the precursors of modern supermarkets (which were firmly established after World War II). However, street vendors were still part of the provision system. In large cities markets took the form of large halls instead of the traditional open-air markets. From the 1880s on, larger German cities also had central market halls for wholesalers similar to *Les Halles* in Paris. Thanks to railway connections and refrigeration, the most perishable goods were available. Advertising gradually replaced bartering and market cries, above all for new products like margarine (the first German margarine factory was founded in 1874) and luxury products. Food slowly underwent a process of democratization, which could be seen as a precursor of the globalization of today. With the exception of economic crises and times of war, the average percentage of the disposable income spent on food decreased steadily after the onset of industrialization.

SOCIALISM AND NUTRITIONAL AWARENESS

As agriculture became ever more commercialized and processed products were redistributed from the cities, the old agrarian social structure was replaced by an urban, modern industrial one that separated the working class from the middle classes. Chancellor Otto von Bismarck (1815–98) from 1880 on gradually introduced the first state social insurance program, thus creating the base of the German social state, or *Vater Staat* (father state). However, very few of the younger members of the population felt like a part of that state, and they were looking for alternatives to their parents' beliefs. The predominant feeling in the youth culture was one of rootlessness, interchangeability, the loss of norms, and social atomization.

Socialism developed in reaction against patriotic *Vaterland* conserva-
tism, and within the larger rubric of socialism a movement formed that had
its roots in the new nutritional awareness. The *Lebensreform* (life reform)
movement, whose early beginnings started in the 1860s, could be sum-
marized under the slogan "back to the purity of nature." Vegetarianism;
temperance (or abstinence) from coffee, tobacco, and/or alcohol; antivac-
cination clubs; idealization of raw food; *Freikörperkultur* or *FKK* (nudism);
scout and hiking clubs; and many more facets (some of them recalling
medieval beliefs, many sounding familiar to modern ears) combined with
various political, cultural, and social ideas as well as myths.[25] The roots
of the green movement today can be traced back to *Lebensreform*. The
anthroposophic philosopher Rudolf Steiner with his *Landwirtschaftlicher
Kurs* (a lecture given to landowners in 1924 in Silesian Kobernitz near
Breslau, today Polish Wroclaw) developed the base of biodynamic agriculture, which has currently witnessed a strong revival. *Reformhäuser* (reform houses) opened and still exist today, in the same vein as the organic
stores. These shops specialized in "whole food," such as the new *Steinmetzbrot* (a special kind of whole-grain bread), or *Kneippkaffee*, a coffee
surrogate made from barley malt that was promoted by the Catholic priest
Sebastian Kneipp (1821–79), who also developed hydropathic treatments
that included walking barefoot on wet meadows.[26] *Sinalco* ("without alcohol"), a citrus lemonade still available today, was developed at that time
(the factory was founded in 1908) to tap into the growing market for
nonalcoholic alternatives to beer and schnapps.

FOREIGN POLITICS, COLONIES, AND WORLD WAR I

Wilhelminismus, named after William II (1859–1941), combined an economic boom with nationalism and originally appeared to be a benign development. German wines, mostly Riesling from the Moselle and Rhine
areas, were among the most expensive wines in the world, next to the famous châteaus from Bordeaux. Royal German cuisine sought to match
their ostentatious French neighbors. For example, Julius Féher, purveyor
of delicacies to the imperial court in Berlin, offered grilled kangaroo tail.
But William II, who took the throne in 1888, was a much less modest
man than his grandfather William I, and German world politics gradually
became more aggressive, leading to political isolation. *Wilhelminismus* had
a cultural interest in food nationalism as well. Calls to Germanize French
and English cooking terminology made themselves heard: sauce was to
be *Tunke*, casserole *Kochtopf*, and beefsteak *Rindsstück*; dictionaries were
published for this purpose.[27] Inner fragmentation resulting from social,

religious, and old territorial divides was hidden under the pompous, neo-baroque façade of this period.

As with many historical developments, Germany was late to the table with colonization, and most of the world had already been split up by the time it arrived. A fleet was built, mainly to protect the sea trade, on the initiative of its most ardent advocate, Admiral von Tirpitz, minister of naval affairs. The *Sektsteuer* (sparkling wine tax) was introduced in 1909 to finance the fleet; it is still levied today: one euro for each 750-ml bottle.

Some distant regions that were already in the possession of German merchants became German state protectorates: German Southwest Africa (today Namibia), New Guinea, German East Africa (today Tanzania, Burundi, and Rwanda), Togo, Cameroon, Samoa, and some other small Pacific islands, as well as Kiautschou (Jiaozhou) on the eastern Chinese coast. Conflicts with the indigenous population led to brutal genocides, especially in Africa. In 1919, the League of Nations undertook the decolonization of the German territories. The impact of these colonies on German foodways was minimal compared with that of England or France.

In July 1914, the assassination of the Austrian heir to the throne in Sarajevo was the trigger for long-smoldering conflicts to erupt into war. The German people saw this as an excuse to unite against an enemy, in spite of all internal conflicts. But what they hoped would be a quick and easy war, like the one in 1870–71, turned out to be miserably long, fatally misjudged, and ill conceived, and, with U.S. involvement in 1917, a war of world scope. Germany had never taken seriously the possibility of a British sea blockade. But as the scale of World War I increased, this hitherto unimagined possibility became a reality. Germany depended on imports for half of its needs in dairy products, a third of its eggs, the majority of its fat, and, most important, concentrated cattle fodder and fertilizer. In spite of increasingly severe rationing of all basic staples, and from 1916 on complete government control of food production and distribution, hunger reached all social classes. Its ravages were even more deeply felt when the much-longed-for potato crop of 1916 failed because of rot. The following winter went down in history as the *Rübenwinter* (rutabaga winter). Rutabagas (swedes) so far had been regarded as cattle feed, and relying on them for survival represented a severe blow to German morale. Even so there was too little to go around. Every available space (including balconies) was used to grow food. All kinds of *Ersatz* (substitute) food had to be eaten to survive, including weeds and beechnuts. After the end of World War I in 1918, the Allied forces worked out a territorial plan—Alsace and Lorraine once more returned to France—as well as severe financial reparations; a treaty was signed, again, in Versailles.

William II resigned and left for Holland, thus making room for parliamentary democracy.

THE WEIMAR REPUBLIC AND THE GOLDEN TWENTIES

However, the new Weimar Republic experienced rebellions and revolutions that never completely desisted; right from the start it had no sound basis.

Because Germany seemed reluctant to pay the reparations exacted following World War I, Belgian and French troops invaded the Ruhr region and took control of its steel plants in 1923. The ensuing inflation threatened to break up the German state. Luckily, calm returned with the introduction of a new currency, the *Rentenmark*, and economic recovery set in, mainly supported by exports. But the newly introduced eight-hour workday made German industry less flexible, and unemployment was higher than in the worst years before World War I. The so-called Golden Twenties constituted above all a cultural upswing for artists and the film industry. These glamorous enterprises set the tone for German society now that bourgeois self-esteem was low following the war. The Golden Twenties had no cultural principles to speak of, nor were they based on any of the old social standards. Nostalgic German emigrants in Prague and Paris, and as far away as New York and California, in their reports transformed the large glittering restaurants and lavish parties of the 1920s into the mythic height of German elegance. Despite its reputation for frivolity, the period was marked by extreme reaction on the one hand and enormous technical and scientific progress on the other.

BLACK FRIDAY, THE RISE OF THE NAZI PARTY, AND WORLD WAR II

The bourgeois middle class was adrift in a sea of change and felt itself in a continual crisis. With Black Friday, the crash of the New York Stock Exchange (October 25, 1929), came the first world economic crisis and unemployment soared even higher. The rising National Socialist Party knew how to exploit people's fears and uncertainties for its own ends. In 1933, Adolf Hitler, the head of the National Socialist Party, became state chancellor and started to make his maniacal vision of a larger, united Germanic state come true. Anything and anyone who did not fit his notion of what a true German should be had to leave or was killed. He declared that the Germanic race needed *Lebensraum* (space to live), so the Reich—the third empire, after the Holy Roman Empire and the *Kaiserreich* of William I—was to be expanded at all costs to provide this space. Besides the enlargement of the German territory by force, land alteration projects also included *Landeskulturmassnahmen* (programs to create new or more usable land from swamps or along the coast). The economy was built up with the goal of self-sufficiency, which in terms of food, for instance, included heavy promotion of the fish industry. From 1936 on Germany even revived its whaling industry, with whale fat also being used for margarine production. Fish was also deep-frozen in factories erected in Denmark and Norway. *Vollkornbrot* (whole-grain bread) was heavily promoted. It not only kept longer than white bread but was also seen as healthier. The average citizen was convinced of the Third Reich's progress by the creation of new jobs (for instance, by the building of the *Autobahn* [highway], although the project itself had been conceived before Nazi involvement) or the *Kraft durch Freude* (power through joy) holiday program. The Olympic Games staged in 1936 in Berlin were exemplary for their seducing mix of extreme modernity and heavy traditionalism (that often lacked deeper historic roots). The whole state and its population were forced into line. Everyday life was organized in an increasingly militaristic, centralist way, and the federal structure of the German *Länder* (states) was replaced by *Gaue* (districts), reviving an older term and installing a centralist structure.

In line with centuries-old European discrimination practices, Jews were proclaimed as the general enemy and scapegoats in Hitler's political doctrine. Gradually, they were stigmatized, expropriated, and persecuted, and those who could or would not leave were deported, tortured, and killed. Along with them, a world of wit and wisdom, as well as a cuisine that was once part of German culture, vanished. Other than in the United Kingdom or the United States, Jewish food until today is virtually nonexistent in German grocery stores and supermarkets.

World War II began with the invasion of Poland in 1939, expanded throughout Europe, then into the north of Africa. At first, German troops had successes on all sides. Food supply had been well planned this time: the conquered territories were forced to feed the Germans. Rationing at home was well in place beginning in 1939. *Eintopf-Sonntage* (stew Sundays) were a general appeal to eat stew for Sunday dinner in order to save food and combined with other campaigns of the same kind to reinforce the feelings of communal war efforts. Hunger really only set in after the surrender of Hitler's troops in 1945.

HUNGER AND RUINS

Most German cities had been reduced to ruins by Allied bombs, and innumerable refugees were streaming in from the east, many fleeing from the Red Army, which had a reputation for merciless brutality. The refugees mostly came from former German regions of East Prussia, Pomerania, and Silesia, as well as the Sudetenland, Hungary, Romania, Yugoslavia, and Poland. A national census in 1950 showed that 16.6% of the population, that is, 9.6 million people, were refugees. Most of them were resettled in the rural areas of Bavaria, Lower Saxony, and Schleswig-Holstein. However, the so-called *Siedlungen* (literally, settlements) at the edge of many towns in Baden-Württemberg also date back to the resettling of *Siedler* (settlers) there. Many German refugees from eastern countries had been strangers in the places they came from and became strangers once again.

It has been calculated that average food rations in the immediate postwar period were between one- and two-thirds below the hunger limit. At the same time, labor was more intense; the *Trümmerfrauen* (literally, rubble women) worked hard with little food, clearing away the rubble from the bombed-out buildings. Epidemics raged as well as criminality, and the particularly cold winter of 1946–47 claimed many lives. There was little on offer in terms of food, but a lot of money around, so inflation reigned supreme on the black market. American cigarettes were as highly valued as any currency, as were the contents of parcels sent by the Cooperative for American Remittances to Europe (CARE). CARE was mainly a privately funded aid organization seeking to relieve suffering and hunger in Europe following World War II. The CARE packets were sent from 1946 on and contained preserved meat and fat, tinned and dried fruit, honey, chocolate, sugar, powdered eggs and milk, and coffee. The equivalent package in the Soviet zone was the *Stalin-Paket* (Stalin parcel). Rampant hunger meant that every available piece of land was once again used for growing food. Park trees were felled for firewood, and all sorts of seemingly impossible things were (out of necessity) transformed into cookware to replace items that had been lost, stolen, or burned during the war.

OCCUPATION, RESTRUCTURING, AIRLIFTS, AND THE SPLIT BETWEEN EAST AND WEST GERMANY

A widespread reorganization took place once more throughout Germany. The federal structure of the *Länder* (states) was restored, and the result was once again the familiar map of today, with Poland extending to the rivers Oder and Neisse, and Alsace and Lorraine part of France (the Saar region however stayed under French control until a plebiscite in 1956; only after that did it join the German *Länder*). The Allied forces— the United States, the United Kingdom, France, and the Soviet Union— divided Germany into four occupation zones, with a special status placed on the former capital Berlin, which was situated in the Soviet zone but was divided into four separate Allied zones. A crucial turning point in the restructuring process was the currency reform introduced in 1948 by the Western Allied forces in the Western zones, including Berlin. In combination with the official abolition of rationing and price controls, it made for a sudden end to the black market. The Soviets' response, however, was to mount a complete blockade of Berlin, whereupon 1.5 tons of food, coal, and building materials were flown in by the planes of the Western Allies, an act that also represented their refusal to give up "their" part of Berlin. During the *Luftbrücke* (airlift) between June 1948 and May 1949, the so-called *Rosinenbomber* (raisin bombers) landed every two or three minutes.

In the Western zones, the U.S.-organized Marshall Plan (or European recovery program) helped the economy to recover from 1948 on, by means of loans and gifts of food as well as raw materials. The political divide between the East and West deepened. In May 1949 the *Bundesrepublik Deutschland* (Federal Republic of Germany) was founded, consisting of the Western zones with the government headquarters located in Bonn. This was followed by the declaration of the *Deutsche Demokratische Republik* (German Democratic Republic) in October 1949, which comprised the Soviet zone and set up its headquarters in the eastern part of Berlin. Both were limited in their sovereignty and explicitly temporary, the ultimate goal on both sides then being a unified Germany.

WEST GERMANY: POSTWAR TIMES AND *WIRTSCHAFTSWUNDER* (ECONOMIC MIRACLE)

In 1949 mass unemployment still held sway. But the worldwide economic boom in the following years also included West Germany. Food rationing was abolished in 1950, and a social state formed with the belief in never-ending economic growth. However, the Bonn republic was sensible and sober, consciously the opposite of Weimar and other historic precedents. With backing from the United States, West Germany gained international credibility. It was made a NATO member in 1955 and was included in the economic communities that were the precursors of the modern European Union. The integration of refugees, including those from East Germany, was helped along by the *Wirtschaftswunder* (economic miracle) under Ludwig Erhard (1891–1977), minister of trade and commerce. The main political slogans of the time were "*Wohlstand für alle*" (prosperity for all) and "*keine Experimente*" (no experiments). People in general longed for normalcy instead of political daring, and retired to their private homes.

Several waves of food consumption set in after restructuring was under way. The first and most pronounced was the *Fresswelle* (wave of gluttony) in the 1950s. The definite end of the hunger period was celebrated with unrestrained indulgence in cream, butter, alcohol, and meat. Between 1950 and 1960, the consumption of pork in West Germany rose from 19 to almost 30 kilograms (41.89 and 66.1 lb., respectively) per person annually; consumption of poultry tripled, whereas potatoes fell from 184 to 132 kilograms (405.65 to 291 lb.).[28] However, meal structures seem not to have changed significantly as compared to before the war. This wave of gluttony was followed by a less decadent wave with an emphasis on house and home, then came travel, above all bringing German tourists to Italian beaches and leading to a vast increase in the consumption of Italian food in Germany. Finally, health became the priority, and today, restraint seems to be back on the menu.

Since the end of the nineteenth century, Italian ice-cream makers, mainly from the region of the Dolomites, had been a feature of all major cities during summers, but during the 1950s and 1960s many of them moved to Germany for good. Tourism not only created a demand for *wurstel con kraut* (sausage with sauerkraut) along the Italian coastline, it also widened the German culinary repertoire back home with pasta, pizza, and the like—although often in Germanized versions. The first pizzeria, Sabbie di Capri, opened in Würzburg in 1952. Beyond Italian food, the longing for distant shores expressed itself in an internationalization of dishes and recipes of the "Toast Hawaii" variety. This consists of a toasted, buttered slice of white bread topped with boiled ham, a slice of canned pineapple and cheese, all of it then passed under the broiler and often decorated with a bright red cocktail cherry or a dollop of ketchup. It is exemplary for the pseudo-international cooking-style that reigned high at that time.

With growing general prosperity, *Gastarbeiter* (guest workers)[29] were recruited through state agencies, mostly for lower-paying jobs in mining and the car industry. They first came from Italy in 1955, but guest worker visas quickly extended to many more of the less industrialized Mediterranean states: Spain, Portugal, Greece, Yugoslavia, and Turkey. This scheme had been planned as a temporary solution, with workers to be replaced in a rotation system. But as industry requested more experienced laborers, many of them were soon joined by their families. By the 1970s, more than 5 million foreign workers had moved permanently to West Germany, making it a de facto immigration country, although this was only acknowledged officially at the end of the 1990s. Berlin, for instance, is the second-largest Turkish city after Istanbul, with its own Turkish open-air markets and grocery stores.[30]

Among younger West German intellectuals of the 1960s, the perceived pragmatism, apparent cultural stagnation, and ignorance of the Nazi past of older generations led to a wave of antifascism.[31] Civil war–like riots spearheaded by students in 1968 and the violent actions of the terrorist association *Rote-Armee-Fraktion* (Red Army Faction) shook the nation until the end of the 1970s. The oil crisis of 1973 further shattered the belief in never-ending economic growth, progress, and technology that had been generally accepted since the beginning of the 1960s. Refrigerators (and increasingly freezers) were a standard feature in private kitchens, and supermarkets outnumbered traditional grocers. Especially in cities and among students *Wohngemeinschaften* (groups sharing an apartment) or *Kommunen* (communes) superseded patriarchal family structures. Accordingly meals changed: one-pot dishes and spaghetti became favorites. The journalist Wolfram Siebeck wrote his first articles on food in a magazine called *Twen* (1958), laying the basis for a modern, quality-conscious food culture. In 1971, Eckart Witzigmann started to work at the restaurant Tantris in Munich and in 1979 went on to become Germany's first chef with three Michelin stars.

LIFE IN EAST GERMANY AND THE WALL

In East Germany, food was just as important to people as in the West, but supplies were patchy and uneven. Inadequate distribution methods worsened these unreliable offerings. Ironically, legend has it that the Socialist United Party (SED) was founded at Borchardt, a delicatessen cum restaurant and ex-purveyor to the court, still more or less intact in 1946 (and today once again a meeting place for the political establishment). The whole country was divided into centralized administrative districts. A planned economy, collectivism, and a ministry of state security (complete with an extended system of informers, spies, and snoops) were introduced to mimic the Soviet model. The government set extremely high production goals so as to be totally self-sufficient and free of all imports, but neglected consumer goods and the quality of daily life. Growing discontent led to the revolt of June 17, 1953, which was put down by Soviet tanks. After 1.65 million people had voted with their feet and left the "Workers' and Peasants' State" for good, on August 13, 1961, the Berlin Wall was built, strictly and abruptly dividing East and West. Families and friends were separated, as visits from West to East became possible only after some years and under strict conditions.

The socialist economic system, however, did not work any better with the wall in place. Queuing was a fact of life for anybody not among the small political elite who indulged in luxuries imported with foreign currencies that East Germany was notoriously short in. The Central Committee theoretically understood how important food was in order to keep everybody happy. Rarely, however, plans were as successful like the invention of the *Goldbroiler*, a chain of diners selling grilled chicken, and they were not enough to offset the general lack of quality food and the disillusionment with life in general. There was no shortage in calories and basic staples, but one could not be picky. Buying whatever was available, out of sheer frustration and possibly exchanging with neighbors or friends later on, became normal. Berlin as the capital was much better supplied than the rest of the country, but even here only good connections with notoriously unfriendly sales people paved the way to the *Bückware* (bending ware), merchandise that never made it onto the shelves and was instead kept under the counter for favored customers. Special shops, *Delikatläden*, offered better-quality chocolate, coffee, and specialties if one had *Deutschmark*, which many people were given by West German relatives from the other side of the wall, just as Christmas food packets from "the West" were part of life for many. Restaurants played by the same rules: waiters were surly at best, rude at worst. Restaurant offerings were very limited and unpredictable, although typically some sort of *Soljanka* soup and something with *Letscho* was available although those often were very liberal variations on the Eastern European originals.[32] Again, somewhat better service and food were available in special restaurants in exchange for Western currency.

East German cookbooks were as inventive and international in their creations as in the West, although the actual dishes people consumed were just as pedestrian. Cooking was a necessity more than a source of fulfillment, and hearty, down-to-earth food was generally preferred. East German wine was extremely hard to come by and unreliable in quality. Imports from Bulgaria and Romania (*Rosenthaler Kadarka*, *Stierblut*) were also rare and very sought after, whereas beer and spirits were plentiful and widely consumed.

REUNIFICATION AND A NEW NORMALCY

Beginning with the Solidarity movement in Poland (founded in 1980), a new political era dawned. From 1985 on, Mikhail Gorbachev in the Soviet Union started perestroika reforms. In May 1989 the border between Austria and Hungary opened. Beginning in October 1989, marches took place each Monday in Dresden, Berlin, and Leipzig, with protesters chanting "We are one people." On November 9, 1989, the wall fell. On October 3, 1990 (since then *Tag der deutschen Einheit* [German unity day] and a public holiday), Germany was reunified with Berlin as the capital. Federalism was restored with the five new *Länder* of Mecklenburg-Vorpommern (Mecklenburg-West Pomerania), Brandenburg, Sachsen-Anhalt (Saxony-Anhalt), Thüringen (Thuringia), and Sachsen (Saxony) joining the formerly West German states of Schleswig-Holstein, Hamburg, Bremen, Niedersachsen (Lower Saxony), Nordrhein-Westfalen (North Rhine-Westphalia), Hessen (Hessia), Rheinland-Pfalz (Rhineland-Palatinate), Saarland (the Saar), Baden-Württemberg, Bayern (Bavaria), and Berlin.

Chancellor Helmut Kohl, known as *"Kanzler der Einheit"* (the unity chancellor) promised *"blühende Landschaften"* (flowering landscapes) in the east. But equalizing living standards has proved to be a much more lengthy, difficult, and expensive process than hoped. Reunification coincided with the first economic depression of postwar times in Germany. It hit most people as a shock and became psychologically connected to the falling of the wall. This resulted in a long, moody low for the collective German temperament. Once again significant internal migrations took place, mostly from East to West, for reasons of employment and general standard of life. Identity problems had to be dealt with. The initial inebriation that East Germans felt about all the products of the West, so long familiar from television and now finally available, led to many East German products disappearing. With privatizations taking place, an "Ostalgia" (nostalgia for the East) arose within the psychologically displaced population. Thus, after reunification, Spreewald pickles came to international fame with the film *Goodbye Lenin*.

In 2002 the introduction of the euro, the currency of most of the European Union, was felt as another economic obstacle for Germany. It took until 2006 with the election of chancellor Angela Merkel, a scientist from former "East" Mecklenburg, for the economy to pick up again and the mood to normalize. Recently, depopulation of the East seems to have halted; normalization is setting in there, too, at least to a certain degree.

Italian, Spanish, and Turkish ethnic food shops and restaurants have been joined by Thai, Vietnamese, and lately Polish and Russian ones. At the same time, a growing interest in regional and artisanal food products and cuisines has developed as a countertrend to the ubiquitous international brands and chains of globalization helped along by European common standards as well as the influence of the large discounters.[33] This new sensitivity about food production could well be seen as another sign of normalization in Germans' feelings about their own identity. German wines have overcome the stigma of their nationality as well as the industrialization in the 1960s of erstwhile successes like *Liebfraumilch*. A new generation of winegrowers is focusing on *terroir*, the wines' origin in the vineyard.

However, this new approach to food also results from health scares. The agricultural crisis following the outbreak of bovine spongiform encephalopathy (BSE) in Germany led to a significant strengthening of the green movement. The political party *Die Grünen* (today *Bündnis 90/Die Grünen*) had formed in 1980 out of numerous citizens' groups, women's groups, and peace movements. In many ways, it can be traced back to the nature-dominated ideologies of the *Lebensreform* movement a century ago. In 2001, the Green Renate Künast replaced her socialist, but nevertheless conservative, predecessor as federal minister for nutrition, agriculture, and forestry, thus marking a turning point in German agricultural politics. The first woman on this post in history, she put the consumer first and made transparency and organic methods in agriculture one of her priorities. Organic grocers, farm shops, and supermarkets are flourishing. Although Künast herself had to leave in 2005 because of the political shift in government, the new name of her post remains: the Ministry for Consumer Protection, Nutrition, and Agriculture. Germans spent only 13.9% of their income on food in 2003, but it is partly thanks to Künast's efforts that the value and importance of food has increased at least among the higher-ranking social groups.

NOTES

1. With regard to wine in Germany after the Roman period, Phyllis Pray Bober points out that the alleged slow destruction of vineyards that had been fostered by classical civilization is unfounded, but that winemaking certainly transferred from the large estates to small landowners, nobles, and monks in the developing monastic communities, all for private and local consumption. Phyllis Pray Bober, *Art, Culture, and Cuisine: Ancient and Medieval Gastronomy* (Chicago: University of Chicago Press, 1999), 195–96.

2. Bober, *Art, Culture, and Cuisine*, 208, 213–14.

3. How far those bans were observed even in monasteries is a matter of discussion among historians, who speculate that a church decree exempting eggs and milk from that rule in 1491 might have sanctioned an already-existing practice.

4. The word *Deutschland* (Germany) did not appear until the fifteenth century, but *diutsch/deutsch* (German) developed in the eleventh century from the Latin *theodiscus* to refer to the popular languages spoken by the common person on the street, such as Alemannic, Old Saxon, or Bavarian, as opposed to scholarly Latin and Slavic or Romance languages. The *deutsche Länder* (German countries) were the countries with similar popular languages. There was no connection with

the pejorative *teutonic,* which originated in the Italians' contempt for the Germanic barbarians.

5. Accordingly eggs were abundant. Linguistically, an egg stood for "a nothing." Hans Wiswe, *Kulturgeschichte der Kochkunst: Kochbücher und Rezepte aus zwei Jahrtausenden mit einem lexikalischen Anhang zur Fachsprache von Eva Hepp* (Munich: Moos, 1970), 77.

6. The abundant use of spices, their medical significance, and their symbolism as originating from distant, legendary countries equivalent to paradise on earth have been discussed extensively elsewhere.

7. Like all over Europe, blancmange made from almond milk was popular among all who could afford that luxury dish. According to Melitta Weiss Adamson it is first mentioned in a German text around 1300. Melitta Weiss Adamson, *Daz buch von guter spise (The Book of Good Food): A Study, Edition, and English Translation of the Oldest German Cookbook* (Krems, 2000), 29.

8. Decline set in with increasing piracy in the fifteenth century (the most famous pirate was Klaus Störtebecker) and the Thirty Years' War. The last official Hansa members' gathering took place in 1669, but up to the present a number of those German cities call themselves *Hansestadt.*

9. That may be changing with the advancing effects of global warming, however. The German wine regions in 2004 have been enlarged by the region of Stargarder Land in Mecklenburg-West Pomerania, north of Berlin.

10. Ken Albala counts 150 mentions of buckwheat in Sebizius. Ken Albala, *Eating Right in the Renaissance* (Berkeley: University of California Press, 2002), 281.

11. Günter Wiegelmann, *Alltags- und Festspeisen in Mitteleuropa: Innovationen, Strukturen und Regionen vom späten Mittelalter bis zum 20. Jahrhundert,* 2nd ed., with Barbara Krug-Richter (Münster: Waxmann, 2006), 28.

12. On the subject of table manners see the work of the German sociologist Norbert Elias (1897–1990), above all *Über das Verhalten beim Essen,* first published in 1939. Norbert Elias, *Über das Verhalten beim Essen in Gesammelte Schriften* vol 3.1 *Wandlungen des Verhaltens in den weltlichen Oberschichten des Abendlandes* (Frankfurt am Main: Suhrkamp, 1997), 202–65.

13. They were not the only ones suffering that fate; wide migrations took place at that time. Württemberg, Holland, Switzerland, England, and Russia welcomed Huguenots, whereas Protestants from Salzburg (1731–32) migrated to southern Germany, East Prussia, Holland, Hanover, and Georgia (United States). Other religious groups suffering persecution included the Bohemian Brethren, Hutterites, Calvinists, and Mennonites.

14. However, at the beginning of the nineteenth century the Swiss French writer Madame de Staël (1766–1817) still complained about the lack of *joie de vivre* in Berlin, where everything seemed to be rational and organized in a military way. Germaine de Staël, *De l'Allemagne* (Paris: Garnier-Flammarion, 1968).

15. In 1768 more than 90% of the wheat and rye bread consumed in Berlin was made by bakers; home-baked bread was already the exception. Karl-Peter

Ellerbrock, *Geschichte der deutschen Nahrungs- und Genußmittelindustrie 1750–1914* (Stuttgart: Franz Steiner, 1993), 65.

16. Hans Jürgen Teuteberg, ed., *Die Revolution am Eßtisch: Neue Studien zur Nahrungskultur im 19./20. Jahrhundert* (Stuttgart: Franz Steiner, 2004), 117–18.

17. Migration mainly occurred from the south of Germany to eastern Europe and beyond: Volga Germans in 1762–63; to Hungary, Siebenbürgen, and areas on the Black Sea in 1804–24.

18. Schleswig was part of Denmark but wanted to become German. Poland had been divided between Prussia, Russia, and Austria and had to be re-formed as a nation. South Tyroleans felt themselves to be German but were presently of Italian nationality.

19. Ironically, the English jam industry of the time mostly used fruit imported from Germany. Ellerbrock, *Geschichte der deutschen Nahrungs- und Genußmittelindustrie*, 368–69.

20. For example, the German production of pig iron in 1840 corresponded to the English production in 1780.

21. Ellerbrock points out the dominant position of the food industry among the German joint-stock companies in 1889, at the height of the *Gründerboom*, with on average the highest dividends (*Geschichte der deutschen Nahrungs- und Genußmittelindustrie*, 283).

22. The first German factory for chemical fertilizer was founded in 1855.

23. The *Schrebergärten* (allotments/community garden plots) in and around German cities were originally for food production but nowadays are mostly used as recreational retreats.

24. According to Teuteberg, until 1870 significant numbers of livestock were still kept in the cities. For him this is also the turning point for the mercantilization of food. Hans Jürgen Teuteberg, "Studien zur Volksernährung unter sozial- und wirtschaftsgeschichtlichen Aspekten," in *Nahrungsgewohnheiten in der Industrialisierung des 19. Jahrhunderts*, ed. Hans Jürgen Teuteberg and Günter Wiegelmann (Münster: Lit Verlag, 2005), 13–210.

25. Some points were well founded, though: For instance, from the beginnings of the modern food industry, artificial coloring was used. Karl-Peter Ellerbrock, *Lebensmittelqualität vor dem Ersten Weltkrieg: Industrielle Produktion und staatliche Gesundheitspolitik* in Hans Jürgen Teuteberg, ed., *Durchbruch zum modernen Massenkonsum: Lebensmittelmärkte und Lebensmittelqualität im Städtewachstum des Industriezeitalters* (Münster: Coppenrath, 1987), 127–88.

26. About reform cooking see also Ursula Heinzelmann, "Children's Cookery Books: Nurturing Adults' Ideas about Society," in *Proceedings of the Oxford Symposium on Food and Cookery*, edited by Richard Hosking (Bristol: Footwork, 2004), 112–23.

27. This continued until the end of World War II. For instance, Coca-Cola invented the brand Fanta, a new orange lemonade, deriving its name from *Fantasia*, to avoid the economic effects of anti-American tendencies during the Nazi era.

28. Hans Jürgen Teuteberg, quoted in Gunther Hirschfelder, *Europäische Es-skultur: Geschichte der Ernährung von der Steinzeit bis heute* (Frankfurt am Main: Campus, 2001), 242.

29. Nowadays this term is considered derogatory, the correct one being *ausländische Arbeitnehmer* (foreign workers).

30. In East Germany, foreign workers were recruited mainly from Vietnam, Cuba, Mozambique, Poland, and Angola. They were not expected to integrate and definitely had to return after five years.

31. That generation has commonly been christened the *Alt-68er*, who championed very liberal and antiauthoritarian methods in education and favored Provence as their Shangri-La—although with age and increasingly bourgeois attitudes they went on to become the *Toskana-Fraktion*, joining, for instance, British Prime Minister Tony Blair in Chiantishire.

32. *Soljanka* originated as a Russian/Ukrainian soup made with pickled mushrooms, cucumbers or vegetables, tomato, lemon, and sour cream. Hungarian *Letscho* is a spicy dish of bell peppers, tomato and onions somewhat in the style of an Italian Peperonata.

33. The German Slow Food movement tries to save and revive traditional regional food products (www.slowfood.de).

2

Major Foods and Ingredients

HOME PRODUCTION AND SHOPPING

The natural conditions for agriculture in Germany are good: of the 137,838 square miles (slightly less than the area of Montana), more than half is agricultural land. Soil quality varies considerably from very light sand, fertile loess, and loam to heavy clay of differing depths. Broadly speaking, soil conditions are better in the south than in the north. Further diversity comes with climatic variation: Germany is situated in a temperate zone, stretching almost 500 miles from north (55°N) to south (47°N) and about 370 miles from west (6°E) to east (15°E). The maritime influence of the gulf stream diminishes toward the east; that means gradually less precipitation, more hours of sunshine, and more marked temperature differences between summer and winter. The differences in altitude throughout the country are vast as well. Lowland plains characterize the north. Ranges of moderately high mountains mark the center, with the higher Alps and their foothills to the south. The Rhine region is a wide rift valley in the southwest along the eastern side of the French Vosges mountain range.

Although grain is the most common crop, the geographic diversity of Germany traditionally makes for highly specialized agriculture: cattle in the north and the Alps, asparagus in light soils around Schwetzingen in Baden or Beelitz near Berlin, apple trees on the elevated shores of Lake Constance and in the *Altes Land* (old country) near Hamburg. Cherry trees are rampant near Ingelheim along the Selz Valley (a tributary of the Rhine), and wide lettuce and vegetable fields dominate the fertile Rhine valley west of Mannheim. Cabbage is grown around Stuttgart as well as Bremen and Hamburg and in the Dithmarschen region further north.

Nevertheless, Germany is no agricultural idyll—with more than 81 million inhabitants it is densely populated, thoroughly urbanized (72% of Germans live in towns of more than 10,000 inhabitants, 32% in large cities of more than 100,000), and heavily industrialized. Although the general standard of living is high, differences in income are rising steadily. Competition is steep because of the European single market as well as imports from non–European Union countries.[1] With strong trade unions, labor is expensive and, in spite of high unemployment, difficult to find (today, viticulture and asparagus cultivation, for instance, would be unthinkable without foreign workers from Poland and Russia), which leads to further attempts to increase efficiency through concentration, mechanization, and rationalization.

In addition, the concentration of food retailers (increasingly spilling over national borders) takes its toll in Germany just as it does in the United Kingdom or the United States. A small number of stores and chains demand ever-higher levels of availability, hygiene, flexibility, and extended shelf life for the food they are willing to trade. With only a small minority of the population actually involved in food production, the reality of seasons and weather is often ignored. Instead, expectations for fresh produce and variety all year round at affordable to low prices have been rising with globalization and progress in transport and preservation. Producers (as well as consumers) who are willing to invest in individual quality, character, and taste increasingly create their own market niches, especially in the organic sector.

Food shopping in Germany mostly takes place at discounters on the edge of towns and supermarket chains with outlets of varying sizes in towns. These major chain markets offer a vast array of food from all over the world, mostly of reliable industrial quality. Traditional independent butchers and bakers who used to be found in every village and neighborhood have largely been replaced by meat counters or prepackaged meat in supermarkets and *Backshops* (baking chain outlets), where centrally produced wares are just finished or crisped up. The small neighborhood grocery stores of old have become rare. In the cities they are mostly run by immigrants or reappear in luxury retro versions as delicatessens cum cafés.

In the 1970s, France was seen as culinary heaven by most Germans— *baguettes, Camembert, herbes de Provence,* and the like seemed like rare treats, but mass distribution of these foods has since made them widely available, and they are now taken for granted. In the 1980s, foodies' interest moved on to Italy—spaghetti, *Parmigiano* cheese, mozzarella, *Parma* ham, as well as olive oil and fresh basil were introduced and have now become naturalized as well. In the 1990s, East Asia became the new focus. Germany has seen an increase in Asian food markets as well as Turkish, Russian, and Polish stores that offer food from their various countries and cultures, including bread, pastries, meat, and fish.

The health-conscious and those seeking higher-quality food shop at weekly open-air markets (some of them *Ökomärkte*, all-organic markets), farm shops, and *Bioläden* (organic stores), and/or subscribe directly to (mostly organic) farms for a regular delivery of fresh produce from farm to doorstep. A few independent butchers and bakers remain, and new enterprises are being started by highly motivated food idealists coming from other sectors and rapidly moving into the quality end of the market. It is mostly through this local food shop movement that a new feeling for regionality is burgeoning as a countertrend to industrial homogeneity and purely nominal local specialties.

When considering typical, local food it is important to bear in mind that anything regional and special happens on a small scale compared

Organic vegetables at an outdoor organic market, Dresden, 2006. AP Photo/ Matthias Rietschel.

with the ubiquitous Western world food: New Zealand apples, Dutch tomatoes, and Kenyan beans as well as pizza, pasta, and fries. Still, because of the resurgence in regional products, much of what seemed destined to be reduced to pure folklore only a couple of years ago is experiencing a new breath of life.

Shop hours used to be strictly regulated until the end of the twentieth century, with shops closing at 6:30 P.M. on weekdays, 1:00 P.M. on Saturdays, and staying completely closed on Sundays and public holidays. In the past decade or so, things have become more relaxed; most stores stay open until 8:00 P.M. (6:00 P.M. on Saturdays), and some are even open on Sundays.

STARCHES

Brot (Bread)

Bread, arguably the most significant German food, has always played an important role in the folklore and superstitions of old and still has a central place in modern German food culture. Meals called *Abendbrot*—the traditional cold evening meal in northern and central Germany of bread spread with butter, cheese, cold cuts, and the like—and *Brotzeit*, a similar in-between meal mostly found in Bavaria (where it can either be a mid-morning or an afternoon snack) point to bread's key position in the diet. *Brotsuppe* (bread soup) made from stale bread is one of the last remnants of the old gruel. It was still widely eaten in the 1960s but with increasing prosperity has become a nostalgic specialty.

The traditional multitudinous variety of bread and rolls is based on different grains (wheat or rye, pure or in all possible mixtures with oat, spelt, buckwheat, linseed, and millet), coarse or finely ground flours, varying fermenting methods (sourdough or yeast) and baking methods, and shapes and seasonings in the form of nuts, seeds, or spices, all developed through specific regional conditions. This variety still survives on bakery shelves all over Germany, although the bread often comes from factories (usually baked beforehand and finished on site).

Dark and white bread historically were markers of social differences as well as based on geographical conditions. Rye contains less gluten than wheat and therefore requires a long sourdough fermentation to rise. This results in a decidedly sour taste in the finished bread, as well as a heavier, more compact texture. Before the arrival of chemical fertilizers, wheat could only be grown in better soils. This meant that rye and darker whole-grain sourdough loaves mainly belong to the traditions of northern Germany.

A historic bakery in Nuremberg. AP Photo/Frank Boxler.

The darkest and most extreme of those northern breads is Westphalian *Pumpernickel*. Originally it was called *Swattbraut* (black bread); in spite of many stories, historians are divided as to the roots of its seventeenth-century name. It is still made from coarsely ground whole-grain rye with water and salt in large, long, rectangular loaves that steam rather than bake for 24 hours in a sealed oven to produce a sweetish, syrup-like taste. Traditionally Pumpernickel was also fed to poultry and horses, but in its most elegant form it is eaten alongside coffee as a kind of black-and-white sandwich with *Stuten* (white yeast bread), thickly spread with butter and thus taking the place of cake.

Seasoning bread dates back to the Middle Ages and marks another difference between north and south. In the north, from the fifteenth century on, bread was eaten with (often salted) butter and other savory and sweet accompaniments, later alongside tea or coffee. Therefore, until today, only white yeast bread here is seasoned for special occasions with sugar, raisins, cinnamon, and sometimes cardamom and then is treated almost like cake. In the south, however, bread is seen as a separate food item and often has the same status as potatoes in the north. Caraway, fennel, coriander, and aniseed are commonly used in the south to season large loaves made from a finely ground mix of rye and wheat, using yeast or a mild sourdough. The sweet bread version in the south is called *Hutzel-*, *Kletzen-*, or *Früchtebrot* (fruit bread), which is made in autumn with dried pears as well as other dried fruit.

All over Germany, darker, whole-grain breads during the last decades have seen a renaissance through the organic and health movements. A similar trend became apparent about a century ago. Back then it was triggered by Justus von Liebig's findings in nutritional chemistry and the subsequent industrialization of food production. Healthier whole-grain breads were promoted by the *Lebensreform* (life reform) movement against a background of growing consumption of white bread by workers, mostly in the form of *Brötchen* (rolls). But those often highly philosophical ideas reached very few among the lower classes, and rolls are still highly popular today. They come in all versions, dark or white. For breakfast, fresh *Semmeln, Brötchen,* or *Schrippen* (the basic versions and names vary according to regions) are for many people almost a necessity. There are numerous variations or upgrades including *Mohn-* or *Sesambrötchen/semmeln* with poppy seeds or sesame, flaky *Splitterbrötchen* (literally, "flaky rolls"; in texture, they resemble French croissants), all kinds of *Vollkornbrötchen* (whole-grain rolls), as well as *Rosinenbrötchen* (raisin rolls) made with richer yeast dough. *Laugengebäck* also is an important bread tradition in German culinary history. Originally from the south, the white pretzels or sticks are sprayed with lye and sprinkled with salt. A *Laugenbrezel* from the Black Forest or Swabia has to be thick and moist on the lower side (which is slashed to split open during baking into white, pouting lips) and very thin and crispy around the knot. The *Bierbrezel* (beer pretzel) sold at the *Oktoberfest* in Munich is a much softer, larger affair. In Swabia (around Ulm and south to Lake Constance), *Seelen,* long, flat, white breadsticks that are formed with wet hands and sprinkled with salt and caraway seeds, are eaten as a sandwich with butter, cheese, or ham. In the Rhineland around Cologne, *Röggelchen,* a small, shiny flat roll from a mixture of predominantly wheat and some rye flour, is eaten as *halve Hahn* (half a rooster) with mature Dutch cheese and mustard. In and around Berlin *Schusterjungen* (literally shoemaker's apprentices) are small, flat rye rolls, traditionally eaten with lard and/or *Harzer* (cheese made from low-fat sour milk).

Dinkel (Spelt)

Dinkel (spelt) is an older, more robust form of wheat traditionally cultivated in the north of Baden, where it is also made into beer. When harvested half-ripe, it is called *Grünkern* (literally green grain) and is used as gruel for soups. Both are seeing a revival in the organic and health food scene and appear mostly in the form of bread and pasta.

Kartoffeln (Potatoes)

After Germans had overcome their initial distrust toward a newcomer from a newly discovered, distant continent, potatoes went on to drastically change food culture in Germany. Belonging to the *solanum* (nightshade) family, the floury tubers were at first suspected to be poisonous, and then around 1600 they were regarded in noble circles as decorative and medicinal plants. A century later, they were discovered by the lower classes, introduced by wandering soldiers and field workers from England and the Netherlands. They spread fast (in Prussia they were promoted by the government) because they reliably yielded large crops, thus helping with tithes. They contained much more water and less fat than any grain but were superficially nourishing and could go directly from the soil to the stove—for the simplest meals, until today they are boiled in their skins as *Pellkartoffeln*. Potatoes soon replaced the gruel made from cereal grains on most low-income family tables, henceforth disrupting the centuries-old unilateral dependency on grain crops. Flourishing in soils too poor for grain cultivation, potatoes formed the basis of the diet and enabled rapid population growth from the beginning of the nineteenth century. Slowly, they worked their way up to more affluent kitchens. Although a substantial part of the potato crop was distilled into spirits or fed to cattle, potato consumption rose from 262 lb. on average per person annually in 1850–54 to a peak of 628 lb. in 1900–1904. With the exception of war times and economic crises, consumption subsequently declined. In the 1950s, it was still over 330 lb. but dropped to just under 154 lb. after the millennium. By this point, the potato repertoire included ever more finished products like chips, fries, dumplings, ready-to-serve fried potatoes, or dried mashed potatoes.

Germans still see themselves as potato eaters and distinguish between *fest, halbfest,* and *mehlig kochend* (waxy, semiwaxy, and floury) varieties. More recently, German gourmets have also started to discuss the hierarchy of potato varieties. As with wine, soil, climate, and cultivation methods play a decisive role in determining the resulting product, but the *Sieglinde, Linda,* and small *Bamberger Hörnchen* varieties generally are rated highly. The first new potatoes of the year are imported from Mediterranean countries to go with the first asparagus in spring. Broadly speaking, in the north, potatoes are regarded as a staple food, a starch in the same league as rice or pasta, traditionally served with every warm meal on principle. In the south, however, they are treated as a vegetable. For instance, (waxy) potato salad dressed with oil and vinegar (or, in thrifty Swabian households, the brine from the pickle jar) is a standard feature on a plate of mixed salads and often accompanies warm dishes that usually include another starch element such as noodles. Potato soup is perhaps the most German of all soups, sometimes refined with cream and often served with small rounds of *Frankfurter* or *Fleischwurst* (a larger type of scalded sausage). In and around the Palatinate region, it is traditionally eaten for Thursday or Saturday lunch with *Quetschekuche*, a flat plum cake with a yeast dough.

Kartoffelsuppe (Potato Soup)

- 2 tbs. butter
- 1 onion, diced
- 2 tbs. bacon, diced
- 1 carrot, diced
- 1 small leek, sliced
- 2 tbs. celeriac or celery, diced
- 1 tsp. dried marjoram
- sea salt
- white pepper
- nutmeg
- 1 lb. floury potatoes, peeled and diced
- 1 qt. water
- 1/2 c. heavy cream (optional)
- fresh parsley, chopped

Sauté onion and bacon in butter until translucent, adding carrot, leek, and celeriac or celery after a little while, together with seasonings. After some minutes, add potatoes, cover, and let cook for 10 min. Add water and bring to a slow boil. When vegetables are soft, add cream if desired and puree the soup in a blender to the desired consistency—it should not be too smooth. Serve with parsley—and possibly sliced frankfurter sausages.

Quetschekuche (Plum Tart)

- 3 1/4 c. flour
- 1 oz. fresh yeast (or dry yeast according to the instruction on the packet)
- 1 1/4 c. lukewarm milk

- 1/3 c. granulated sugar
- 4 1/2 tbs. butter, softened
- 1 pinch of sea salt
- about 4 lb. plums, preferably *Zwetschgen* (see glossary)
- about 1/4 c. confectioners' sugar for sprinkling after baking

Sift the flour into a bowl. Make a well in the center; add the dry yeast or crumble the fresh yeast into it, then add 3 tablespoons of the milk and a pinch of the sugar. Mix with a little of the flour. Cover with a cloth and let rise in a warm spot for about 10 min. Add the softened butter, sugar, and salt, and knead into a homogenous, soft dough. Cover and let rise again until doubled in volume. Knead dough again and roll out evenly on a buttered and floured baking sheet. Pit the plums and quarter them without cutting all the way through, so that they spread open. Place them skin-side down in tight rows on the dough. Cover and let rise again for about 30 min., then bake in a preheated hot oven (200°C/400°F/gas mark 6) for about 30 min., until golden brown. Sprinkle with sugar.

Klöße, Knödel, Nudeln (Dumplings, Noodles, Pasta)

A leading German food ethnologist believes flour dumplings developed in the sixteenth century as a simpler, more affordable version of fish and meat dumplings.[2] They are still a dominant food of south and central Germany. In their countless versions and variations, they are comparable to the multitude of pasta shapes and uses in Italy. It is extremely difficult to distinguish between the two categories of dumplings, *Knödel* (in the south) or *Klösse* (in the center) on the one hand, and *Nudeln* (noodles) on the other, which also designates Italian-style pasta (also widely consumed in Germany: 15.65 lb. per person in 2006). Although German noodles often come in small dried pasta shapes (always made with eggs) and are eaten in clear soups and stews, arguably most important in this category are Swabian *Spätzle*.[3] They are traditionally scraped by hand from a wooden board into boiling water but can also be bought dried or vacuum-packed. A slightly rounder, more compact version is called *Knöpfle*. Both can be made with the addition of finely ground fresh liver. *Knöpfle* and *Spätzle* often accompany meat and generally demand large amounts of gravy. With cheese or sauerkraut they can form a meal on their own. The same is true for *Schupfnudeln* or *Buabespitzle*, which are made from boiled potato and a little egg, then shaped into small, pointed, finger-sized rolls; they are first boiled, then often fried like Italian gnocchi.

Dampfnudeln (steamed noodles) are fist-sized dumplings (usually Bavarian) made with wheat flour, eggs, and yeast, cooked side by side in a covered pan with a little milk and butter. Another version known as *Rohrnudeln* is baked uncovered in the oven, then eaten with all kinds of steamed fruits or custards. The northern counterparts, which possibly spread with the migration of Silesian workers, are steamed *Hefeklösse* (yeast dumplings) made from wheat flour and yeast and traditionally eaten with steamed prunes or dried apples and pears. *Zwetschgenknödel* (plum dumplings) are yet another sweet dumpling from Bavaria: fresh plums are covered with a potato dough and boiled. Still another Bavarian dumpling is made with stale white rolls, which are thinly cut (or bought as such), mixed with milk and eggs, sometimes with the addition of chopped parsley and fried bacon, then shaped into individual *Semmelknödel* (bread dumplings). The same preparation is used for *Serviettenknödel* (napkin dumplings); the mixture is shaped into a large roll and wrapped in a cloth napkin; after boiling, it is cut into slices. Either *Servietten-* or *Semmelknödel* are a must with roast pork but are also popular with *Schwammerl* (wild mushrooms) in cream.

Semmelknödel (Bread Dumplings)

- 8 small stale plain white rolls, thinly sliced
- 1 1/4 c. hot milk
- 2 tbs. fresh parsley, chopped
- 3 eggs
- 1 small onion, diced
- 1/2 tbs. butter
- sea salt
- pepper
- nutmeg
- 3 tbs. bread crumbs

Pour the milk over the sliced bread, and let soak for about 30 min. Fry the onion in the butter. Mix parsley, onion, and eggs with the bread-milk mixture, and season well. Add as much of the bread crumbs as needed to obtain a dough that can be shaped with wet hands into round dumplings (about 8). Poach in plenty of barely simmering salt water for about 15 min.

To the north, in Franconia and Thuringia, but also in the Rhineland, dumplings are generally made from potatoes. The famous, almost small fist-sized *Thüringer* or *Grüne* (green) *Klösse* are usually made entirely from raw, grated tubers (not an easy task, and ready-made *Klossteig* [dumpling dough] is available in stores). Each dumpling is filled with a few croûtons made from fried bread. Countless versions of dumplings that mix varying amounts of boiled and raw potatoes, as well as wheat flour, can be found throughout the center and north of Germany. There are also recipes that integrate quark[4] or sour cream, with favorite seasonings such as nutmeg or marjoram. All those dumplings need plenty of brown gravy on the plate. Any leftover larger dumplings of that kind can be cut in slices when cold and fried. Leftover *Maultaschen* (literally, gob pockets) are prepared similarly in the southeast (Swabia). *Maultaschen* are a kind of square ravioli filled with a finely ground mixture of pork and veal, some bread, egg, and spinach and/or parsley; when fresh they are eaten either in a clear broth or *geschmälzt* (larded), with fried onion rings.

Finally, three unusual dumpling varieties demonstrate the breadth of the category: *Mohnpielen* (poppy seed dumplings) are an old-fashioned Silesian import to Berlin. They are actually a kind of mush (shaped into dumplings on the serving plate) made from sliced white rolls, soaked with milk, raisins, and ground blue poppy seed and eaten on Christmas Eve. *Quarkkeulchen* (small quark clubs) from Saxony are small dumplings made from a mixture of quark, egg, and wheat flour and deep-fried in lard, then sprinkled with sugar; they are often found at fairs and street stalls. *Mehlbeutel* (flour bag) is a modern version of French *boudin* that made its way to England originally and from there spread over the North Sea to Hamburg, Schleswig-Holstein, and East Friesland as a form of pudding. In *Mehlbeutel*, the meat of the original *boudin* is transformed into a large flour dumpling (sometimes with yeast) and either boiled in or steamed over water with (traditionally) smoked pork in a napkin or a basin, then eaten with fruit and sugar.

Reis (Rice)

Rice is not grown in Germany but has long been imported, initially as a luxury food in the Middle Ages; when it was eaten mainly with spices and sugar. Today, German stores carry all the usual varieties of mostly Italian and Asian rice, with risotto being very popular. *Milchreis* (milk rice), a homely dish similar to American rice pudding, is a child's food and is topped with cinnamon and sugar or steamed fruit, thus still referring to medieval practice.

Samen und Nüsse (Seeds and Nuts)

Walnüsse (walnuts) and *Haselnüsse* (hazelnuts) are grown in Germany and are widely used in baking. *Mandeln* (almonds) play an important role as well but are mostly imported. *Pinienkerne* (pine nuts) are above all used in ethnic cuisines, whereas *Erdnüsse* (peanuts), cashews, macadamia nuts, pecans, and *Pistazien* (pistachios) are usually roasted with salt and eaten as a snack. Sesame seeds, *Kürbiskerne* (pumpkin seeds), *Sonnenblumenkerne* (sunflower seeds), and *Leinsamen* (flax/linseed) are used in breads and pastries. In the southwest, *Maronen* or *Eßkastanien* (sweet chestnuts) are a local specialty, roasted and eaten with young wine, or used to enrich red cabbage and to accompany venison dishes of all kinds.

Mohn (poppy seed) is especially popular in eastern Germany and historically came with immigrants from even further east, that is, from Bohemia, Silesia, or the Sudetenland. Mostly blue seeds (the white varieties are rare to find) are used for cooking and baking. They originate from the same plant, *Papaver somniferum latex*, that, when refined, is the source of morphine, laudanum, and codeine—all of which are opiates.

Poppy cultivation was of some importance in the nineteenth century and up until the middle of the twentieth century in Thuringia, Saxony, Württemberg, and Baden but has been strictly regulated by German narcotics laws since 1978 in West Germany and since 1992 in the rest of reunified Germany. In recent years, a variety with a very low morphine content has been granted a license to be grown for culinary use. Historically, poppy seeds were associated with many legends: chickens were said to lay more eggs when given poppy seeds, and poppy seeds (as a high-yielding plant) were supposed to bring luck, hence the many poppy seed dishes that still today are eaten near the end of the year. They were even thought to keep away vampires. Poppy seeds have a very high oil content and therefore become rancid quickly. To reveal their full aroma, they need to be (freshly) ground in a special grinder, which is mostly done at the bakery or grocery store selling them. *Überbrühen* (scalding poppy seeds with hot water or milk) is a common method in older recipes and is only necessary when the seeds are crushed in a mortar as was the habit back then. Poppy seeds today are not only used for cakes and desserts but also appear in yogurt, bread, and rolls.

FLEISCH (MEAT)

Historians believe that meat was a staple food from the Germanic period on. The consumed meat came from domestic animals like horses,[5] sheep, pigs, goats, and geese on the one hand and wild animals on the other (although game hunting quickly became a privilege of the ruling classes). Today Germans eat about 180 lb. of meat per year (and on top of that 67 lb. of sausage). It is still a symbol of affluence and general well-being—except for vegetarians who, as around the turn of the last century with the *Lebensreform* movement, are currently seeing a revival.

With the general introduction of potatoes and later on the expanding milk industry, pigs soon became the favored domesticated source of meat (instead of goat and mutton) and provided the basis for the general increase in meat consumption during the 1850s.[6] Pigs were undemanding in terms of space, could be fattened on household leftovers and whey, and could be made into winter supplies using every part from nose to tail, including the blood, all the inner parts, and the skin. However, prior to the arrival of modern transportation, preserving, and cooling technologies, meat for ordinary people had to be preserved and therefore was mostly eaten salted, smoked, or dried. Except for around the autumnal slaughter period, roasted meat of any kind was a festive dish, as it required fresh meat. The extraordinary variety and popularity of cured meat in the form of ham and sausages in Germany partly date back to these practices.

Animals' dressed weights have more than doubled since the beginning of the nineteenth century and the time needed to reach that weight has been reduced significantly. Since World War II, beef and poultry consumption has risen with affluence and health awareness, and mutton and goat meat are slowly gaining ground—but pork is still the favored meat of Germans.[7]

Schwein (Pork)

In general pork today is worryingly cheap, be it as ground meat, chops, schnitzel, or fillet. However, as in other food sectors, there is a movement back to older (almost extinct) breeds such as *Schwäbisch-Hällische* and *Bunte Bentheimer*, as well as less intense (industrial) raising methods, in order to obtain meat with more fat, more taste, and lower water content. So far this movement is limited to a small elite group. Nevertheless, *Schweinebraten* (pork roast, frequently a leg) with crackling crust is still considered something special in Bavaria, as is *Spanferkel* (suckling pig). One could generalize that pork is more present in the traditional festive dishes of the southeast, whereas beef is more common in the north, center, and west. *Speck* (bacon), however, is an essential ingredient all over Germany, until a few decades ago in an all-fat, that is, all-white fat version, but now rather streaky. *Schlachteplatte* is the German version of Alsatian *choucroûte*, which combines all kinds of salted and boiled pork cuts, served with sauerkraut and boiled potatoes.

Geflügel (Poultry)

Following the same model as sugar, poultry was once considered a high-prestige item, but its consumption has soared with cheaper, industrial production. Since the 1950s, the Sunday roast chicken has become industrially produced everyday fare, and erstwhile festive dishes like *Hühnerfrikassee* (chicken fricassee) are still popular but have become much less special. In the north around Bremen and Hamburg there is a tradition of eating *Stubenküken* (very young chicks) that were originally raised in the *Stube* (living room) or the kitchen. In gourmet circles, rarer variations of fowl such as *Wachtel* (quail), *Perlhuhn* (guinea fowl), or *Barbarie-Ente* (Barbary duck) are mostly being imported for consumption. Besides venison, *Gans* (goose) and *Ente* (duck) account for a large part of festive winter roasts and often take pride of place on Christmas dinner tables. Goose traditionally is highly regarded because, as with pigs, all parts of the animal can be used. The northern areas along the coast still enjoy a great reputation for raising the best geese and ducks.

Kalb und Rind (Veal and Beef)

Although the gusto for eating steak in modern Germany rivals Texas or Chicago, there is no particular tradition for raising and maturing beef that corresponds to that in the United States. Traditionally, veal is pan fried as *Wiener Schnitzel* and roasted as *Kalbshaxe* (shank). A popular roast is *gefüllte Kalbsbrust*, breast of veal filled with ground meat (in the north) or a bread stuffing (in the south). Veal is also made into *Ragoûts* with white sauce or darker *Gulasch* (goulash). Beef is braised, whether in smaller pieces for *Rindergulasch* or rolled up in thin, large slices around a filling of onions, pickles, and mustard as *Rindsrouladen* (beef roulades). All kinds of larger *Schmorbraten* (pot roasts) yield abundant amounts of gravy to accompany *Spätzle*, *Knödel* or *Klösse*, or potatoes.

Töttchen (Veal Ragout in White Sauce)

- 1 onion, chopped coarsely
- 1 carrot, in thick slices
- 1 clove
- 1 bay leaf
- 1 1/2 lb. veal shoulder or breast
- 1 1/2 qt. water

Slowly simmer the meat with the vegetables and seasonings, until tender, about 1 1/2 hrs. Reserve 1 pint of the cooking liquid. Cut meat into cubes of about 1/2 inch.

- 1 onion, diced
- 5 tbs. butter
- 2 tbs. flour
- sea salt
- white pepper
- Worcestershire sauce
- zest of 1/2 lemon
- 1 tbs. Dijon mustard
- 2 tbs. capers (rinsed in water if salted)
- 2 tbs. crème fraîche (could be substituted by sour cream)
- 1 tbs. parsley, chopped

Sauté onion in butter until translucent; sprinkle with flour, stirring continually until smooth and clear. Still stirring, gradually add the reserved cooking liquid to make a white sauce. Season with salt, pepper, Worcestershire sauce, lemon zest, and mustard. Add capers, crème fraîche, and parsley. Gently reheat the meat in this sauce.

Lamm und Ziege (Lamb and Goat)

Sheep in Germany traditionally are above all wool suppliers, so that mostly the meat of older animals was eaten. Because of its often-pungent taste, *Hammelfleisch* (mutton) does not enjoy a very good reputation (and has, for instance, traditionally been served in a broth seasoned with caraway seed to counteract the meat's flavor in and around Berlin). Today it is almost exclusively sold in ethnic markets. However, with imports from New Zealand, lamb in recent decades has become more important and is now very popular as pan-fried loins, chops, and fillets or leg roasts. The north coast nowadays furnishes exquisite *Salzwiesenlamm* (salt-meadow lamb), the German equivalent of French *pré-salé*. The *Rhönschaf* (Rhön sheep), an old breed from the Rhön mountain region northeast of Frankfurt, is also being revived, and *Heidschnucken* (moorland sheep) from the heath around Lüneburg yield aromatic, venison-like darker meat. Goat is almost invisible as meat and was traditionally regarded as the poor man's beef. Only in Thuringia does a certain tradition exist for eating goat. However, both sheep and goat have seen a revival with the organic/green movement, as a younger generation, often newcomers to the farming world, take over or start estates and search for market niches.

Heidschnucke (moorland sheep)

Wild (Game)

Although it is widely available and affordable today—also with imports of farmed venison from New Zealand—the meat of roe, red, and fallow deer, as well as wild boar, is still seen as special, and a venison roast is a marker for festive occasions. This exclusivity undoubtedly goes back to the royal directives of Charlemagne, a passionate hunter, who sought to protect game hunting for his sport alone. Over time, hunting rights became the ruler's privilege and emphasized his territorial claims over peasants. Organized hunts served as a means of self-presentation as well as practice for wartime. A distinction between *Hochwild* and *Niederwild* (higher and lower game) paralleled that between the higher and lower aristocracy. The exact makeup of these categories seems to have varied depending on royal preferences and regional differences, but the *Hirsch* (stag) certainly symbolized utter noblesse. Nowadays, *Rehrücken* (rack of venison from fallow deer) is the culinary highlight, often served with poached pears and cranberry sauce.[8] The *Jagdgesetz* (hunting law) in Germany today is more democratic but still much stricter than in France, for instance. Fallow deer and wild boar are plentiful and often end up on the tables of winegrowers, who hunt them in order to protect their vineyards from voracious animals. *Hase* (hare) is mostly imported, whereas *Kaninchen* (rabbit) is traditionally considered a poor man's substitute and is above all made into ragoûts and stews.

Rehrücken (Roast Rack of Venison)

- a rack of venison, about 5 lb.
- sea salt

- black pepper
- butter

Cut off any silver skin (you can make gravy of this) as well as the small fillets that would be overcooked by the time the rest of the meat is ready (they make an extra special treat for a salad or in a soup). Make cuts on both sides along the backbone for even cooking. Salt and pepper the meat and then cover the whole roast carefully with thin slices of cold butter to prevent the very lean meat from drying out. Put into the preheated oven (180°C/350°F/gas mark 4) for about 20 min. The meat should be cooked medium (a bit pink inside). Let it rest in a warm corner, covered with foil, for another 15 min. before cutting. Serve with red cabbage.

Innereien (Offal or Variety Meats)

On German plates, offal can be everything from a lowly substitute for "real" meat to an expensive delicacy. *Kalbsleber* (calf's liver), for example, is served in large slices with mashed potatoes, fried apples, and onion rings as *Kalbsleber Berliner Art*. Kidneys and sweetbreads are highly regarded, and occasionally even found in the north where traditionally offal is judged as too ordinary and therefore undesirable. In the south, however, there is a rich tradition for kidney, lung, and liver as well as *Kutteln* (tripe) from all butchered animals, often served *sauer* (sour) as small strips in a roux-based brown sauce with vinegar. Liver is also used for all kinds of dumplings eaten in soups or with sauerkraut such as *Lewwerknepp* (liver dumplings) in the Palatinate.

Kalbsleber Berliner Art (Calf's Liver Berlin-Style)

- About 1/4 lb. calf's liver per person, sliced 1/4 inch thick
- 1 medium onion per person, thinly sliced
- 1/2 apple per person, sliced in rings 1/4 inch thick
- 1 tbs. butter per person
- flour
- sea salt
- black pepper

Slowly fry onion and apple slices in half of the butter until golden and soft but not disintegrating, and season. Remove and keep warm. Add the rest of the butter to the pan. Toss liver in flour, shake off excess, and fry at medium heat until just done but still pink. Season, and top with onion and apple. Serve with mashed potatoes and all the buttery juices from the pan.

Hackfleisch (Ground Meat)

The handling of raw ground meat in shops and restaurant kitchens is strictly regulated by law (the *Hackfleischverordnung*), as is the maximum content of bread in the pan-fried meat patties that are called *Buletten* (in Berlin), *Frikadellen* (all over Germany), or *Fleischpflanzerl* (in Bavaria). These meat patties are eaten warm or cold, often as a snack with beer. They are always made from a mixture of pork and beef and on principle taste best when homemade, with just the right amount of (white) bread to achieve a light texture. The same mixture in the form of a larger, oven-roasted meat loaf goes by the name of *Falscher Hase* (mock hare). *Mett* or *Hackepeter* (in Berlin) is coarsely ground pork eaten raw on bread, seasoned with raw onion, pepper, and salt. *Schabefleisch* or *Tartar* is the same dish made from very lean, finely ground beef, with the addition of raw egg yolk and capers. Ground meat is also made into all kinds of dumplings served in sauce. The most famous of these without a doubt are the *Königsberger Klopse* or *Saure Klopse*, a mixture of beef and veal in a roux-based white sauce flavored with capers, salted herring, and lemon juice.

CURED MEAT

The variety of sausages and ham in Germany is overwhelming and dominated by pork. Initially, sausage developed as a means of preserving meat before the arrival of modern refrigeration. Traditionally, slaughtering took place in autumn because feed was scarce during the winter. Curing, salting, boiling, smoking, grinding, and stuffing meat in skins were easy ways to ensure meat supply in the following months. In the course of time, countless variations, mixtures of different cuts, and seasonings developed.

With the often-characterless quality of industrially raised meat on the one hand and market pressure for low prices on the other, variety can seem today purely nominal, and real quality and taste hard to find. However, as in other food sectors, through regional initiatives and the organic movement, pioneers are returning flavor and real quality to cured meats. Ham and sausage are mostly eaten as cold cuts with bread, but some varieties are also served warm.

Wurst (Sausage)

Very broadly speaking, *Wurst* (sausage) in the north tends to be made from raw meat. It can be the equivalent of Italian salami: *Zervelat, Schlackwurst, Katenrauchwurst, Plockwurst,* or the excellent *Ahle Worschd* (literally old sausage) from around Kassel that has recently seen a revival. *Mettwurst* is softer in consistency, whereas *Rügenwalder Teewurst* (originally from this town on the Baltic coast, today part of Poland) is very fine and spreadable. In the south, many sausage varieties are made from finely cut meat, possibly with larger pieces of ham or pickled tongue added afterwards, and scalded in a fashion similar to mortadella or bologna. Examples of this type include *Fleischwurst* (meat sausage), *Lyoner*, *Gelbwurst* (yellow sausage), *Bierschinken* (beer ham), *Jagdwurst* (hunting sausage), *Zungenwurst* (tongue sausage), and *Bierwurst* (beer sausage). *Fleischkäse* (literally, meat cheese) is baked in large loaves. Sliced and served on a roll it is popular street food. *Fleischkäse* is also called *Leberkäse* (liver cheese) and may contain some liver, but legally does not when designated as *Bayerischer* (Bavarian) *Leberkäse* (its confusing name is derived from *Leib*, which means loaf or body, not liver).

Würstchen (smaller, individual sausages) are served heated and whole, often in pairs. They range from some raw ones like *Landjäger* (literally, country hunters) and *Debrecziner* to a multitude of scalded (parboiled) ones. *Frankfurter* undoubtedly are the best-known variety outside of Germany, although Germans tend to eat the more or less identical *Wiener*, *Halberstädter*, or *Schüblinge*. This divergence may be explained by the fact that one of the very first sausage-canning factories opened in Frankfurt am Main at the very end of the nineteenth century, so that the delicate ware could be shipped and thus became known worldwide. *Bockwurst* is a thicker Berlin version, and Bavarian *Regensburger* are even sturdier in shape and much shorter. All of these were originally made from pork. However, modern versions made from turkey or beef can be found. Bavarian *Weisswurst* (white sausage) is made from veal and eaten with sweet mustard, traditionally as a midmorning snack before noon. *Bratwürste* (grilled sausages) range from skinless, finely textured Swabian *Geschwollene/Wollwurst* to coarser *Nürnberger* and *Thüringer*.

All over Germany, sausage is also made from cooked meat, often seasoned with marjoram and/or onion. *Leberwurst* (liver sausage) is always spreadable (resembling chopped liver) and can be fine or coarse, with the addition of herbs, truffles, and the like. All kinds of *Blut-* or *Rotwurst* (blood or red sausage) may also contain some ham or tongue in addition to blood. Headcheese-like *Preßsack* (pressed bag) and *Schwartenmagen* (literally, rind or skin stomach) are made using gelatinous meat cuts and the skin, whereas *Schweinskopfsülze* (pig's headcheese) is made from pig's head. *Ochsenmaulsalat* (literally, beef's mouth salad), the same dish made from beef, is usually finely sliced and dressed as a salad with oil and vinegar.

Some very traditional cooked sausage varieties like *Grützwurst/Knipp*, *Beutelwurst*, *Panhas*, and *Pinkel* developed during times of meat scarcity and contain various cereals (such as oats, buckwheat, barley, or rye), bread, or potatoes, like the famous *Pfälzer Saumagen*, which uses a cleaned pig's stomach for a casing. They are eaten warm, usually accompanied by some form of cabbage.

Schinken (Ham)

Ham is mostly made from pork leg or shoulder and smoked or cooked, as the climate only permits air drying for smaller sausages rather than larger cuts like in Italy or Spain. There are versions matured on the bone—*Westfälischer Knochenschinken, Holsteiner Katenschinken*—and deboned varieties like *Schwarzwälder Schinken* from the Black Forest. Others are boiled or baked, and in Bavaria *Schwarzgeräuchertes* (black smoked ham) is salted, boiled, and smoked black over resiny wood. *Geräucherte Gänsebrust* (smoked goose breast), originally a Pomeranian specialty, is highly valued in the north and east. *Lachsschinken* (literally, salmon ham) is a completely fat free, deboned, cured, and lightly smoked pork loin, rolled in a thin slice of fat bacon.

SCHNECKEN, FROSCHSCHENKEL UND SCHILDKRÖTE (SNAILS, FROGS' LEGS, AND TURTLE)

Schnecken (snails) are a specialty of the southeast, with creamy *Schneckenrahmsüpple* (snail cream soup) as a preferred preparation. Snails currently are back en vogue around Ulm and toward Lake Constance, where several farms have started raising them. In the rest of Germany, snails are seen as a French specialty and eaten with plenty of garlic herb butter. *Froschschenkel* (frogs' legs) are very rarely eaten and are viewed as cruel by animal lovers. In the same vein, real *Schildkrötensuppe* (turtle soup) has been banned by law. *Falsche Schildkrötensuppe* or *Mockturtle* was once popular but now is almost forgotten. Legend attributes its invention to a wealthy farmer from Lower Saxony during the Napoleonic trade embargo (1806–13). Apparently, he did not want to go without his beloved turtle soup, and his cook replaced the unobtainable turtle meat with calf's head.

FISCH (FISH)

Fresh Fish

Germans are not great fish eaters, consuming only about 30 lb. annually, about a sixth the amount of meat consumed.[9] Although with modern transportation, fresh (and frozen) fish of all international varieties

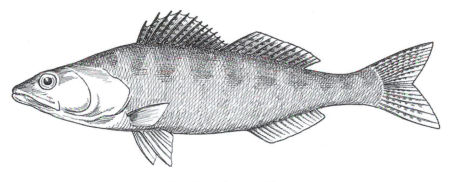

Zander (pike perch)

is readily available throughout Germany, the north still consumes more than the south. Most offerings today come from aquacultures around the world. Of the fish consumed in Germany, 85% is imported, and *Lachs* (salmon) is as common as chicken. Saltwater species include *Scholle* (plaice), which is traditionally eaten in May and prepared fried with bacon and capers as *Finkenwerder Maischolle*. *Kabeljau* or *Dorsch* (cod), *Makrele* (mackerel), *Rotbarsch* (redfish or ocean perch), *Seezunge* (sole), and *Steinbutt* (turbot), along with river fish like *Aal* (eel), *Hecht* (pike), and *Zander* (pike perch), are all popular. *Karpfen* (carp) is mostly bred in ponds and still plays a role on special occasions, especially those histori-cally related to fasting. *Forelle* (trout) from aquaculture is very common, whereas the more aromatic, wild *Bachforelle* (river trout) is an extreme rarity. In the south, *Waller* (catfish) is popular. *Lachsforelle* (salmon trout), *Egli/Kretzer* (perch), and *Felchen* (a trout-like whitefish) are specialties from Lake Constance. The latter is known as *Renken* on the Chiemsee. Since the mid-1970s, *Austernzucht* (oyster farming) has been successfully reintroduced on the island of Sylt. However, most of the oysters consumed (mostly raw) in Germany are imported from France. All along the north coast *Nordseekrabben* (tiny brown shrimp) are a specialty. Local *Krebse* (small crayfish) are a highly valued traditional specialty that had almost disappeared, but with better water quality in small streams and rivers is making a tentative comeback.

Gratinierte Austern auf Sauerkraut (Oysters au Gratin in Their Shells on a Bed of Sauerkraut)

For Oysters

- 32 oysters
- 1 small onion, finely diced

- 1 tbs. butter
- a little dry vermouth
- 1/2 c. dry white wine
- oyster liquid, quantity according to saltiness
- 1 c. plus 3 tbs. heavy cream
- white pepper
- cayenne pepper
- 2 egg yolks

For Sauerkraut

- 1 small onion, finely diced
- 2 tbs. butter
- 0.3 lb. (about 1 c.) raw sauerkraut, squeezed dry
- 1/2 c. dry white wine

Open oysters, reserving liquid in a bowl. Clean deeper shells and arrange them on a baking sheet (possibly using rock salt to stabilize them). Sauté onion in butter until translucent, then add vermouth, wine, oyster liquid, and cream and reduce by a third. Season, and remove from the heat. Whisk egg yolk with cream and fold into the sauce. For the sauerkraut, sauté onion in butter until translucent, then add sauerkraut and wine. Simmer until the sauerkraut loses its rawness. Put some sauerkraut (without any liquid) in each shell, place an oyster on top, and cover with some of the sauce. Place the baking sheet with the oysters under a preheated broiler until the sauce is a nice golden brown and the oysters are just starting to stiffen. Serve immediately.

Smoked, Pickled, and Salted Fish

Salzhering (salted herring), *Klippfisch* (dried cod), and *Stockfisch* (dried and salted cod, stockfish) were generally the most widely consumed and affordable fish, because they kept well and thus could be transported from the northern coasts inland. Today salted herring mostly survives as *Matjes* (caught young and fat) and is usually imported from the Netherlands. It is often served in a sauce made from sour cream mixed with apple, onion, and pickled cucumbers, or accompanied by green beans, fried bacon, and boiled potatoes. Besides all kinds of canned pickled herring in sauces, *Brathering* (fried herring) is coated in bread crumbs, fried, and then marinated in vinegar. *Bückling* is herring smoked whole, whereas herring that has been filleted and marinated in a vinegary brine is called *Bismarckhering* (if served flat) or *Rollmops* (if rolled around a piece of pickled cucumber)—both are traditionally also seen as a hangover cure. *Makrele* (mackerel) is mostly eaten smoked, as is a lot of *Aal* (eel). *Räucherlachs* (smoked salmon) is quite common, also enriching breakfast buffets, but today is rarely of truly excellent quality. Golden *Kieler Sprotten* (smoked sprats) from the towns of Eckernförde and Kiel are packed in flat wooden crates, whereas *Schillerlocken* (literally, Schiller locks) have nothing to do with the locks of the famous German writer and poet Friedrich von Schiller, but rather consist of the smoked belly of *Dornhai*, a variety of shark.

Grünkohlsalat mit Geräucherter Forelle (Kale Salad with Smoked Trout)

- about 8 c. kale leaves (de-stemmed)
- 2 tsp. Dijon mustard
- 2 tbs. balsamic vinegar
- 2 tsp. apple jelly
- sea salt
- black pepper
- 4 tbs. olive oil
- 8 smoked trout fillets (or another kind of smoked fish)

Wash kale thoroughly, then very quickly blanch it in salted boiling water. Immediately rinse in cold water and pat dry or dry in a salad spinner. Combine mustard, vinegar, jelly, salt, pepper, and oil to make a vinaigrette, and dress the kale with it. Serve with the trout.

MILCHPRODUKTE (DAIRY PRODUCTS)

Milch und Sahne (Milk and Cream)

According to the Roman writer Tacitus (around 55–after 115), the Germanic tribes' main staples were fresh meat and *lac concretum* (curdled milk or quark). Fresh milk as a drink is a rather modern idea that only took hold in Germany with the advent of modern dairy farming during the agricultural reforms in the 1870s and subsequently pasteurization. Apart from Schleswig-Holstein in the north and the Alpine regions in the south (which still enjoy a special reputation for dairy products), milk until then was almost seen as a by-product. Cattle were considered a source of meat and pack animals. Milk was consumed domestically, mostly in soured or curdled form. The farmer's wife and daughters made it into butter, considered a luxury product, or into very simple cheese. Both were often sold to yield some pocket money, whereas buttermilk and whey were kept for home consumption and animal fodder. However, with urbanization and industrialization, demand for milk rose because cows and goats (the poor man's cow, sheep being almost exclusively for wool production) gradually disappeared from the cities. Agricultural labor became more expensive, so that pastures were more attractive than labor-intense fields. New animal breeds with higher milk yields, as well as the introduction of cooling and modern dairy technologies (like the centrifuge to separate cream) made for a new industry unconcerned with weather conditions and long distances. This industry was quickly dominated by dairy cooperatives. From 1887 on, pasteurization was generally introduced for milk, and important efforts from the official side were made to avoid the common practices of adulteration and dilution. Milk was promoted as a healthy alternative to coffee and alcohol.

Today dairy farming in Germany is generally highly industrialized. Except for a very small number of estates, that, under strict controls, offer untreated *Rohmilch* (raw milk) and *Vorzugsmilch* (special milk) for sale, milk in Germany (by definition cow's milk, other kinds have to be designated as such and do not play an important role)has to be pasteurized and most often is homogenized as well. Milk is still seen as a healthy product, important for infants and children, whereas adults consume less than 0.53 pints per day (significantly below the 1.6 pints officially considered ideal for vitamin and calcium needs). Consumers can choose between *Vollmilch* (full-fat, min. 3.5% fat content), *fettarm* (low-fat, 1.5% to 1.8% fat), and *entrahmt* or *Magermilch* (skim, less than 0.5% fat). All varieties are available as either fresh milk or *H-Milch* (heat-treated for longer shelf-life without the need of refrigeration). Apart from the current fad for lattes and cappuccino, Germans traditionally drink *Filterkaffee* (filter coffee) with *Kaffeesahne* or *Kondensmilch*, that is, condensed and sterilized milk in small glass bottles (formerly tins, hence the common name of *Büchsenmilch* [tinned milk]) and portion-sized plastic tubs. *Schlagsahne* (whipping cream) is used for cooking and eaten with cake.

Joghurt und Quark (Yogurt and Quark)

Yogurt in all its modern forms is a favorite for breakfast and snacks and seen as very healthy. At a typical German grocery store, yogurts of all fat percentages, combined with every conceivable fruit, flavoring, and even whole wheat kernels, line the shelves. Yogurt packaging has become a marker of wealth, with handwritten labels and glass jars at one end of the spectrum and cheap plastic tubs at the other.

Most of today's quark is produced industrially with fermenting bacteria and rennet added, whereas the *lac concretum* of Tacitus' times might have been left to coagulate in animal skins. In more recent history, quark was made from sour milk that was skimmed and left to coagulate in a warm place. The milk solids were then hung up in a linen towel without any pressure so that the *Molke* (whey) could drain out. When this process was completed, some sweet or sour cream was added back in, as well as salt, and possibly some seasonings. In contrast to American-style cottage cheese (in Germany less common and called *Hüttenkäse*), quark is smooth and homogenous in texture. It has a more or less pronounced acidic tang. Similar to milk, it can be found with various fat contents.

Kräuterquark mit Pellkartoffeln is a popular dish consisting of quark mixed with fresh herbs such as chives, parsley, and dill, eaten with potatoes boiled in their skins. A multitude of regional names for quark, such as *Weisskäse, Bibbeleskäs, Glumse, Klatschkäse, Lückelekäs, Matte, Sibbkäs, Topfen,* or *Schichtkäse,* attest to its importance in the daily diet. It is used for *Käsekuchen* (cheesecake), which is either baked or made with gelatin, and combined with all kinds of fruit for desserts.

Pellkartoffeln mit Kräuterquark (Potatoes Boiled in Their Skin with Quark with Fresh Herbs)

- potatoes, preferably new ones, quantity depending on appetite
- quark, about 1 c. per person
- milk or cream to your liking
- fresh herbs, such as parsley, chives, dill, and/or tarragon, all finely chopped
- sea salt
- pepper
- butter

Scrub potatoes and boil in their skins until tender. Mix quark with plenty of herbs, adding some milk or cream to achieve desired consistency; season with salt and pepper. Serve with the potatoes and some fresh butter.

Käse (Cheese)

Germans eat 48.28 lb. of cheese per capita annually; the cheese ranges from industrial, rubbery slices to the most sophisticated imports from France and Italy. Traditionally, cheese is consumed on bread as cold cuts, but more and more it is also taking the place of dessert. German cheese culture was so quickly overwhelmed by industrial production at the end of the nineteenth century that it has only very recently begun to search for a distinctive character.[10] A growing number of German dairy farms, predominantly small and organic, are developing new regional cheeses. Because there are no patterns for artisanal cheese production to follow, as there are in France, modern artisanal cheese makers work not only with the traditional cow's milk but also with sheep, goat, and even buffalo milk. The only traditional German goat cheese comes from Thuringia. *Altenburger Ziegenkäse* resembles a milder Camembert and is made from a mixture of goat's and cow's milk.

The most basic and most traditional cheeses of Germany are made from salted, pressed sour-milk quark: *Handkäse* originally was a simple, domestic way to prevent skimmed milk's precious protein from spoiling. This developed into a small industry. In the Palatinate, around Mainz, and in the Harz region (where it is made to develop a white rind), it is still popular with beer or wine. It is often served *mit Musik* (with music), which means that it is marinated with onion, oil, and vinegar and often seasoned with caraway seeds. *Handkäse*, or *Harzer*, as it is also called, is shaped in small flat discs or finger-thick sticks and with maturation goes from crumbly white and mild to gooey, yellow, and pungent.

Cheese making using rennet came to Germany with the Romans and survived in monasteries. It only developed where dairy farming yielded enough milk, that is, mainly on the north coast and in the Allgäu, the foothills of the Alps. *Tilsiter* is the trademark cheese of the north. It developed from a Swiss dairy worker's recipe in the then–East Prussian town of Tilsit into the rectangular shape of today. Mature versions can be full of character. *Allgäuer Bergkäse* (mountain cheese) and *Allgäuer Emmentaler* are its equivalent in the south. These large, round, hard cheeses follow the Swiss examples with their aromatic, sweet, nutty flavor. They were originally produced in the summer dairies up in the mountains. Nowadays, they come mostly from large dairies in the valleys and are difficult to find in high quality. Smaller, softer with a sticky washed rind, and more pungent are *Limburger* and *Romadur*, also from the Allgäu. Both were developed in the 1830s through the influence of a Belgian dairy worker (along with *Steinbuscher*, a variation based on an East Prussian recipe). The strong-tasting small white cubes of *Weisslacker* are a Bavarian specialty meant to go with beer, whereas *Liptauer*, *Obatzda*, and *Spundekäs* are some examples of cheese preparations using quark, cream cheese, and sometimes other cheese varieties, mashed and mixed with all kinds of spices, onions, and herbs.

FETT UND ÖL (FAT AND OIL)

Before slimness became the ideal with the ideas of the *Lebensreform* movement, fat was a marker of living standards. The motto seemed to be the more the better, be it in meat cuts, in dishes, or spread on bread.

Butter (Butter)

Prior to industrial farming methods, butter was considered a luxury product. With the onset of modern technology, it became more affordable but kept its high reputation. Around the end of the nineteenth century, Germany went from exporting to importing butter (as well as cheese), back then from Galicia (a region situated today partly in Poland, partly in the Ukraine) and the United States. Nowadays, imported butter comes from the Netherlands, Denmark, and Ireland, and some more expensive types (and arguably the best quality) come from France.

Traditionally, German butter was almost exclusively *Sauerrahmbutter* made from cream that had turned sour while being collected from the large, shallow milk containers. Only with modern cooling technology and the invention of the centrifuge to quickly separate sweet cream from fresh milk did *Süßrahmbutter* become an option. Today most German butter (always made of cow's milk and rarely salted) tastes rather bland and is quite soft to assure good spreadability. It is made in ever-larger dairies and is *mildgesäuert* (mildly soured). This method uses fresh cream, then adds acidic cultures for flavor later on. Beta-carotene is often added during winter months for more intense color. Germans consume 14.77 lb. of butter per person per year, spreading it on bread and rolls with jam and cold cuts, as well as using it in baking and cooking.[11] Although most butter today is affordable, this still is a very sensitive issue for the majority of Germans (similar to coffee prices). Most are very reluctant to pay a premium for top quality, so that truly excellent butter of German origin is very rare (the more affluent, middle-aged Germans still are more willing to pay more for French food).

Schmalz (Lard)

Until butter became widely affordable, most of the fat consumed was in the form of *Talg* (suet) and *Schmalz* (lard). *Schmalz* in Germany is made from the rendered flare, back, and belly fat from pigs as well as the much softer goose fat. It is still popular, often homemade, but also commercially available. Apples, onions, marjoram, and *Grieben* (small cracklings) are often added, and it is eaten spread on bread. However, it is kept pure for cooking (it is considered essential for cabbage and sauerkraut) and baking. With the contemporary view on saturated fats, it is not seen as particularly healthy. Nevertheless, *Schmalzgebäck* (small pastry originally deep-fried in lard), such as *Eberswalder Spritzkuchen, Berliner* (called *Pfannkuchen* in Berlin), or *Quarkkeulchen*, has not lost its appeal, although today other fats can be used to produce these pastries.

Margarine und Öl (Margarine and Oil)

Margarine, introduced as a cheaper butter alternative in the 1870s, now covers all sorts of lower-fat spreads and butter substitutes and is mostly promoted as a healthier alternative to butter. However, in that respect, it cannot beat *Olivenöl* (olive oil) in German kitchens. Olive oil is seen as very healthy and offered at all price levels. Consumption of olive oil stands at 1.8 pints per person per year, which puts Germany significantly behind Mediterranean countries. In kitchen practice, though, olive oil also sees strong competition from *Sonnenblumenöl* (sunflower seed oil). The reputation of *Rapsöl* (rape seed or canola oil), which contains even more unsaturated fats than olive oil and is increasingly produced locally, suffers from the fact that it is also used for technical purposes and is therefore seen as industrial. Dark green Austrian *Kürbiskernöl* (pumpkin seed oil) from roasted pumpkin seeds is quite popular in salad dressings or drizzled over pumpkin soups. An old specialty, above all in the eastern regions like the Spreewald south of Berlin, is *Leinöl* (linseed or flax oil), mostly eaten cold with boiled potatoes and quark, drizzled over *Kartoffelpuffer* (latke-style potato pancakes), or simply eaten with white rolls and salt.

EIER (EGGS)

Similar to what was done with milk and butter, farmers' wives made "pocket money" by selling eggs, which had a rather large profit margin. Generally, though, before urbanization egg consumption was based on self-production and only significantly rose after World War II with modern production methods in large factories. Today consumption is at an average of 290 eggs per person per year. Eggs are constantly surrounded by concerns about production methods and scares about food safety, raw egg now being considered very risky. Eggs are used in pastries and desserts, but are also eaten *gekocht* (boiled) or as *Rühreier* (scrambled eggs) for breakfast, or as an alternative to meat. Traditional dishes are *Bratkartoffeln mit Spiegeleiern* (fried potatoes with fried eggs) or *Saure Eier* (sour eggs), which are poached in a roux-based white sauce seasoned with sugar and vinegar. In traditional Berlin pubs, *Soleier*, unshelled hard-boiled eggs marinated in brine in large glass jars, are offered with beer.

GEMÜSE (VEGETABLES)

Prior to industrialization and modern ideas about nutrition, fresh vegetables were seen as not very filling and therefore more a luxury than a daily necessity. Transport and storage were difficult and prices consequently high (as compared to much less perishable, nourishing dried legumes). Availability depended on regions, seasons, and, to a large extent, private gardens. Vegetables were mostly pickled or salted. However, during the second half of the nineteenth century, consumption of fresh vegetables rose significantly, to 140 lb. in 1913. Consumption then dipped due to wars and economic shakeups, and it took until 1970 to reach that level again. Today, vegetables in general accompany meat or fish, are eaten raw as *Rohkost*, or made into salads or soups. *Leipziger Allerlei*, a very elegant dish conceived sometime during the nineteenth century (possibly in Leipzig), represents a true highlight of German vegetable cuisine. It is a springtime or early summer dish, when asparagus, green peas, carrots, kohlrabi, cauliflower, and morels are at their tender best. Cooked separately, they are then combined in a white sauce flavored with crayfish butter, adorned by small crayfish, and served with veal chops or unbreaded schnitzel.

Kohlrabi

Schrebergärten (allotments/community garden plots) in and around cities still exist today but are used mostly for recreational purposes instead of vegetable production. With rising vegetable consumption (211.64 lb. per person in 2004–5), the area used for large-scale commercial vegetable growing is increasing. Most vegetables are sold through nationwide wholesale structures. Increasingly, foil is used to speed harvest time and compete with imports from less northerly climates.

Frozen vegetables and herbs are regularly consumed in Germany. From the 1980s on, freezing replaced cans and jars as the most popular preserving technique. In 2005 Germans consumed 7.72 lb. annually of frozen vegetables on average.

Kohl/Kraut und Sauerkraut (Cabbage and Sauerkraut)

The proverbial Germanic preference for cabbage—*Kohl* in the north, *Kraut* in the south—reaches back at least to the Middle Ages, and likely even earlier, at least for some varieties. *Grünkohl* (curly kale) is the indigenous cabbage of the north, traditionally eaten beginning in mid-November after the first frost, when it is said to taste sweeter, and gradually harvested during the whole of winter. *Weißkohl* and *Rotkohl* (round white and red cabbage) are traditional standard fare all over Germany during autumn and winter. Cut into fine strips they are also eaten raw as salad—a dish the French philosopher Michel de Montaigne remarked on as "unknown to me" in his travel diaries when passing Lindau on Lake Constance in 1580. For *Kohlrouladen* or *Krautwickel* white or savoy cabbage leaves are wrapped around a ground-meat stuffing and braised in the oven.

Sauerkraut is one of the foods most strongly associated with Germany. Although the German poet Ludwig Uhland attributes its invention to his compatriots, the history of pickling vegetables reaches back to the Bronze Age. But sauerkraut is still found throughout Germany. The pointed white *Filderkraut* cabbage heads from around Stuttgart are mostly shredded and salted for *Sauerkraut*, which through malolactic fermentation makes for a less perishable and more digestible result. When eaten raw, it is considered very healthy, but it is also cooked to accompany all kinds of pork in the German versions of Alsatian *choucroûte*.

Blumenkohl (cauliflower) and *Wirsing* (savoy cabbage) arrived with the Romans. They are considered less heavy and less of a winter fare, whereas *Rosenkohl* (Brussels sprouts)—a Belgian cultivate from the end of the eighteenth century—like curly kale are considered best after the first frost. In contemporary Germany, *Brokkoli* (broccoli), although belonging to the cabbage family, is seen as a modern "Italian" vegetable all on its own.

Rotkohl (Red Cabbage)

- 1 3/4 lb. red cabbage, cut in very fine shreds
- 1 eating apple (not too tart), peeled, cored, and diced
- 1 bottle dry, fruity red wine
- 3/8 c. balsamic vinegar
- 1 c. red currant juice, slightly sweetened
- 1 bay leaf
- 4 cloves
- 1 stick cinnamon
- 6 juniper berries, slightly crushed
- sea salt
- black pepper
- 2 tbs. lard
- 1 onion, diced

Heat the spices with the wine, vinegar, and juice. Pour over the cabbage while hot and mix well, then marinate overnight. Strain the cabbage, reserving the liquid. Sweat the onion and apple with the lard until translucent. Add the cabbage and about two fingers' width of the marinade. Cover and cook slowly until the cabbage is soft. Tastes better reheated on the next day.

Kohlrouladen (Cabbage Rolls)

- 1/2 lb. ground meat (half pork, half beef)
- 1 egg
- 1 onion, finely diced
- half a stale white roll, soaked in water or milk, squeezed dry and torn into small pieces
- sea salt
- black pepper
- 1 tbs. parsley, chopped
- 2 small or 1 large head of white cabbage or savoy cabbage
- 2 tbs. butter or lard
- 4 thin slices bacon

- 1 c. water
- 1 tbs. dried porcini mushrooms

Mix the meat with the egg, onion, and bread, and season well. Add the parsley, and divide into four parts. Cut cabbage(s) in halves, cut out stalk liberally, taking out the heart of the cabbage as well as enough to create a hollow for filling. Season cabbage with salt and pepper. If working with two small heads, fill each of the four halves with one part of the stuffing, fold gently to form rolls and tie with string (if using one large head, the halves first need to be gently separated into two layers). Brown rolls on all sides in butter, cover each with a bacon slice, add water and mushrooms, and cover and braise for about 1 hour. Serve with boiled potatoes. Optional: Cooking liquid can be slightly thickened with some potato starch.

Wurzelgemüse (Root Vegetables)

Next to cabbage, *Rüben* (beets), *Rübchen* (turnips), and all other root vegetables play an important role in German cooking. In spite of their bad reputation as cattle fodder, *Kohl-* or *Steckrüben* (rutabagas/swedes) are enjoying a slow comeback, as are *Pastinaken* (parsnips). *Rote Bete* (beets, almost exclusively red) are now being explored in other forms than the traditional sweet-sour pickles. Carrots, called *Karotten, Möhren,* or *Mohrrüben,* are ubiquitous. *Kohlrabi* really belongs to the cabbage family but is often eaten raw and is somewhat similar in flavor to *Rettich* (radish). In its long, white form, *Rettich* is a staple in Bavarian beer gardens, where it is eaten raw, cut in long spirals and salted. *Radieschen* (radishes)

Suppengrün

Teltower Rübchen (Teltow turnips)

are smaller with a red skin and made into salads or used as decoration. The most exclusive member of this family undoubtedly is the small *Teltower Rübchen* (Teltow turnip), from the poor gravel soils just south of Berlin. There it develops a very special spicy taste that had the famous writer and gourmet Johann Wolfgang von Goethe begging his Berlin friend, the composer Carl Friedrich Zelter, for shipments to his house in Weimar.[12] Another special turnip dish is found in the Rhineland: for *Stielmus or Rübstiel* the green stems of white turnips are chopped and cooked in a white sauce to accompany grilled sausages. *Petersilienwurzel* (parsley roots) together with carrot, leek, and celeriac are part of *Suppengrün*, a kind of bouquet garni sold in grocery stores as a bundle and used to make soups.

Steckrübeneintopf (Rutabaga Stew)

- 1 lb. pork belly, fairly finely sliced
- 1 onion, diced
- 1 tbs. pork lard
- 1 qt. water
- 2 lb. rutabagas (swedes), diced
- 1 lb. potatoes, diced
- 0.5 lb. carrots, sliced
- sea salt
- black pepper
- fresh lemon juice

- fresh marjoram
- fresh parsley

Fry pork belly and onion in lard, add water, cover and simmer for about 15 min. Add vegetables, season with salt and pepper, cover and simmer until vegetables are soft. Puree about a quarter of the vegetables in a blender, return to the pot, and add the chopped herbs. Season to taste with lemon juice, salt, and pepper. As with many soups, this one tastes better the next day.

Bohnen (Beans)

Beans are another traditional staple vegetable. *Grüne Bohnen* (green beans) designate French or runner beans and are a common side dish all over Germany. In the north they are also combined in a stew with bacon and small pears—*Birnen, Bohnen, Speck*—or cut up and cooked in a creamy white sauce as *Schnippelbohnen*. Broad beans are rarely found, with the exception of Westphalia, where they are prepared with bacon for *Dicke Bohnen mit Speck*.

Hülsenfrüchte (Legumes)

The dried pods of *Linsen* (lentils), *Erbsen* (peas), and *Bohnen* (beans) have been around since Germanic times. They were never as popular as, for instance, in India but rather represented an answer to the problem of storage and winter food supply. They were always seen as time consuming to prepare and difficult to digest. In the north, gray peas were the most popular legume, whereas in the southwest (and Westphalia) dried broad beans were common; all over Germany, but above all in Bavaria and Württemberg, yellow peas and lentils are used. With the spread of potatoes, a rapid decline in the area planted with legumes set in. Consumption correspondingly went down from 45.64 lb. per capita in 1850 to 1.98 lb. in 1975. Legumes were often associated with hard times. Today this *cucina povera* (poor man's cuisine) survives in some stews and regional dishes, mostly in Swabia. *Linsen mit Spätzle* (lentils with spätzle) is the Swabian version of Italian dishes combining pasta and beans. *Erbsensuppe* (pea soup) is almost a cliché as a working-class soup. However, today most *Erbsen* are consumed fresh or frozen, then called *grüne Erbsen* (green peas).

Linsensuppe mit Preiselbeeren und Äpfeln
(Lentil Soup with Cranberries and Apples)

- 0.6 lb. (1 1/2 c.) large brown lentils
- 4 tbs. dried cranberries, coarsely chopped

- 1 tbs. bacon, diced
- 1 small onion, diced
- 1 small carrot, diced
- 1 tbs. celeriac, diced
- 1 medium parsnip, diced
- 1 firm tart apple, diced
- 1 tsp. thyme
- sea salt
- black pepper
- 1 tbs. butter
- 2 1/2 c. water
- pure cranberry juice to taste

Soak lentils (if necessary) and boil until soft, adding cranberries toward the end. In a separate pot, sauté bacon, vegetables, and apple in butter. When onion is translucent, add water and thyme. Boil until soft, then puree to desired chunkiness. Add the lentil/cranberry mixture, and season to taste with salt, pepper, and juice.

Gurken (Cucumbers)

Long green cucumbers are made into salads, often seasoned with dill, whereas stouter versions are seeded and (especially in and around Berlin) cut up into *Schmorgurken* (braised cucumbers), accompanied by boiled potatoes and *Buletten*. In the Spreewald region southeast of Berlin, renowned for its cucumbers and horseradish, they are pickled with mustard seeds in a sweet-sour brine for *Senfgurken* (mustard pickles). Smaller cucumbers are salted and, like *Sauerkraut*, undergo malolactic fermentation to emerge as *Saure* (sour) *Gurken*, similar to American Jewish pickles.[13] Alternatively, they may be pickled in a brine with vinegar, dill, and onion for *Gewürzgurken* (spiced pickles).

Buletten mit Schmorgurken (Fried Meat Patties with Braised Cucumber)

- 1/2 lb. ground meat (half pork, half beef)
- 1 egg
- 1 onion, finely diced
- half a stale white roll, soaked in water or milk, squeezed dry and torn into small pieces
- sea salt

- black pepper
- bread crumbs
- butter

Mix the meat with the egg, onion, and bread, and season well. Shape with hands into six not-too-flat patties, coat with bread crumbs, and fry in butter.

- 1 long English cucumber
- 1 tbs. bacon, finely diced
- 1/2 onion, finely diced
- 1 tbs. butter
- sea salt
- pepper

Cut the cucumber in half lengthwise, scrape out the seeds with a spoon, and cut into slices about 1/3 inch wide. Sauté bacon and onion in the butter, add cucumber, and cook to your liking. Season with salt and pepper.

Zwiebeln und Knoblauch (Onions and Garlic)

In Germany today, *Knoblauch* (garlic) is associated with Mediterranean cuisine and has found its way into contemporary cooking mostly through the influence of immigrant workers from former Yugoslavia and from

Bärlauch (wild garlic)

Italy. However, it was once cultivated among other herbs in private gardens, and the area around Nuremberg, still referred to as *Knoblauchsland* (garlic country), supplied garlic on a commercial scale. *Zwiebeln* (onions), mostly yellow but some red or white, are omnipresent as a basic ingredient. At open-air markets, they are traditionally sold at the same stalls as potatoes. They are used in many recipes, almost as a condiment, but also made into *Zwiebelkuchen* (onion tart) to go with young wine in autumn. Swabian *Zwiebelrostbraten* (onion roast) pairs fried onions with a steak and gravy. For the past decade, the wild-growing *Bärlauch* (*allium ursinum*) of medieval times has enjoyed a general comeback. This more delicately flavored garlic variety grows in the woods in springtime. Its leaves, which resemble lily of the valley, are used in all kinds of dishes, pesto-like preparations, and cheeses.

Spargel (Asparagus)

Spargel (asparagus) is a national passion in Germany. It is cultivated in all the *Länder* (states), but Schwetzingen near Heidelberg and Beelitz southwest of Berlin arguably enjoy the highest reputation. Although the green version is now produced and eaten as well, and fresh spears are imported from Israel, California, and Peru in the off-season, asparagus in Germany is still clearly defined as white, something special, and strictly seasonal. The asparagus spears are cut and eaten from around Easter (depending on the weather, although some producers are now heating their fields in addition to covering them with foil for an earlier harvest) until

Spargelstecher (white asparagus harvest)

Johannistag on June 24. Traditionally, asparagus does not accompany meat as a side dish like other "ordinary" vegetables but instead plays the main role and is itself accompanied by ham or a small schnitzel, butter or Hollandaise sauce, and boiled potatoes or *Flädle* (small, thin, crêpe-like pancakes). *Schwarzwurzeln* (salsify) are also known as winter asparagus, as they are in season from October until January, but they are much less popular. *Hopfensprossen* (hop sprouts) are a rare local specialty in the hop-growing area around Tettnang near Lake Constance.

Gebratener weißer Spargel mit Poulardenbrust in Estragonsauce (Fried White Asparagus with Chicken Breast in Tarragon Sauce)

- 2 lb. white asparagus, peeled and cut diagonally in 1-inch-long pieces
- 2 tbs. butter
- sea salt
- 4 skinless chicken breasts
- black pepper
- 1 tbs. flour
- 2 tbs. butter
- 5 tbs. dry white wine
- 4 tbs. chicken broth
- 6 slightly crushed juniper berries
- 5/8 c. cream
- 2 tbs. fresh tarragon, chopped

Slowly fry asparagus in butter, so that it partly caramelizes to a shiny golden color. Season and reserve. Season meat and toss in flour. Sauté in butter on both sides. Add wine, broth, and juniper berries, reduce heat, cover, and cook on very low heat for about 10 min., turning meat once. Add cream and tarragon, and cook another 5 min. without boiling. Reheat asparagus and serve with chicken.

Tomaten und Mittelmeergemüse (Tomatoes and Mediterranean Vegetables)

Omnipresent today, albeit mostly in an industrialized, robust, long-life version, *Tomaten* (tomatoes) are a surprisingly new feature on German tables. For a long time they were seen as suspicious—they belong to the nightshade family—and not particularly suited to the German climate. At the turn of the twentieth century, they started to be made into sweet jams, corresponding to ketchups and sweet pickles in English-speaking countries. Mediterranean influences boosted tomatoes' popularity after

World War II, and today tomato soup, spaghetti with tomato sauce, and mozzarella with tomatoes and basil count among the most popular dishes throughout Germany. *Gemüsepaprika* (bell peppers), *Auberginen* (eggplants), *Zucchini*, and *Fenchel* (fennel) are all common and available year-round. These vegetables are often imported from the Netherlands, Italy, or Israel.

Kürbis (Pumpkin and Squash)

Kürbis (designating both pumpkin and squash), like beets, used to be consumed mostly in the form of sweet-sour pickles, but it is experiencing a culinary renaissance. For the younger generation, it is seen as a new discovery, furthered by the offerings of organic gardeners growing smaller, more flavorful varieties like Hokkaido.

Salat (Lettuce)

Salat (lettuce, although in German *Salat* also means salad) is very popular and considered extremely healthy. All the modern varieties are available, increasingly also in ready-to-eat bags. Lettuce is always eaten cold, as a side dish or, enriched with all kinds of meat, cheese, or seafood, as a starter or light meal. The mild-tasting *Kopfsalat* (round green head lettuce) is a favorite in the north, where it is traditionally dressed with sour cream, lemon juice, and sugar. In the south, *Feldsalat* (lamb's lettuce) dominates, dressed with oil and vinegar, sometimes with a little pureed potato added. *Rucola* (arugula) is a hugely successful import from Italy since the 1990s, whereas

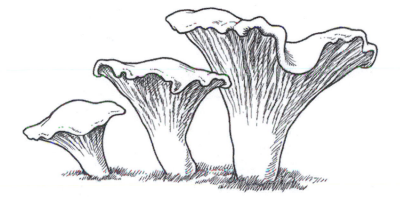

Pfifferlinge (chanterelles)

Maronen (bay bolete mushroom)

Brunnenkresse (watercress), once grown on a large scale around Erfurt, today is a rarity and mostly imported from France.

Pilze (Mushrooms)

Germans love *Pilze* (mushrooms) or *Schwammerl*, as they are called in the south. *Steinpilze* (ceps/porcini), *Pfifferlinge* (chanterelles), and *Maronen* (bay bolete) are seen as very special, either gathered privately or bought in the market, where they are often imported from eastern European countries. They are incorporated into many dishes, especially in autumn. *Champignons* (button mushrooms) are very common and commercially cultivated, as are relatively new varieties such as *Austernpilze* (oyster mushrooms), *Shitake*, and, very recently, various new kinds of *Seitlinge* (Pleurotus/oyster mushrooms).

KRÄUTER UND GEWÜRZE (HERBS AND SPICES)

Küchenkräuter (Green Herbs)

Petersilie (parsley), *Schnittlauch* (chives), and *Dill* are the most common fresh herbs in Germany, grown in gardens and on windowsills, and widely available commercially in small bunches or pots. They are used as a garnish as well as in all kinds of dishes. In the egg-based, cold *Frankfurter Grüne Sauce* (Frankfurt green sauce), they are joined by *Kerbel* (chervil), *Borretsch* (borage), *Estragon* (tarragon), and *Pimpernelle* (pimpernel). Fresh *Basilikum* (basil) is perceived as Italian and since the 1990s has become extremely popular, as dried *Herbes de Provence* from France used to be in

Waldmeister (woodruff)

the 1970s. Thanks to the recent success of Thai and Vietnamese cuisine, fresh *Koriander* (cilantro) will probably be remembered as the fashion of the first years of the twenty-first century. *Majoran* (marjoram) is traditionally used in many sausages and in lard. Green beans are often boiled with *Bohnenkraut* (savory) added to the water, whereas goose is prepared with *Beifuß* (mugwort). These combinations are leftovers from the old holistic medicine school of the time of Hildegard von Bingen (1098–1179). *Waldmeister* (woodruff) used to be a very popular flavor for ice cream. It is still used in private preparations of *Maibowle*, a white wine punch. However, since 1981 it has been banned for commercial purposes because it contains toxic cumarin.

Salz, Pfeffer und Gewürze (Salt, Pepper, and Spices)

Salz (salt), as in other countries, has recently been the subject of many paradoxical discussions. On the one hand, a fashion has developed for exclusive-origin salt varieties like "ancient" Himalayan salt or French *fleur de sel* instead of traditional German *Bad Reichenhaller Salinensalz*. On the other hand, salt is being denounced as the new culprit in nutrition-based diseases. Nevertheless, the *Salzstreuer* (salt shaker) still is an essential part of the table setting in Germany. More often than not it is joined by a pepper shaker or a *Pfeffermühle* (pepper mill)—and sometimes also by a bottle of *Maggi* (a popular brand of liquid seasoning tasting predominantly of lovage, which is often used in soups). Otherwise, *Gewürze* (spices) are used sparingly compared with practices in other countries. *Muskatnuß* (nutmeg) is mostly used for potato dishes. *Piment* (allspice) is important in blood sausage. *Wacholder* (juniper) is used for game roasts and *Sauerkraut*.

Maggiwürze

Nelken (cloves), *Zimt* (cinnamon), *Anis* (aniseed), *Fenchel* (fennel seed), *Kardamom* (cardamom), and *Vanille* (vanilla, often in the form of artificially flavored *Vanillinzucker*) feature mostly in (Christmas) baking or in combination with fruit.

Essig (Vinegar)

Apart from salad dressings, *Essig* (vinegar) is used in traditional cooking for purposes of seasoning, preserving vegetables and meat, or tenderizing. *Rheinischer Sauerbraten* is probably the most popular dish in that respect. Referred to as brisket in Jewish American cooking, *Sauerbraten* is a beef pot roast in a dark brown, vinegary sauce, sometimes with the addition of raisins. Traditionally, game was also marinated in vinegar, but with modern refrigeration that preparation has become less popular. Vinegar used to be mostly *Branntweinessig* of very ordinary quality, made from diluted potato spirits and sometimes flavored with herbs. *Weinessig* (wine vinegar) is more expensive, and *Apfelessig* (apple cider vinegar) is a popular alternative in some regions in the south. Today, Italian *balsamico* is practically a German ingredient, although mostly in somewhat lighter, less expensive versions than the *tradizionale di Modena*. Recently some producers in the Palatinate and Württemberg have specialized in very refined fruit and wine vinegars, also offered as an aperitif or digestif.

Senf und Meerrettich (Mustard and Horseradish)

Senf (mustard), or *Mostrich* as it is known in the east, above all is an important accompaniment for all kinds of sausages. *Scharf* (hot) mustard is the German version of Dijon mustard, the most extreme being from Düsseldorf. *Süss* (sweet) mustard is a Bavarian specialty for *Weisswurst*. Apart from those, mustard exists in all kinds of flavors, which are available from smaller producers. In the south, freshly grated, pungent *Meerrettich* (horseradish) often replaces mustard with boiled beef or sausages. It is used in pickles, made into sauces for meat and fish, and mixed with cream or grated apple (these preparations are also available commercially in jars and tubes). The Spreewald southeast of Berlin and the region around Nuremberg are the main production areas for horseradish.

OBST (FRUIT)

As with fresh vegetables, *Obst* (fresh fruit) was deemed not very nourishing in the nineteenth century and was even more perishable and thus difficult to store and transport. Consumption really only picked up toward the end of the nineteenth century. Until then, fruit was grown in private gardens, as an aristocratic hobby, or in wealthy monasteries. With agricultural reforms, the interest in pomology (the study of fruit growing) swept over from England, and fruit production started on a commercial level. Transregional distribution was made possible by the new railway system. Apples, pears, sweet and sour cherries, and plums dominated the market, mostly dried for storage or as ingredients in other dishes. Only a very small privileged group could afford imported tropical luxuries. The canning industry at the end of the nineteenth century first offered such luxury products as peaches and pineapple. Today these fruits are mostly consumed fresh, as are all kinds of fresh imports from around the world. However, before reunification bananas were extremely rare in East Germany and became a symbol of freedom. Similarly, a can of pineapple rings was once considered a very welcome gift from the West. Today Germans annually consume about 165 lb. of fresh fruit (of which about a quarter is produced in Germany, mostly around Hamburg and on Lake Constance), plus about 88 lb. of citrus fruit (much of it in the form of juice).

Äpfel und Birnen (Apples and Pears)

Äpfel (apples) are probably seen as the most "German" fruit, with local varieties like *Ananasrenette*, *Berlepsch*, *Finkenwerder Herbstprinz*, *Gewürzluike*, *Goldparmäne*, *Horneburger*, or *Jakob Fischer* enjoying a revival. But the bulk of fresh apples are international varieties like Granny Smith, Golden and Red Delicious, Jonagold, or Pink Lady imported from as far away as New Zealand, just as *Birnen* (pears) mostly come from Italy or Argentina. Traditionally, apples are often made into *Apfelmus* (applesauce) to eat with pancakes or other desserts. Pears are poached with cloves or cinnamon for compote or baked into cakes. *Bratäpfel* (baked whole apples) are a popular dessert in winter. In savory dishes apples are combined with blood sausage, such as in *Himmel und Erde* (heaven and earth), which also includes mashed potatoes and fried onions.

Kirschen und Pflaumen (Cherries and Plums)

Süßkirschen (sweet cherries) are mostly eaten fresh, whereas *Sauerkirschen* (sour cherries) are made into compote, baked puddings like *Kirschenmichel/Kerscheplotzer*, or baked into cakes like *Kirschstreuselkuchen* topped with plenty of butter-sugar crumble. *Pflaumen* (plums) are mostly of the medium-sized, oblong, purple *Zwetschgen* variety with yellow meat and are, above all, baked on top of large sheets of yeast dough to make *Pflaumenkuchen*, *Zwetschgenkuchen*, or *Quetschekuche* (plum cake/tart). In some regions this cake is combined with potato soup for a traditional Thursday or Saturday lunch.

Beeren und Rhabarber (Berries and Rhubarb)

Erdbeeren (strawberries) are perhaps the favorite fruit of Germans (at least strawberry is their favored yogurt flavor) and a symbol of spring or early summer. Today strawberries are imported throughout the year but experience the same quality loss as year-round imported tomatoes. The most traditional way to enjoy strawberries is with milk and sugar

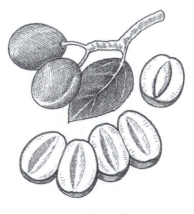

Zwetschgen

or, more luxuriously, with cream.[14] They are also combined with ice cream and made into all kinds of desserts or into *Erdbeerkuchen* (strawberry cake/tart), using a sponge cake or shortbread pastry as a base. In combination with other berries such as *Himbeeren* (raspberries), *Blau-* or *Heidelbeeren* (blueberries), *Brombeeren* (blackberries), *weiße, rote,* and *schwarze Johannisbeeren* (white, red, and black currants), and *Kirschen* (cherries), strawberries are cooked and thickened with potato starch, semolina, or sago (very similar to tapioca) to make *Rote Grütze* (literally red gruel), a semiliquid dessert often served with cream or ice cream. Originally *Rote Grütze* was a specialty of the regions on the northern coast, probably a remnant of the old gruel. *Rhabarbergrütze* is made from rhubarb, which is in season much earlier than strawberries. The long red sticks (the large leaves contain toxic oxalic acid and are discarded) are seen as somewhat old-fashioned and very German. However, they only came to Germany at the end of the nineteenth century from England, where rhubarb cultivation originally started for the pharmaceutical use of the plant's root.

Rote Grütze (Red Berry Dessert)

- Red, black, and white currants—or rhubarb
- Cherries
- Blackberries
- Strawberries
- Raspberries
- Granulated sugar
- Granulated gelatin, potato starch, sago or tapioca pearls
  (whatever you are using, the result should be semiliquid)

This is a dish without a fixed recipe: use the fruit that is available, in quantities that appeal to you—there is no right or wrong with this! Boil the currants or rhubarb with some sugar until soft, and (if using currants) pass though a sieve to get rid of the pips. Thicken this puree with the starch, sago, or tapioca following instructions on the package. Toward the end add the other (more delicate) fruit, and bring to a boil once. If using gelatin, soak and dissolve in the hot fruit. Serve cold with liquid cream, vanilla custard, or vanilla ice cream.

Andere Früchte, Trockenfrüchte und Konfitüre (Other Fruits, Dried Fruit, and Jam)

Pfirsiche (peaches) and *Aprikosen* (apricots) are grown locally to a small extent, but the bulk is imported like all other Mediterranean, tropical, and exotic varieties. Wild fruits such as *Preiselbeeren* (a smaller, local variety of cranberries, mostly served with game dishes), *Holunder* (elderberry), *Hagebutten* (rose hips), or *Sanddorn* (sea buckthorn) play minor roles in German cuisine. *Trockenfrüchte* (dried fruits) are enjoying a certain comeback in health food stores, whereas *Konfitüre* (jam) on buttered rolls or bread is seen as a necessity for breakfast and is often homemade rather than purchased.[15] Again, strawberry seems to top an enormous variety of other flavors in popularity. Apples are mostly made into jelly or *Apfelkraut* (a kind of dark syrup), whereas *Pflaumenmus* is made from plums cooked for long hours with some spices and very little sugar in a slow oven until it becomes a thick, dark, aromatic puree.

SWEETENERS

Zucker (Sugar)

Today, sugar in Germany is commonly white refined *Rübenzucker* (beet sugar). Brown, unrefined *Rohrzucker* (cane sugar) is perceived by some as healthier (although more expensive), and thickened fruit syrup is used in health food. Imports of cane sugar historically replaced honey, until then the only sweetener available, first in the sixteenth century through Venetian merchants, then from the seventeenth century on through northern ports. Reserved initially for medicinal purposes, sugar became a real cult among the upper classes (in his cookbook published in 1581, Marx Rumpolt does not use any honey). In the eighteenth century, for peasants, sugar was still affordable only for special occasions; for example, millet porridge was sprinkled with sugar on festive occasions. Sugar was also combined with the fashionable new hot drinks coffee, tea, and chocolate and was featured in the sweet pastries served with them. It was used in liqueurs, pralines, lemonade, and ice cream. The extraction of sugar from beets first started in Prussia during the trade embargo in the Napoleonic wars, and with modern agricultural techniques, sugar became much more affordable from the 1840s. By 1900, sugar was no longer a luxury product but common among the working classes. In the Rhineland, *Rübenkraut*, a noncrystallizing dark sweet syrup and by-product of sugar production, is today a regional specialty eaten like jam. *Konfekt* (a box of chocolates) is a common gift when invited to someone's house, apart from flowers and, more recently, wine. Sweet snacks, chocolate bars, and the like are readily available at kiosks and vending machines. *Gummibärchen* (gummy bears) made from glucose syrup, sugar, dextrose, gelatin, and flavorings were invented in Bonn in 1922. Their popularity transcends all age and social boundaries. However, as in other Western cultures, sugar generally has a negative image and is seen as a major culprit in obesity and related health problems. Artificial sweeteners are widely available, as are sugarfree diet versions of soft drinks and all kinds of food.

Honig (Honey)

With the introduction and subsequent spread of sugar use, *Honig* (honey) transformed from general sweetener to special ingredient. The two have nearly swapped roles, as honey today is seen as a very healthy alternative to sugar, almost like medicine. Honey is spread on buttered bread as an alternative to jam and used to sweeten herbal tea as well in baking *Honigkuchen* (gingerbread) for Christmas. *Heidehonig* from the heath around Lüneburg is especially aromatic and a valued rarity.

GETRÄNKE (BEVERAGES)

Kaffee und Tee (Coffee and Tea)

Although *Tee* (tea) has a long tradition in the north, where strong, dark *Ostfriesentee* (East Frisian tea) is drunk with cream and rock candy, *Kaffee* (coffee) is the hot caffeinated drink of choice in Germany. It is drunk at breakfast, during numerous breaks throughout the day, and especially for *Kaffee und Kuchen* (coffee and cake) in the afternoon. Italian espresso machines have become fashionable, but the standard is less concentrated *Filterkaffee* (filtered coffee), drunk with milk or *Kaffeesahne* (condensed milk) and sometimes sugar. International coffee chains, as well as most bakeries, offer take-out coffee in all the modern "latte" versions. *Koffeinfreier Kaffee* (decaffeinated coffee) is generally readily available. Similarly to butter prices, coffee prices are a sensitive issue for many Germans, although generally coffee is very affordable compared to in the past. Coffee surrogates such as chicory or malted barley play a much lesser role compared with pre–World War II consumption. With few exceptions, tea is prepared using bags of undifferentiated "*schwarzer*" (black) tea (although *schwarz* [black] in connection with coffee refers to a beverage without milk, with tea it designates the fermented variety in contrast to green or herbal tea). Various types of *Kräutertee* (herbal tea), such as *Kamille* (chamomile), *Hagebutte* (rose hip), *Früchte* (mixed fruit), and *Pfefferminze* (peppermint), are considered a healthy alternative, lately joined by green tea and caffeine-free rooibos tea from South Africa, also available in a multitude of flavored versions.

Bier (Beer)

Whereas coffee as a popular beverage is a relatively recent phenomenon, *Bier* (beer) has been *the* German drink since Germanic times. Today an average of 274.84 pints per person are drunk annually, whether with meals or on its own, at home or in pubs and bars. However, there are great variations in consumption and preferred varieties from region to region. All German beer sold in Germany must be produced according to the German *Reinheitsgebot* (purity law). This originated as a Bavarian law and dates back to 1516 when it only allowed *Hopfen* (hops), *Gerstenmalz* (barley malt), and *Wasser* (water) for beer production. *Weizen* (wheat) has been added to the list, due to the yeast-clouded *Weizenbier* much loved in southern Germany, which is drunk from special tall glasses. Today, stabilizing agents are tolerated as well, as a concession to the large beer companies that dominate the industry. Most beer today is bottom-fermented and sold in bottles, although draughts are more highly valued by connoisseurs. *Pilsner* (frequently shortened to *Pils*) is almost a synonym for beer in the north and tastes (in general) much more bitter than the light *Kölsch* of Cologne. Brown *Altbier* is the specialty of Düsseldorf along with various local specialties like *Gose* in Leipzig or *Berliner Weisse*, both slightly sour wheat beers, the latter served flavored with a dash of red or green fruit syrup. In Bavaria, where beer consumption is highest following Saxony, beer is considered a food more than an alcoholic beverage, and Bavarian varieties tend to be lighter than in the north. However, anything ending in *-ator* (like *Salvator*) and brewed during Lent can be of devastating strength. Shandies, beer mixed with soda, are popular in the north as *Alsterwasser* (with Sprite), in the south as *Radler*, or as *Russ'n* with wheat beer. *Malzbier* (malt beer) is dark and sweet and contains no alcohol.

Wein (Wine)

Generally *Wein* (wine) complements beer in regional consumption, with the exception of the north, where spirits play a more important role in total alcohol consumption. Wine has been produced in Germany at least since the first century A.D. The main wine-growing areas have always been along the Rhine river and its tributaries: the Main, Nahe, Moselle, and Ahr, as well as around the Neckar and the Elbe. The northern climate is balanced by protected microclimates near rivers. Riesling is the most important variety of German wine in terms of quality. Traditionally (and in complete contrast to Roman culture), wine was and to some extent still is drunk by itself, for instance, in the afternoon or after dinner, and in general does not require food. This possibly reflects the fact that German wine tends to contain less alcohol than the products of more southern wine countries. However, since the 1990s, Germans have developed a keen interest in all kinds of wines from around the world, as well as wine and food combinations. Wine service and wine lists in restaurants have become much better. Wine shops with a very good international selection are common now, whereas previous generations used to buy their wine exclusively and directly from "their" winegrower. Contrary to widespread prejudices, German wine is not all sweet, and a considerable percentage of it is even red and very good at that.

Around Frankfurt and in the southwest, traditional *Apfelwein* (apple, sometimes also pear cider), locally called *Ebbelwoi* or *Moschd*, is made and mostly consumed locally like beer. It can be very harsh on unaccustomed palates, although some producers have recently achieved outstanding quality.

Spirituosen und Liköre (Spirits and Liqueurs)

Most spirits, commonly called *Schnaps*, are drunk in the north in the form of *Korn* or *Klarer*, a clear grain spirit often flavored with juniper. They are often accompanied by beer. Their consumption in public, even by respectable elderly ladies (and even in the afternoon), is totally socially acceptable. In the southwest, all kinds of fruits are distilled to make *Obstbranntwein* (fruit brandy), the simplest being *Obstler*, which is made from apples and pears, whereas *Kirsch(wasser)* is perhaps the best known. *Zibärtle* is a brandy made from a wild plum variety and reminiscent in taste of marzipan. *Topi(nambur)* from Jerusalem artichokes is another specialty brandy with a very unique taste. Liqueurs are seen as old-fashioned today and mostly relegated to cocktails, with *Eierlikör* (eggnog) made of egg yolks and cream enjoying a special retro fashion status.

Mineralwasser, Fruchtsäfte und Softdrinks (Mineral Water, Fruit Juice, and Soft Drinks)

In 2006 Germans drank 627.27 pints of alcohol-free beverages on average (up 3% from the previous year, and second behind Spain for all of Europe) and spent slightly more on them than on alcoholic beverages. Although *Leitungswasser* (tap water) is perfectly safe everywhere and unchlorinated, today many prefer to buy bottled *Mineralwasser* (mineral water). Traditionally, only *Sprudel* (sparkling mineral water) was purchased, above all to mix with fruit juice or wine for refreshing, lighter

Schorle. Apfelsaft (apple juice) is a big favorite, followed by *Orangensaft* (orange juice), often available freshly squeezed. Besides that, a multitudinous variety of fruit drinks is available, which are mostly seen as an alternative to alcoholic beverages, the other alternative being soft drinks of all kinds. Recently, *Bionade*, a less sweet lemonade with "alternative" flavors like ginger, elderflower, or lychee, has become a huge success, above all in health food circles and the club scene.

NOTES

1. Domestic fruit varieties in 1982–83 had a market share of almost 80%, which in 1994–95 had sunk to under 40% (tropical and citrus fruits included). Not even a quarter of the fruit consumed was home grown. Bundesministerium für Ernährung, Landwirtschaft und Forsten, ed., *Der Gartenbau in der Bundesrepublik Deutschland* (Bonn: Köllen, 1997), 73.

2. The most common meat versions today probably are *Leberknödel* with liver; *Königsberger Klopse* made of pork, served in a white sauce with capers; and fried meat patties like *Buletten, Frikadellen, Fleischpflanzerl,* and so on. Günter Wiegelmann, *Alltags- und Festspeisen in Mitteleuropa: Innovationen, Strukturen und Regionen vom späten Mittelalter bis zum 20. Jahrhundert,* 2nd ed. with Barbara Krug-Richter (Münster: Waxmann, 2006), 233.

3. The simplest version of this are *Flädle,* crêpe-like pancakes cut into thin stripes or served with asparagus. They belong to a whole family of "flat dumplings/ noodles": *Eierkuchen* or *Pfannkuchen* are pancakes eaten with sweet or savory accompaniments. *Reibekuchen* or *Kartoffelpuffer* are made from grated raw potatoes, often eaten with applesauce. In contrast, small dumplings made of meat, semolina, or marrow are eaten in soups.

4. Quark is a soft white cheese, similar to sour cream in texture. In America, quark is available at some health food stores and many German delis and restaurants. If unavailable, fresh soft farmer's cheese can also be used. See also section on yogurt and quark.

5. Today horsemeat is very rare in Germany, found almost exclusively in the southeast at specialty butchers. Undoubtedly this is linked to the fact that in 736, the Benedictine missionary Boniface prohibited the eating of horsemeat.

6. According to most historians, pigs had already enjoyed great popularity until the thirteenth century, when they were mostly fattened in oak forests. When those became more scarce, pig raising could not keep pace with population growth. In 1900 Germans consumed about twice as much pork (then more affordable) as beef (more expensive), and total meat consumption was significantly higher in the generally more affluent cities than in poorer rural areas. Hans Jürgen Teuteberg, "Studien zur Volksernährung unter sozial- und wirtschaftsgeschichtlichen Aspekten," in *Nahrungsgewohnheiten in der Industrialisierung des 19. Jahrhunderts,* ed. Hans Jürgen Teuteberg and Günter Wiegelmann (Münster: Lit

Verlag, 2005), 105; and Hans Jürgen Teuteberg and Günter Wiegelmann, eds., *Unsere tägliche Kost: Studien zur Geschichte des Alltags* (Münster: Coppenrath, 1986), 70.

7. In 2003 Germans ate about 121 lb. pork per person, as compared to 95 lb. average for the European Union. Beef and veal: Germany 29/European Union 44 lb. Poultry: Germany 40/European Union 51 lb. (Gross human apparent consumption, data published by the European Commission in *Food: From farm to fork statistics [Luxembourg: Office for Official Publications of the European Communities, 2006]*). Given that pork was regarded as an indulgence and "distempered" during the Renaissance, Tacitus would still be right about Germany being an uncivilized country without self-control. Ken Albala, *Eating Right in the Renaissance* (Berkeley: University of California Press, 2002), 181.

8. For a more detailed discussion, see Ursula Heinzelmann, "Rumohr's Falscher Rehschlegel: The Significance of Venison in German Cuisine," *Gastronomica: The Journal of Food and Culture* 6, no. 4 (2006): 53–58.

9. Statistisches Bundesamt, *Statistisches Jahrbuch 2006 für die Bundesrepublik Deutschland* (Wiesbaden, 2006), figure for 2004, http://www.destatis.de/jetspeed/portal/cms/Sites/destatis/SharedContent/Oeffentlich/AI/IC/Publikationen/Jahrbuch/Wirtschaftsrechnungen,property=file.pdf.

10. Another aspect is the 1933 Nazi law forcing all farms to deliver their entire milk production to a dairy, hindering individual cheese-making (and butter-making) culture.

11. Statistisches Bundesamt, *Statistisches Jahrbuch 2006*, figure for 2004.

12. Goethe, for instance, wrote in a letter on September 28, 1807: "I would then be very obliged if you could send me a bushel of genuine Teltow turnips," then in another letter on December 21, 1809: "the delicious [Teltow] turnips strike me firstly, to forget them would be very hard since they, once again, stand deliciously upon the table." Hans-Günter Ottenberg and Edith Zehm (ed.), *Briefwechsel zwischen Goethe und Zelter in den Jahren 1799 bis 1832* (München: Carl Hanser, 1991), 166, 221. For a detailed study of the history of Teltow turnips, see Ursula Heinzelmann, "The Teltow Turnip," *Slow: The Magazine of the Slowfood Movement*, Engl. ed., no. 55 (2006): 98–109.

13. For a detailed study of their history, see Ursula Heinzelmann, "Spreewälder Gurken: Pickled Cucumbers from the Spreewald," *Gastronomica: The Journal of Food and Culture* 4, no. 3 (2004): 13–17.

14. The Alsatian physician Melchior Sebizius (1578–1674) complained about that habit and remarked how much more digestible they would be when eaten with wine, sugar, cinnamon, or ginger (quoted in Albala, *Eating Right in the Renaissance*, 282).

15. *Marmelade* is the more popular designation, but since an EU law of 1982 that word is reserved for English-style marmalade.

3

Cooking

In Germany, as in most societies and cultures worldwide, the private kitchen where cooking and related tasks take place has traditionally been women's domain. Recent studies have shown that food- and meal-related work is still distributed according to gender. Women invest significantly more time in nutrition-related household tasks than do men, no matter whether and to what extent they contribute to the family income.[1] But women's status in the family as well as in German society as a whole clearly has changed during the last century.

WOMEN'S STANDING IN THE KITCHEN AND STATE

Until about 200 years ago, a strict patriarchal system in heaven, on earth, and in the home was assumed. The father was at the top of the household and its sole legal representative. He was followed in ranking order by the mother, their natural children, and possibly the servants. The mother and mistress of the house had clearly designated responsibilities of her own, overseeing the daily running and administration of the household, the size of which depended on their social class and thus the husband's occupation. She could make money of her own only in a very limited way (for instance, by selling eggs or butter). Thus women had internal power, but neither legal nor financial means for an independent position in society.

At the onset of the industrial revolution, because of growing urbanization, household structures changed and German women became more aware of gender role imbalance. Beginning around 1848, some of them organized in clubs to fight for political, social, and cultural equality. Due to the economic and social upheavals during and following World War I, more and more women took paid jobs and gradually became more integrated in politics and society. Equal rights legislation introduced in 1918 brought the right to vote as well as eligibility for holding office but failed to redefine women's role in marriage. Household work remained her unpaid, legal duty, and the husband as provider ruled over any legal and financial decisions. The Nazi ideology of the woman as solely wife and mother was a severe hurdle, even a throwback, on the road to independence.

The path to a man's heart leads through his stomach, this is an old, never questioned truth. . . . The man at noon returns home from his office or any other working place and wants to get new strength at the family table. . . . The social question will be solved quickly, as soon as all women know how to cook well and make the home feel cozy, so that the man feels better at home than at the inn.[2]

This quotation from one of the most important middle-class cookbooks of the 1930s typifies the attitude toward gender roles throughout Germany. What is striking is that compared with the following excerpt from a "modern" cookbook of 1965, not much seems to have changed:

Although throughout time women were expected to cook "with love," this is especially true today, as we have come to understand that the family's health lies in the woman's hands. However, for the love for her family, she has to make a genuine effort.[3]

In spite of the significant role women played in the everyday economy during the immediate postwar years, at least in West Germany they were soon expected to return to the prewar gender pattern as nice, caring, submissive *Hausfrauen* (housewives). Only in 1977 did political pressure from the German feminist movement (inspired by the American civil rights movement and the European-wide students' movement), as well as from associations like the *Deutscher Hausfrauen-Bund* (German Housewives' Alliance, founded in 1949) and the *Deutscher LandFrauenverband* (German Countrywomen's Society, founded in 1898), lead to legal reforms in West Germany. Male dominance was replaced by partnership, and a married woman no longer needed permission from her husband to take a paid job outside the household. By now, the most extreme representatives of the new women's movement saw anything related to kitchen and household as discriminatory and antifeminist. In the communes and shared apartments at the end of the 1960s and through the 1970s, cooking as well as other household tasks tended to be strictly shared.

In East Germany, equal rights for women were part of the 1949 constitution from the start: "Through the Republic's rights the necessary institutions will be created which guarantee that a woman can reconcile her tasks as citizen and worker with her duties as woman and mother" (paragraph 18). But neither kindergartens nor socialist ideas managed to suddenly change traditional role models. In the reality of everyday life, women were merely expected to perform a double role, one paid and one not. And most of them did: in 1989, 91% of East German women went out to work and 92% had at least one child. Most women without doubt enjoyed the recognition and self-affirmation that came with a paid job. But most of them were also probably too tired for extravagant cooking in the evening. Combined with the never-ending problems of food supplies, it is difficult to take the following statements from the introduction of East Germany's most important general cookbook very seriously:

For many, kitchen and stove have become epicurean fields of experiments. Both housewives and housemen are striving for "good cooking," for a carefully and nicely laid table, for ever new, temptingly presented dishes. Grandmother's recipes are being fished out again, and just for the fun of cooking, even some complicated dishes are being tried.[4]

According to a time budget study from 2001–2, German women on average still invest one hour and six minutes daily in household tasks, of which 45 minutes are spent on food preparation. German men spend just 23 minutes daily on food preparation and directly related tasks like setting the table and washing the dishes.[5] In families with children and working mothers, fathers contribute even less time, and almost half of the male population is being looked after by women. Young people show the same gender pattern, with 72% of young men between 20 and 25 years of age not getting involved at all in food preparation, most of them undoubtedly taking advantage of "Hotel Mama." At least there seems to be a tendency for retired (pensioner) couples to share food-related tasks more evenly.

Obviously, these numbers would have been much higher in the past. However, the basic premise of shared kitchen labor is not making new strides. The decrease in food preparation time is on the one hand related to the availability and use of prepared food and meals—ever less is prepared from scratch or made into preserves—and on the other hand to the logistics and technicalities of the kitchen and its equipment. With time won through efficiency, women's double role has become ever more accepted.

THE KITCHEN

In German apartments and houses, the *Küche* (kitchen) is seen as the second most important room after the living room: it is often described as used most, with the best atmosphere or feeling, and it is the room most used to receive visitors.[6] Younger Germans especially use the kitchen in a very multifunctional way; many a party ends there.

Throughout history, the tendency in German home architecture was to make the kitchen a separate room whenever possible, because of smoke and noise. Only poorer peasants and workers lived in the kitchen or even slept around the fireplace. The famous *Katenrauchschinken*, a smoked ham from the Holstein region, originally was smoked in the small, single-room *Katen* (cottages), which had no chimney so that the smoke escaped through the thatched roof under which the ham was hung.

Smokefree, closed *Herde* (ranges) were developed from the sixteenth century on for convenience as well as because of acute wood shortages. On these tiled or iron *Sparherde* (saving ranges) or *Kochmaschinen* (cooking machines), with a separate oven for baking, several dishes could easily be cooked at once. But they spread only slowly, first in the large kitchens of the nobility, monasteries, and hospitals, and then more widely in the second half of the nineteenth century. In rural areas it took until the beginning of the twentieth century for this trend to catch on. Most urban apartments were not equipped with full kitchens, and with migrations due to massive urbanization, the mobility of the kitchen was important— although in Berlin, kitchens in rented apartments tended to be equipped with a stove and a sink.

Poorer working families in the large tenement houses in the cities were forced to live in the kitchen, next to stove, sink, and trash bin. The middle classes however were highly aware of the new scientific findings concerning food hygiene. The ideal of the *Gründerzeit* (the founding years after 1871) was the white tiled kitchen at the far end of the apartment (a long way from the dining room). It had a separate entrance for the servants, an airy *Speisekammer* (pantry) for supplies, and utensils all stored away in cupboards. When servants became more difficult to find around the turn of the century, women in middle-class households gradually became more actively involved in the kitchen, so that efficiency in food preparation was a must.

Gas for lighting and cooking arrived in 1860, whereas running water on a large scale only appeared at the beginning of the twentieth century, and electricity took until 1930 to become widespread. In newly built tenement houses the kitchen became a small, separate room where the housewife was on her own to perform her duties. The model of the *Frankfurter Küche*[7] was commissioned by the head of Frankfurt am Main's building department for the numerous new council flats. It was designed by the Viennese architect Margarete Schütte-Litotzky in 1926. She intended to make the housewives' work easier and increase food hygiene, both on a very affordable level. The small kitchens were a rectangular space of 6.5 square meters (about 70 square feet). They were furnished according to the Taylor system and modern efficiency studies in home management. Inspired by the minuscule kitchens in train dining cars, they included an ironing board that opened out from the wall, moveable lamps, and *Schütten* (small aluminum drawers) for flour, sugar, and so on. Their simplicity has its own aesthetic, but critics of the time attacked the design for its tendency to keep housewives isolated. Soon, another model with a glass wall toward the *Wohn-* or *Eßzimmer* (living room and dining room) was developed in Munich. After World War II the blue-painted wood for the cabinets (a color with a hygienic "anti-fly effect" according to Schütte-Litotzky) was replaced by plastic—seen as *praktisch, sauber, pflegeleicht* (handy, clean, easy to take care of).

The *Einbauküche* (fitted kitchen) still is the ideal for the majority of Germans today. However, most of them like to combine its functionality and technical potential with more *Gemütlichkeit* (homeyness). The passthrough of the 1950s and 1960s gave way to a *Sitzecke* (corner seat with a table) in the kitchen. In students' communes at the end of the 1960s

Frankfurter Küche (Frankfurt kitchen)

and 1970s, a large table was one of the most important pieces of kitchen furniture, to counteract the isolation of the one at the stove.

Today, Germany's highly specialized kitchen builders are renowned worldwide. At the luxury end, even the open fire that was once a necessity and then was technically superseded, has returned as the ultimate in elegant comfort and coziness. But also on a more normal level, German kitchens are fitted out well. Styles range from rustic oak-paneled fronts to laboratory-like stainless steel. Since the 1950s, gas or electric stoves have been a standard feature, depending on what services are provided by the town. Electric stoves now often feature a ceramic stovetop, preferred by many because of ease of cleaning. Induction cooking so far is found almost exclusively in professional kitchens, as are separate high-pressure steamers—with rare exceptions, above all among ambitious hobby chefs who also own copper pans and are into the latest so-called molecular cuisine. However, 67% of all German households own a *Mikro* (microwave). With more open kitchen plans, *Abzugshauben* (extractor hoods) have become the norm. The *Backofen* (oven) used to be directly under the stove top but is increasingly separate and located at eye level. Most ovens feature an *Umluft* function (a fan), so that several dishes or cakes can be cooked or baked at once, and a *Grill* (broiler). *Abwaschbecken* (sinks) are mostly stainless steel and have shrunk in size with the growing popularity of electric *Geschirrspüler* (dishwashers) since the 1970s: in 2005 almost 60% of all German households had one.[8] *Kühlschränke* (refrigerators) have replaced the pantry everywhere, often combined with a *Gefrierschrank* (freezer). However, these are much smaller than the average American refrigerator. Filter coffee machines are a standard feature (although younger households prefer Italian-style *Espressomaschinen* [espresso machines]), as is a *Wasserkocher* (electric kettle). A radio and sometimes a small TV set enliven the atmosphere. Most people have at least breakfast in the kitchen, and often a separate dining room is used only for more formal or festive occasions or when guests are invited. *Geschirr* (dishes) and *Besteck* (silverware), the latter generally in *Cromargan* (stainless steel), tend to come in two versions as well: simpler and heavier for everyday use and more expensive china and perhaps silver cutlery *für gut* (for special occasions). Obviously, there are large variations in kitchens and their equipment according to regional preferences, income, and social standing.

TECHNIQUES AND TOOLS

The techniques used to prepare food in Germany are by and large the same as in other Western cultures. *Kochen* or *sieden* (boiling in a large amount of salted water, the latter term used in the south) is used for pasta, potatoes, dumplings of all sorts, vegetables, and *Siedfleisch* (larger cuts of meat). *Pochieren* or *garziehen* (poaching) is the slower version just under boiling point for more tender items like fish and eggs. *Dämpfen* (steaming) in a special double pan is much less common in Germany than in English-speaking countries and is either associated with the energy- and time-saving *Schnellkochtopf* (pressure cooker) or, more recently, with Asian cuisine and its woven bamboo steamer baskets. *Dünsten*, which is stewing in its own juice with a little fat and some liquid like wine, stock, or simply water added, is perhaps the method most commonly used for vegetables and meat. It combines dry heat for roast flavors with wet heat to tender-ize and yield some sauce. This is also the case with *schmoren* (braising), most often used for ragoûts, goulash, and large cuts of meat: the meat is browned, and then some vegetables like carrots, celeriac, and onions are added and lightly sautéed as well before the *ablöschen*, when a little liquid is added. Then a lid goes on the pan, and the meat is slowly finished, often in the oven, where it yields the gravy deemed essential for a tradi-tional "real" meal. Somewhat paradoxically, the finished dish is called a *(Schmor-)Braten*, a roast, although strictly speaking *braten* (roasting) only comprises dry heat in a *Pfanne* (pan), with a little fat, either on the stove or in the oven. *Schnitzel* (often covered in bread crumbs), *Kotelett* (cutlet), steaks, and fish fillets, but also the famous Christmas goose or duck, are examples of meats and fish that are roasted. *Frittieren* (deep-frying) is not very common in private households; the popular *Pommes* (French fries) or *Fritten* are mostly eaten at street stalls or in restaurants. *Backen* (baking) is the Austrian term for deep-frying, but in Germany, the term stands for the sweet staple of cake baked in the oven.

Töpfe (pans) are mostly of stainless steel, as the aluminum widely used after World War II today is deemed a health risk. Cast iron, copper, and other materials can be found as well. *Backformen* (cake pans) and *Back-bleche* (baking sheets) often are enameled white or black. Cake pans also come in glass and all kinds of traditional and modern shapes.

Undoubtedly, food preparation, which entails chopping, pounding, and the like, used to be a more physically demanding task and has been made much easier today with the aid of electricity. Germans love electri-cal kitchen gadgets. The *Mixstab* (handheld blender), *Handquirl* (electric whisk), *Mixer* (standing blender), and *Küchenmaschine* (food processor) with all kinds of functions are common features in German kitchens. Besides that, anything from herb and garlic choppers, egg cookers, can openers, knives, knife sharpeners, lemon squeezers, and bread slicers to cheese graters and even pepper mills can be found in electrically powered

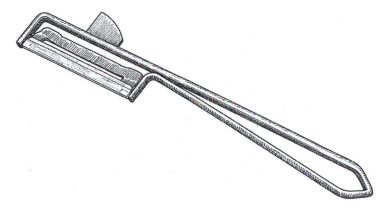

Sparschäler (peeler)

form. Most households own a liter measure as well as (electric) scales for baking, as recipes are given in (kilo)grams and (milli)liters. Cutting boards are made of wood (old-fashioned), plastic, or glass. The familiar battery of *Messer* (knives) in all qualities, shapes, and sizes and other tools like wooden spoons, slotted spoons, sieves, and most probably a rolling pin and cookie cutters are stored in kitchen drawers, sit in some kind of containers, or hang on the wall. But there are some German peculiarities: the *Spätzlebrett* is a handheld wooden board on which the almost-liquid egg noodle dough is spread with a palette knife in order to be scraped in thin strips into boiling water—or for the lazy or less dexterous there is the *Spätzleschwob,* a kind of press. A *Kartoffelstampfer* is a wooden or metal implement used to mash potatoes in the pan, and the *Sparschäler* (literally, an "economic" peeler with a swivel blade) speeds the peeling of potatoes, carrots, and asparagus. As with all these implements, several versions are available, from inexpensive but perfectly usable simplicity to high-priced, high-tech stainless steel.

COOKING AS LIFESTYLE

In spite of the dominant pattern where women are responsible for the food, cooking and eating are changing from a pure necessity to a freely chosen option of how to spend one's time. Even in very traditional households, families spend more time around the dinner table during the weekend, no matter what the amount of actual cooking work is. Similarly, food that can be prepared or eaten quickly, fast food or take-out options, frozen or instant meals, and all kinds of prepared ingredients have been taken

Spätzlebrett (Spätzle board)

for granted during the last decade, at least in urban environments. Pizza has long been a German favorite and today tops the list of ready-made frozen products sold in Germany, having doubled in quantity in the decade since 1994. In 2006, each German on average ate 6.61 lb. of frozen pizza, in addition to the pizza consumed during frequent visits to the numerous pizzerias. To cook, to cook a little, or not to cook at all for most Germans has largely become a question of income and inclination.

Likewise, traditional preservation methods have become hobbies or are used exclusively to deal with fruit from one's own garden, since jam, preserves, and fresh and frozen fruit are readily available. A jar of homemade jam is a very popular present to bring when invited to someone's home. Although bread as a general rule is bought, bread baking is springing up again in some rural areas, possibly as a reaction to the often-unsatisfactory quality of the commercial offerings.

In the 1970s, partly due to food journalist and gastrocritic Wolfram Siebeck's (born 1928) weekly writings and recipes in various newspapers and magazines, men have discovered cooking as a hobby of high prestige. Most of these *Hobbyköche* (hobby cooks) are not interested in the everyday routine of the kitchen but instead plan and produce complicated meals on the weekend, preferably according to glossy volumes written by Michelin-starred professional chefs. They chase down exclusive ingredients beforehand, roast bones for sauces and stocks, and grind meat for sophisticated terrines to impress friends. In recent years, cooking schools and courses have become very popular.

Younger Germans have a different, more relaxed approach. They see cooking not as a task but as a trendy, relaxed, and delicious pastime of choice, to indulge in during free time or on the weekend. Meeting with friends to cook or inviting them for meals is a popular social activity.

COOKING ON TELEVISION

Since the mid-1990s, cooking has also become a popular subject in the media. Various TV shows like *Ready, Steady, Cook/Kochduell* or *Hell's Kitchen/TeufelsKüche* have been imported from English-speaking countries; others were developed in Germany, and some successful TV hosts, like Alfred Biolek or Johannes B. Kerner, use cooking as a background to present and interview guests. For ambitious restaurant chefs, a successful marketing campaign now seems on principle to include books and a TV show. Tim Mälzer with his early evening show *Schmeckt nicht, gibts nicht* (*Doesn't Taste Good, Doesn't Exist*) is comparable to the British star Jamie Oliver. Mälzer embodies the general tendency of cooking in modern media in Germany: everything is to be quick, fun, and easy. In contrast, Michelin-starred Johann Lafer and Lea Linster with their shows stand for classic cuisine, and Vincent Klink prefers organic ingredients and an almost anarchistic technical approach.

Although all TV chefs emphasize their professional background and success as credentials, most of them simultaneously declare their recipes to be perfectly simple and easy enough to repeat in a private kitchen—there are no studies yet as to how many people are actually motivated to cook themselves by watching cooking shows on television. These shows could also be seen as the ultimate incarnation of the ancient Roman formula of bread and games to keep the masses happy.

KOCHBÜCHER (COOKBOOKS)

Although many everyday dishes are made without consulting a recipe, Germans consider cookbooks essential. The oldest known German cookbook, *Daz buch von guter spise* (*The Book of Good Food*) from around 1350, was part of a handwritten household companion and probably intended for family use. The recipe collection is preceded by texts on general knowledge and followed by love poems, thus balancing advice on spiritual and physical well-being. In contrast, the first printed German cookbook, the *Kuchen maysterey* (*The Mastering of the Kitchen*), published in 1485 in Nuremberg, was directed at professionals and apparently very successful, just as was (roughly a century later) Marx Rumpolt's *Ein New Kochbuch* (*A New Cookbook*), published in Frankfurt in 1581. This large-format book could be regarded as the precursor to the aforementioned works by contemporary celebrity chefs. The many vignettes and wood-cuts that illustrate the book are from artists highly regarded in their time: the sixteenth-century equivalent of full-color, glossy printing. With its emphasis on the relationship between cookery and medicine, Rumpolt's work is still very much in the spirit of the Middle Ages. However, the inclusion of a recipe for a potato dish, almost certainly the first in German culinary literature, marks him as a member of the avant-garde.

In 1598, Anna Weckerin of Basel was the first woman to have a German cookbook published. The *Nürnberger Kochbuch* (*Nuremberg Cookbook*) of 1691 and that of Maria Schellhammer in 1723 are examples of a whole series of cookbooks with a more regional accent. Slowly the French culinary influence also became noticeable, with important French and English works being translated into German. The former emphasis on housekeeping advice almost disappeared. Nevertheless, Karl Friedrich von Rumohr's *Geist der Kochkunst* (*The Essence of Cookery*), published in 1822, is not so much a cookbook, but a work comparable to the French *La Physiologie du Goût* by Brillat-Savarin, which was published slightly later. They are almost philosophical treatises on cooking and eating.

In the course of the nineteenth century, the category of cookbooks as a whole changed significantly. New kitchen equipment, the growing separation of work and home with industrialization and urbanization, the increasing scarcity of servants, and a tendency away from traditional rural self-reliance—all these changes created a demand for new cooking advice of unprecedented dimensions. Authors like Henriette Davidis (1801–76) were aware of the fact that the traditional transfer of cooking skills from one generation to the next needed to be supplemented or replaced altogether. From its first edition in 1845, her *Praktisches Kochbuch* (*Practical Cookbook*) was aimed at helping young women cope with the new situation. Guidance was offered to middle-class households that had to make do with fewer servants. Many more authors could be mentioned who made similar progress and were equally successful with numerous new editions, among them Sophie Wilhelmine Scheibler, Marie Susanne Kübler, Mary Hahn, and Katharina Prato.

Toward the end of the nineteenth century, with the new scientific findings concerning health and nutrition, cookbooks became more technical, and hygiene was an increasingly important topic. Less and less basic knowledge (formerly transferred from mother to daughter through everyday practice) was assumed by the authors: cooking times, temperatures, quantities, and the like were indicated with exactitude. This new form of cooking knowledge corresponded to the rise of housekeeping schools and cooking courses for young women, which were also co-opted by modern food industries to promote their new products. The pharmacist August Oetker from Bielefeld thus pushed the use of his baking powder and other products by offering lectures on baking, founding Dr. Oetker schools, and publishing cookbooks. *Dr. Oetker Schulkochbuch* (*Dr. Oetker's School Cookbook*) sold extremely well from the first edition in 1911. It is still in print today and counts among the classics.

In spite of often being addressed to the "modern housewife," cookbooks did not change much in style well into the 1960s, and children's cookbooks reflect the same tendency. The irreverent, antiauthoritarian *Comic-Kochbuch* (Comic-cookbook) by Evi and Hansjörg Langenfass,[9] published in 1979 as a paperback, could be seen as a marker that the profound political and social upheavals had finally reached this medium as well. Cooking had entered the public domain, also witnessed by the appearance of two food magazines. In 1972, the first modern German food magazine for the general public was published. The monthly *essen & trinken* (*eating and drinking*), still published today, focuses on recipes and practicality, with reports from the world of wine and food and information about new products as well as restaurant recommendations. Three years later it was followed by the glossier *Der Feinschmecker* (*The Gourmet*), which today is more about lifestyle than everyday cooking. The *Gourmet* series, a lavishly produced quarterly by photographer Johann Willsberger, presented the best of modern German restaurant cooking from its start in 1976 until the last issue in 2005.

A multitude of cookbooks directed at all social groups, ages, and budgets are published in Germany every year. Every possible regional or ethnic cuisine, seasonal theme, and historical subject is covered. A good portion are translations, especially from the United Kingdom and the United States. Celebrities, actors, or persons of supposedly public interest like to pose as cookbook authors as well, and it is not always easy to tell where cooking as such stops and lifestyle takes over. As already mentioned, it is almost a must for ambitious restaurant chefs to add their own contributions to the cookbook craze.

However, does the proliferation of cookbooks and cooking shows mean that people are cooking? Furthermore, does cookbook fare represent what people cook and eat, or rather what they like to read about and look at? Public opinion in Germany tends to be concerned that not enough "real cooking" is happening in private households and that children especially are not getting involved enough with it, thus missing opportunities to learn about food. Recently, there have been government initiatives to incorporate food and cooking into the school-day schedules of children in elementary school.

NOTES

1. Deutsche Gesellschaft für Ernährung e.V., ed., *Ernährungsbericht 2004* (Bonn: Deutsche Gesellschaft für Ernährung e.V., 2004).

2. Mary Hahn, *Praktisches Kochbuch für die bürgerliche Küche*, 16th ed. (Berlin: Mary Hahn's Kochbuch-Verlag, n.d. [1930]).

3. Maria Schmitz, *Wir kochen praktisch: Neuzeitliches Tabellen-Kochbuch*, 36th to 38th ed. (Cologne-Braunsfeld: Müller, 1965), 118.

4. *Kochen*, 6th ed. (Leipzig: Verlag für die Frau, DDR, 1983).

5. Deutsche Gesellschaft für Ernährung, *Ernährungsbericht 2004*.

6. Alphons Silbermann, *Die Küche im Wohnerlebnis der Deutschen* (Opladen: Leske + Budrich, 1995).

7. A replica is in the Museum für Angewandte Kunst (MAK) in Vienna.

8. Statistisches Bundesamt, *Statistisches Jahrbuch 2006 für die Bundesrepublik Deutschland* (Wiesbaden: Statistisches Bundesamt, 2006), www.destatis.de.

9. Ursula Heinzelmann, "Children's Cookery Books: Nurturing Adults' Ideas about Society," in *Proceedings of the Oxford Symposium on Food and Cookery*, ed. Richard Hosking (Bristol: Footwork, 2004), 112–123.

4

Typical Meals

The notion of meals comprises two different aspects: when and under which circumstances food is consumed on one hand, and what those meals consist of on the other hand, the composition of specific dishes, their ingredients, and preparation. For both aspects in Germany as in other countries and cultures, only generalizations are possible. Just as contemporary cultural sociology speaks of trends and habits, dishes are subject to continuous change and appear clear and stable in their development only in hindsight, through the filter of time. There are several reasons for this.

First of all, borders between cultural regions do not necessarily follow administrative demarcations. Second, differences once defined by the close relationship between technology and local food resources (and originally climate and geography) now involve complex layers of migrations, trade, and cultural exchange. Therefore, the rough geographic division used here is more an approximation to the complex reality of how and what kind of food is consumed every day in Germany than a precise analysis. Third, this geographic dimension is further differentiated by other factors: disposable income and social standing on the one hand, and demographic structure on the other, that is, the contrasts between rich and poor, urban and rural.

However, in contrast to the past when poverty and/or rural locations tended to be linked to regional and seasonal constraints in food whereas being rich and/or urban meant more freedom of choice, modern industrialization and globalization have almost led to a reverse situation. Urban surroundings still make for a greater mix of cultural influences and therefore food habits, but through the predominance of modern food industries, erstwhile regional and seasonal mainstays are becoming a pecuniary and intellectual privilege.

Finally, an eminent German food historian stresses an important point regarding the history of national, regional, and favored dishes. He notes that it is a "naïve reverse projection" to accept the contemporary predominance of a certain dish as proof for its long historic past. He argues against assuming a one-dimensional, linear development and maintains that, above all, everyday foods (in contrast to those consumed on special occasions) are subject to rapid changes.[1]

MEAL STRUCTURE

Since the mid-1990s it has often been assumed, in connection with discussion of globalization in Germany, that the perceived rapid rise of fast food and snacking was eroding German food culture and the associated social structures. However, the analysis of two comparable surveys of Germans' use of time in 1991–1992 and 2001–2002 proves this theory wrong.[2] Between the two surveys, the daily amount of time Germans dedicate to the activity of eating actually increased by 22 minutes from 1 hour 21 minutes to 1 hour 43 minutes. Furthermore, this increase was mainly due to meals consumed in the home rather than out. On weekends, with more free time available, Germans on average spend 24 minutes more on eating. Admittedly, the time Germans spend eating between meals also increased during that decade (especially among employed young people between 20 and 25 years old), but the classic structure of three daily meals persists in spite of the frequently mentioned modern phenomenon of "grazing," that is, snacking around the clock without fixed mealtimes. On average 56 minutes are still devoted daily in total to breakfast, lunch, and dinner, and more than 60% of all Germans older than 12 years have these meals between 6 and 9 A.M., 12 and 2 P.M., and 6 and 8 P.M., respectively. Also, the results of the surveys do not confirm the often-heard assertion that the main meal has moved from midday to evening; 20 minutes are spent on average on each meal. But the evening meal is socially more important: more people come together, and families where both parents are working clearly spend more time on dinner than on lunch.

Frühstück (Breakfast)

Frühstück (breakfast) is mostly eaten at home. It is widely thought to be unhealthy to leave home without eating breakfast, although working people in an urban environment might get coffee and a sandwich or pastry on their way to work. Breakfast in Germany consists at its most basic of a hot beverage, more often coffee than tea (with milk and hot chocolate as alternatives, in particular for children), and some kind of starch. This can be—depending on the preference for sweet or savory—bread or rolls spread with butter, then jam or honey, cheese, quark (sometimes with herbs), sausage, ham, or, more luxuriously, smoked salmon. Sweet pastries are also popular as are various cereals with milk. Other options (or additions, when there is more time on the weekend and breakfast often extends into brunch) are orange juice, eggs (mostly boiled), yogurt (plain or with fruit), and fresh fruit. Special occasions might be marked by a glass of *Sekt* (sparkling wine).

Midmorning Break

At school or at work, a break is taken during the morning around 10 A.M. It could be just a *Kaffeepause* (coffee break) for a cup of coffee and perhaps a cigarette. Schoolchildren might have a sandwich they brought from home, but in rural areas, where there is a greater number of manual laborers, more solid fare is consumed. *Brotzeit* in Bavaria might consist of *Weißwurst und Brezel* (scalded white veal sausages and a pretzel), or in Swabia of a slice of freshly baked *Leberkäse* (baked meat loaf) in a roll. Both might be washed down with a beer.

Mittagessen (Lunch)

In rural areas and traditional households, *Mittagessen*, the meal around noon, is on principle a warm meal, and more importance is given to it than to dinner. At its most classic, *Mittagessen* consists of meat or fish accompanied by a vegetable and a starch, often preceded by soup or a salad and followed by a dessert like *Kompott* (stewed fruit), yogurt, custard, or ice cream. Traditionally, meatless dishes, like soft-boiled or fried eggs on spinach with boiled potatoes, are served on Fridays, although today they are probably chosen by vegetarians rather than for religious reasons. In urban surroundings and among office workers, long breaks for an extended meal at lunchtime are rather unusual. Most people only have time for a snack—the business lunch offered by many restaurants is by definition quick.[3] Larger companies and universities run cafeterias for their employees or students. All-day schooling used to be the norm only in East Germany; in West Germany schools typically ended around midday with no meals provided. Therefore school cafeterias are still the exception, but currently are on the rise throughout the country. Sunday lunch tends to be a more sumptuous and family-oriented affair than meals during the week, often accompanied by a glass of wine.

Spinat mit Ei (Spinach with Eggs)

- 1 lb. fresh spinach leaves, whole or coarsely chopped
- 1 small onion, diced
- 1 garlic clove
- 3 tbs. butter
- sea salt
- nutmeg
- 8 eggs

Sauté onion in butter, and add the spinach (still slightly wet from rinsing). Stir with a fork on which the garlic clove is skewered, until spinach has wilted and is cooked to your liking. Season with salt and very little nutmeg. Serve with soft-boiled or fried eggs on top, as well as boiled potatoes.

Coffee- or Teatime, Afternoon Snack

In the afternoon, two very different in-between meals are possible. On the one hand, between 3 and 4 P.M., it is time for *Kaffee und Kuchen*, that is, coffee (or exceptionally tea, mostly in the north) and cake. This can be an occasion to go out and meet friends in a café or a *Konditorei* (pastry shop). Alternatively, cake is bought there or homemade, and friends are invited over. This practice is very popular on the weekend and treated more extensively in chapter 6. Most households have a special china coffee set for this occasion. On the other hand, a bit later, between 4 and 5 P.M., especially in the southern, more rural areas, *Vesper* or *Brotzeit* is taken after the day's work (traditionally between the day's work on the fields and the evening milking of the cows). The cold snack can consist of all kinds of sausages, ham, or brawn (headcheese-like sausage); bread, rolls, or *Brezeln*; sliced and salted long white radish (in Bavaria); and/or cheese and is often accompanied by beer or wine.

Abendessen (Evening Meal)

Abendessen or *Abendbrot*, the evening meal, can either be cold, resembling the afternoon snack described earlier, or warm, above all on days and occasions when lunch has "only" been cold. It tends to be structured similarly to a warm meal at lunchtime but will probably evolve in a more leisurely fashion and be eaten in a larger group, with family or friends. This is the occasion for enjoying food and drink in a relaxed way.

TABLE MANNERS

Table manners became much more relaxed in Germany during the last decades of the twentieth century. However, some basics still apply. It is considered bad taste to start eating before the head of the family (or the person of highest rank at the table) says "*Guten Appetit*" (bon appétit), wishing all an enjoyable meal. Saying grace has become the exception nowadays. No noise should be made while eating and drinking, and talking with a full mouth is considered bad manners. Generally, food is eaten with the *Messer* (knife) in the right hand and the *Gabel* (fork) in the left one (vice versa for left-handers). The fork is held in the right hand only for pasta dishes, which Germans tend to eat with a *Löffel* (spoon) in the other hand. For fish a special, blunt *Fischmesser* (fish knife) is used, although in a less formal situation two forks might do the job. Contrary to what is considered appropriate in English-speaking countries, both hands should be above the table while eating, and a finished plate is indicated by placing knife and fork diagonally on the plate parallel to one other.

MEAL CONTENT

As an eminent German food historian points out, rapidly changing living conditions (or conditions perceived as such) can lead people to cling to some traditional cultural element to compensate, and often this element is food.[4] So it should be no surprise that a recent survey of favorite dishes among Germans aged 14 to 60 years produced a hit parade that is headed by global dishes but dominated by regional fare:[5]

1. Spaghetti Bolognese
2. Spaghetti with tomato sauce
3. *Schnitzel*
4. Pizza
5. *Rouladen* (beef roulades)
6. *Spargel* (asparagus)

 7. *Sauerbraten*

 8. Lasagna

 9. Steak

10. *Nudelauflauf* (pasta dish in the style of macaroni and cheese)

11. *Kohlrouladen* (braised cabbage roulades with a ground-meat stuffing)

12. Fish

13. *Kasselerbraten* (cured and smoked pork roast)

14. *Spinat* (spinach)

15. *Königsberger Klopse* (meatballs in a white sauce flavored with lemon, capers, and herring or anchovies)

16. *Grünkohl mit deftigem Fleisch und Kartoffeln* (curly kale with meat and potatoes)[6]

MEALS OF ETHNIC AND RELIGIOUS MINORITIES AND CHILDREN

Before moving on to an overview of the traditional specialties of different regions of Germany, it is important to note that on some dinner tables different food is served because the people sitting around them are from another ethnic background. Roughly every ninth person in Germany is not of German nationality and thus probably eats differently, to varying degrees. The Turkish are by far the most numerous of this group, making up more than 25% of immigrants, followed by immigrants from Asia (12.2%), Italy (8.0%), and Greece (4.6%).[7]

Most Germans are of Christian background, and Christian traditions still dominate foodways, although religious rituals, especially in urban surroundings, are superseded by a secular lifestyle. Only 0.013% of all Germans are Jewish, and their influence on the food available and consumed in Germany is hardly noticeable. This number is currently increasing, however, because of Jewish immigrants, mainly from Russia. In cities like Berlin, Frankfurt am Main, and Munich, Jewish specialty food shops and restaurants are slowly appearing.

As for children, no clear pattern of food habits and preferences is apparent in Germany today. In contrast, for instance, with France, where children from a very early age join adults at the table and eat the same food, or England, where nursery food consists of a whole range of simpler dishes especially for children, German parents' behavior is very diverse in this area. After they outgrow the ready-made jars and packets of baby's food, children either join the family at the table, eating some of the normal offerings, or they are fed separately before regular mealtimes with simpler, favorite dishes like pasta and mashed potatoes.

TRADITIONAL REGIONAL SPECIALTIES

The North

Along the shores of the North and Baltic Seas, fish and seafood are natural staples of the cuisine, and on the lush pastures, cattle and pigs flourish. Bitter-tasting pilsner beer and *Korn* (clear schnapps made from grain) are the favored beverages. They are drunk with all kinds of pickled herring and also *Kieler Sprotten* (smoked sprats)—originating in fact not from the town of Kiel but from Eckernförde. Scrambled eggs with smoked eel or *Bückling* (whole, non-gutted smoked herring) as well as *Matjes* (young salted herring), which is often served with green beans, some fried bacon, and boiled potatoes, are all popular. Beer and *Korn* also help to digest *Holsteiner Schinken* (smoked Holstein ham), all kinds of sausages, and *Grünkohl* (curly kale), which is cooked slowly and served with all kinds of bits of pork and potatoes. There are many complex gastronomic rituals involving kale (these are described in chapter 6).

At the country's northern tip in Schleswig-Holstein, German food elements mingle with Danish influence, and some medieval touches are still recognizable. Fruit and sugar mix with the savory, milk and cream with meat and vegetables. *Birnen, Bohnen, Speck* (pears cooked together with green beans and bacon) is a favorite dish with a sweet touch as is *Fliederbeersuppe* (elderberry soup) prepared with apples and plums and served hot or cold. Even *Schnüsch*, a vegetable stew with milk and butter, is generously sweetened with sugar. *Pannfisch*, a skillet of potatoes boiled in their skin, bacon, boiled or smoked fish, and onions, all sliced and sautéed in butter, with beaten eggs and parsley added at the end, is a traditional way to use leftovers. Another is *Plockfinken*, made from all kinds of boiled meat (including some cured meats), onions, carrots, and apples, thickened with a white roux and seasoned with sugar and vinegar. *Grosser Hans* or *Mehlbeutel* is a dumpling the size of a young child's head; it is made of egg, milk, butter, flour, and prunes and steamed like a British-style pudding, tied in a napkin. It is eaten with all kinds of steamed fruit and/or smoked pork. *Rote Grütze* (literally, red gruel), a dessert made of all kinds of red berries and cherries thickened with starch or sago (very similar to tapioca), is eaten with milk, liquid cream, or cold custard.

Lower Saxony to the southwest reaches from the river Elbe to the Dutch border, from lowland plains on the North Sea to the low mountain ranges of the Harz. In the north, there is a marked preference for buttermilk, cured meat, and all kinds of sweet or savory pancakes. In the heath around Lüneburg, schnapps is flavored with local juniper. Trout and eel from the ponds and streams are smoked, and aromatic heather honey is a valued specialty. The sandy soils make for very good potatoes as well as asparagus, which is accompanied by a thick slice of smoked ham served separately on a wooden board (instead of thin slices as in the south). *Heidschnucken*, the moorland sheep with black heads and feet and long, shaggy gray coats, still roam this beautiful landscape, guarded by a shepherd and his dogs, and yield highly appreciated dark, almost venison-like meat. For more everyday fare, *Steckrübeneintopf* is a stew combining rutabagas (swedes) and potatoes with some pork. *Harzer*, the characteristic sour-milk cheese traditional to all of central Germany, is covered here with a white, Camembert-like rind. It is served with gray rye bread and *Schmalz* (goose or pork lard).

The four Hanseatic port cities—Bremen, Hamburg, Lübeck, and Rostock—combine the culinary influences of their respective surroundings with faraway elements through their centuries-old mercantile traditions. Thus wine enjoys a special role, and the wealthy and proud bourgeois value the best meat and the freshest fish. For *Scholle Finkenwerder Art*, plaice is fried whole with fatty bacon and served with potato salad. *Hamburger Stubenküken* (young chicks roasted with a stuffing of white bread, button mushrooms, and chicken liver) and *Bremer Kükenragout* (resembling a chicken fricassee) are prepared from very young chicks (*poussin*). But there is also a more down-to-earth side to the cuisine. *Labskaus* is a dish that originated as sailors' fare: boiled potatoes are mixed with corned or salted beef, onions, and pickled beets and served with pickled gherkins, fried eggs, and pickled herring. In Bremen, kale is called *Braunkohl* in reference to an ancient brown-leafed variety and is often served with *Pinkel*, a coarse, smoked pork sausage containing oats, or *Knipp*, a more spreadable, larger version containing offal. *Erbsen mit Snuten und Poten* is a stew combining yellow split peas with pork snouts and feet. The famous *Hamburger Aalsuppe* (literally, eel soup) may contain some eel but originated as a stew in which *all* kinds of meat, including a ham bone, mingled with various vegetables and dried as well as fresh fruit, enriched with herbs and small flour dumplings.

Mecklenburg-West Pomerania in the northeast borders on the Baltic Sea. Its chalk cliffs on the island of Rügen match those of Dover in England but lead to romantic forests beside the sandy beaches. The gently rolling, green hinterland sometimes seems almost untouched, with more lakes than inhabitants. Fish and cattle, fruit, vegetables, cured meat, venison, and poultry, especially geese, are all found here. However, owing to the decades of standardized agriculture and foodways during communist times, cooking is only slowly finding its way back to its regional roots. Traditionally, goose was not only roasted whole and its breast smoked, but it was also prepared as *Gänseweisssauer* in aspic and *Gänseschwarzsauer*, a ragoût including the giblets and dried fruit, thickened with blood and seasoned with cinnamon, cloves, allspice, lemon, and sugar. Another specialty is *Schnippelbohnen*, diagonally sliced green beans in a creamy white sauce.

East Central

The regions that comprise the eastern central parts of Germany include Brandenburg around Berlin, Saxony around Leipzig and Dresden, and Thuringia with Erfurt and Weimar. They lead from the northern plains to the mountain ranges of central Germany. From a culinary point of view, these areas are loosely connected by the complex contrasts between abundance and scarcity on the one hand and Slavic and Silesian influences on the other.

Berlin is the largest German city and historically a melting pot of cultural influences. These come from all over Germany (with a particular influx from the old eastern provinces until World War II) as well as worldwide, reaching from the Huguenots at the end of the seventeenth century to Turkish, Vietnamese, and Russian immigrants today. Just as it is rare to come across a true, born-and-bred Berliner, it is difficult to define and actually get hold of "real" Berlin cuisine. *Buletten* (flattened pan-fried meatballs), *Kalbsleber Berliner Art* (pan-fried slices of veal liver topped with fried apple slices and onion rings and served with mashed potatoes, called *Quetschkartoffeln* in Berlin), and *Eisbein mit Sauerkraut und Erbspüree* (boiled cured pork knuckle served with sauerkraut and mashed dried green peas) are probably the best-known examples of Berlin specialties. *Hühnerfrikassee* (chicken fricassee) is another favorite, as are *Kohlrouladen*, braised cabbage rolls with a ground-meat stuffing. An import from former East Prussia (like Silesia, today part of Poland), *Königsberger Klopse* (meatballs in a white sauce flavored with lemon, capers, and herring or anchovies) have recently seen a revival. For equally everyday fare there is also blood and liver sausage on sauerkraut, *Schmorgurken* (braised cucumber) to accompany the *Buletten*, or *Kartoffelpuffer mit Apfelmus*, latke-like pancakes made from grated raw potato and served with applesauce. Potatoes have played an important role here ever since their promotion by Frederick the Great, as they are particularly well suited to the sandy soils. *Kartoffelsuppe* (potato soup) could even be called *the* German soup. *Kartoffelsalat* (potato salad) in Berlin is always made with mayonnaise and eaten with frankfurter sausages. From the numerous lakes and streams in and around Berlin come fish like *Zander* (pike perch), *Aal* (eel), and *Maränen* (a small variety of perch). As befits the city's cosmopolitan ambitions, Berlin procures beverages from all around the world, be it wine or spirits. However, *Berliner Weisse*, a top-fermented, light, sour-tasting wheat beer delights tourists as a specialty and is served *mit Schuss*, with a shot of raspberry or green woodruff syrup.

The Saxon equivalent of *Berliner Weisse* is the *Gose* of Leipzig, although the Saxon drink per se (besides wine made along the river Elbe between Pillnitz and Meissen of porcelain fame) is coffee, always accompanied by cake or pastries, where the habit of *didschen*, dunking them into the coffee, is widely popular. Following the same principle, Saxon and Thuringian dumplings have to be accompanied by plenty of gravy. Local specialties that are less well known than the famous *Thüringer Klösse* are *Schälkliessl*, a kind of rolled-up noodle dough with a stuffing, cut in thick slices, and *Wickelklösse*, a rolled-up potato dough with bacon stuffing. *Kliess mit Birnen* extends the category of dumplings to a sweet pie with pears under a yeast dough. *Stupperche mit Sauerkraut und Speck* are finger-shaped potato noodles served with sauerkraut and bacon and a good example of how one dish can be traced throughout many regions—it is called *Buabespitzle* in Baden and the Palatinate and *Schupfnudeln* in Swabia. The earlier-mentioned *Leipziger Allerlei*, a refined courtly composition of spring vegetables, including morels, in a white cream sauce flavored with crayfish butter, has become nationally famous, as have the well-seasoned, aromatic *Thüringer Bratwürste*, grilled sausages from coarsely ground meat. More local still is *Bautzener Topfsülze*, cured pork knuckle with pickles in aspic, served with fried potatoes. Carp and trout are also local to these regions and served in numerous variations. The various pumpkin recipes in the Vogtland on the border to Franconia have a special tradition. Finally, *Plinsen* merit a special mention: these are small pancakes made with flour, yeast, milk, and eggs, eaten with all kinds of fruit.

West Central

Westphalia, the Rhineland, and Hessia form a loose culinary block in the west. From Münster down to Koblenz, Kassel, and Frankfurt, pork and potatoes are perhaps the two most important elements. In Westphalia, pigs were traditionally fattened in the oak woods. They yielded *Westfälischer Knochenschinken*, the famous ham cured and smoked on the bone, as well as all kinds of sausages and related dishes once made only at slaughtering time. *Pannhas* is a very fine-ground meat loaf thickened with *Buchweizen* (buckwheat) flour and seasoned with cloves and allspice; *Möppkenbrot* is its counterpart using blood and rye flour. *Wurstebrei* is a kind of gruel of ground pork meat and heart, thickened with pearl barley.

As further to the north, curly kale is eaten with the usual pork decorations. In the Hunsrück mountains, *Spiessbraten* or *Schwenkbraten* is roasted
pork shoulder, originally cooked over an open fire and on a spit—a method
gem cutters from Idar-Oberstein are said to have brought back from South
America in the nineteenth century. *Schnippelbohnen*, the diagonally sliced
green beans, here are served not only fresh but also salted like sauerkraut,
and are eaten with pork, mostly *Kasseler*, a cured and smoked loin roast.
The so-called *Dortmunder Rosenkranz* (Dortmund rosary) combines sliced
potatoes in a meat broth with small smoked pork sausages; *Plaaten in de
Pann* is another version of the same dish, made with fresh sausages.

Among the many potato dishes that mark this culinary region, *Gräwes*
combines sauerkraut (boiled in white wine) with mashed potatoes, topped
with fried onion and bacon. *Potthucke* consists of a mix of raw and boiled
potatoes with eggs and sour cream that is baked in a dish. *Döppekooche* is
a variation of this casserole particular to the Eiffel Mountains, with grated
apple and sliced bacon added. With its many variations it takes the place
of the dumplings of other regions. *Leineweber* and *Pillekauken* are large
pancakes with boiled potatoes in slices or strips. *Kastenpickert* is a sweet
potato-based cake with raisins, whereas *Lappenpickert* are small pancakes
made with grated raw potato, served with all kinds of sweet or savory
accompaniments.

Before chemical fertilizer made growing wheat and rye a viable option
on poor moorland soils, *Buchweizen* (buckwheat) flour was used instead
of wheat flour. A culinary legacy of that time is *Bookweten-Janhinnerk*,
thin, blini-like buckwheat pancakes made with cold coffee including the
grounds. They are served with *Rübenkraut*, dark syrup made from sugar
beets. Rutabagas (swedes) are served as a vegetable side dish, as is *Rübstiel*,
the green tops of turnips.

Beef plays an important role here as well, as witnessed by the classic *Sauerbraten* (literally, sour roast) of the Rhineland around Cologne,
which is marinated with vinegar, wine, and spices before braising. Its
dark sauce is often enriched with raisins. On the same scheme of sweet
and savory meat dishes, fried slices of blood sausage are served on a
bed of mashed potatoes mixed with stewed apples for *Himmel und Erde*
(heaven and earth). *Pfefferpotthast*, another famous beef dish, is a dark,
strong-flavored goulash. *Töttchen* from around Münster is a rare example
of a veal dish in this region, as well as being notable for its use of head,
lung, and heart, finely sliced in a sour-sweet, roux-based white sauce,
reminiscent of some southern German or Austrian dishes.

All this food is washed down with copious amounts of beer, more bitter
in the north, lighter and ale-like in the form of pale *Kölsch* in Cologne

and darker *Altbier* in Düsseldorf, Dortmund, and environs. More to the south and west along the Moselle River as well as in the famous Rheingau, wine—in Hessia also *Äppel-* or *Ebbelwoi* from apples—replaces beer and schnapps. The cooking here becomes a touch lighter, with more vegetables and herbs, and sour cream is often used instead of pork fat. The famous *Frankfurter Grüne Sauce* (Frankfurt green sauce), made from finely chopped hard-boiled eggs, vinegar, and oil, must contain at least seven fresh herbs. It originated as a meatless dish served on *Gründonnerstag* (Maundy Thursday) or *Himmelfahrt* (Ascension Day), but today is served with all kinds of meat and fish. Leeks, cabbage, salsify, celery, and radish are only some examples of the favorite vegetables of this region. *Handkäs*, a small round sour-milk cheese, is often served *mit Musik* (with music), the music consisting of chopped onion, vinegar, and oil. The traditionally favored pork cut here is *Rippchen*, slightly cured pork ribs cooked in one piece and often served with sauerkraut.

For dessert, in Westphalia the black *Pumpernickel* bread is used in all kinds of puddings, and waffles are a favorite, whereas in Hessia *Kirschenmichel*, a cherry pie, as well as apples in all variations, are served. A sabayon-like dish is made using apple or grape wine.

The South

Southern Germany sweeps broadly from Rhenish Hessia, the Saar, and the Palatinate, down to the foothills of the Alps on the borders of Austria and Switzerland, covering Bavaria, Baden, and Württemberg. This is mostly wine country. Compared with northern regions, the climate here is mild, in some corners almost Mediterranean, so that even tobacco, figs, and almond trees flourish. Especially in the Palatinate and Rhenish Hessia, French influence is often clearly noticeable, both historically through the numerous invasions and today because of geographic proximity. *Coq au vin* here becomes *Gockel in Wein* (chicken in wine). *Dippehas* is hare braised in red wine, the sauce thickened with dark bread; it is served with potato dumplings. Sliced potatoes are baked and gratinéed with sour cream and fatty bacon for *Backesgrumbeere*, sometimes seasoned with cinnamon, and served with a green salad. *Eingemachtes Kalbfleisch* is veal blanquette.

However, most of the meat consumed here is pork. In *Fleeschknepp* (meatballs), pork is mixed with some beef, but *Leewerknepp* are pure pork liver dumplings. Both are eaten with horseradish sauce. The most famous Palatinate dish is *Saumagen* (pig's stomach). It is often described as a German version of the haggis of Scottish fame, but they only share the casing method. Instead of the lamb offal found in haggis, finely ground pork sausage, diced ham, and potatoes seasoned with marjoram are poached in a cleaned pig's stomach, sliced and served with sauerkraut. *Pfälzer Bratwürste*, grilled sausages, are coarse in texture and well seasoned. They help to drain the *Pfälzer Schoppen* glasses, which contain half a liter, that is, just over a pint, of wine.[8] However, they are traditionally not drunk by a single person but instead passed around, typically at one of the numerous wine festivals.

Franconia, the northern part of Bavaria, is dominated by beer in the east but by wine in the region around Würzburg. The extensive forests yield diverse game, wild fruit, and mushrooms, whereas countless lakes, ponds, rivers, and streams make for an abundance of fish, especially carp, pike, trout, catfish, and eel. Very small fish from the river Main are deep-fried whole for *Meefischli*. Cabbage is not only salted for sauerkraut but also prepared fresh as salad; stuffed, rolled, and braised for *Kraut-wickerle*; or mixed with ground beef and pork for *Bamberger Krautbraten*, a kind of meat loaf. *Nürnberger Rostbratwürste* are small grilled sausages. Slightly larger sausages are also poached with onions in white wine with vinegar for *Blaue Zipfel*. Potato dumplings come in countless variations and are also served with *Kärrnersbraten*, a beef rib roast with a bread stuffing. *Pichelsteiner Eintopf*, a stew with beef, veal, pork, and mutton, potatoes, and various vegetables, is often attributed to the small town of Büchelstein on the Czech border but is mostly served in Franconia.

Farther south around Munich, in Bavaria proper, beef and veal historically are the standard meats, with all inner and outer bits used, including the lungs and udder. Liver is above all made into dumplings and served in a clear broth, called *Leberknödelsuppe*. Pork here used to be the exception, making *Schweinebraten* (pork roast) a Sunday treat. The dumplings to go with it are made from bread, *Semmelknödel*. Potatoes generally only appear in the form of salad (always dressed with oil and vinegar, as opposed to the mayonnaise used in Berlin) or occasionally as *Reiberdatschi*, savory pancakes made from grated raw potatoes (in other regions called *Reibekuchen* or *Kartoffelpuffer*). Game and wild mushrooms from the *Bayerischer Wald* (Bavarian Forest) on the Czech border are often served together. Although Bavarians feel quite patriotic about "their" wine (from Franconia), this is above all beer country. Snacks to go with Bavarian beer include *Weisswürste* or *Leberkäs*. Traditionally, the cuisine of Bavaria is quite down-to-earth. Instead of the small sour-milk cheeses typical of the central parts of Germany, larger-volume hard cheeses come from the Alpine dairies. For sweet dishes, the Bohemian/Austrian influence is noticeable in the form of strudels and dumplings.

The part of Bavaria that lies west of the city of Augsburg, together with most of Württemberg even farther west, culturally forms one region, called Swabia. Foodwise it is mostly characterized by the rough climate and poor soils of the *Schwäbische Alb*, a low mountain plateau between Stuttgart and Ulm. Thrift is a virtue, and the cooking is dominated by flour. Most often, it takes the form of numerous variations of *Spätzle*, small egg noodles scraped in strips from a wooden board into boiling water. *Leberspätzle*, with liver added to the dough, *Krautspätzle*, which are pan fried with sauerkraut and bacon, and *Kässpätzle*, which are baked with cheese and topped with fried chopped onion, are meals in their own right. *Linsen* (lentils) *mit Spätzle* or *Saure Spätzle* (sour spätzle, served in a vinegar-seasoned sauce based on a dark roux) are other great Swabian favorites. *Maultaschen*, a kind of ravioli served either in a clear broth or *abgeschmälzt* with chopped onion fried in butter, is another specialty of the region. Potatoes, as in Bavaria, appear only as salad, in stews like *Gaisburger Marsch* (consisting of some beef, potatoes, and spätzle), or as *Schupfnudeln* made from boiled potato and a little egg, which are shaped into small, pointed, finger-sized rolls that are first boiled and then often fried. Meals often start with a clear soup with some kind of noodles or pancakes cut into thin strips, *Flädlesuppe*. On special occasions the richer *Hochzeitssuppe* (literally, wedding soup) with three different (varying) kinds of small dumplings is served. As for meat, *Saure Kutteln* (sour tripe) in a dark roux-based sauce seasoned with vinegar is a favorite. *Gemischter Braten*, that is, pork, veal, and mutton roast, as well as *Zwiebelrostbraten*, steak with fried onion rings, are considered Sunday fare. Near the shores of Lake Constance, the lake-fish *Kretzer/Egli* (perch) and *Felchen* (a trout-like white fish) are served, mostly fried. *Zwiebelkuchen* (onion tart) is the favored snack to accompany young wine in autumn, whereas *Tellersülze* (meat in aspic) and *Wurstsalat* (literally, sausage salad, dressed with onions, vinegar and oil, sometimes with chesse added) are eaten year-round as a starter or snack and also with beer. *Laugenbrezeln* (pretzels) are omnipresent.

Baden in the southwestern corner of Germany has perhaps the richest cuisine of all. It shares Alemannic traditions with Alsace in France and the northwest of Switzerland. Many Swabian dishes reappear here in a version enriched with butter and cream. *Brägele* (fried potatoes) play an important role. The fertile Rhine Valley yields all kinds of vegetables including asparagus, typically served with *Chratzete*, a thin savory pancake rich in eggs, torn up in the pan with two forks. The Black Forest mountains historically provided trout, the famous ham (smoked over resiny pine wood), and all kinds of wild mushrooms and fruit. Meat of all kinds is highly valued, including *Schüfeli* (pork shoulder) as well as veal tongue and sweetbread. Snails and frogs' legs compete with brawn (headcheese), boiled breast of beef, and diverse game, all washed down with lightish beer, fruit schnapps, and wine.

NOTES

1. Günter Wiegelmann, *Alltags- und Festspeisen in Mitteleuropa: Innovationen, Strukturen und Regionen vom späten Mittelalter bis zum 20. Jahrhundert*, 2nd ed., with Barbara Krug-Richter (Münster: Waxmann, 2006), 2–4.

2. Deutsche Gesellschaft für Ernährung e.V., ed., *Ernährungsbericht 2004* (Bonn Deutsche Gesellschaft für Ernährung e.V., 2004), 72–82.

3. Business breakfasts and dinners are the exception—the former are considered uncivil and the evening is regarded as family or private time.

4. Wiegelmann, *Alltags- und Festspeisen*, 105.

5. For further reading on the history and concept of regional cuisine, see Kirsten Schlegel-Matthies, "Regionale Speisen in deutschen Kochbüchern des 19. und 20. Jahrhunderts," in *Essen und kulturelle Identität: Europäische Perspektiven*, ed. Hans Jürgen Teuteberg, Gerhard Neumann, and Alois Wierlacher (Berlin: Akademie Verlag, 1997), 212–227.

6. Survey conducted by Emnid on behalf of the Dutch company Podomedi, http://www.podomedi.com/Downloads/Pressemitteilung6.rtf.

7. Statistisches Bundesamt, *Statistisches Jahrbuch 2006 für die Bundesrepublik Deutschland* (Wiesbaden: Statistisches Bundesamt, 2006), figures from 2005, http://www.destatis.de/jetspeed/portal/cms/Sites/destatis/SharedContent/Oeffentlich/AI/IC/Publikationen/Jahrbuch/Bevoelkerung,property=file.pdf.

8. The regional variations in the size of the *Schoppen* reveal the differing attitudes toward wine: in the Palatinate wine was always plentiful and the standard beverage, so they are large, just over a pint. In Württemberg, it was more precious as more labor was needed for its production: the *Schoppen* here is a *Viertele*, a quarter (of a liter), just over half a pint.

5

Eating Out

For most Germans, eating out in a restaurant is not just another everyday meal option but is widely regarded as something special. Generally it is a luxury to be indulged in only when the most important status symbols like a nice home, car, and vacations are already guaranteed, and thus it is a sign of affluence and achievement. A restaurant meal marks special occasions and ranks higher than a meal prepared at home. This attitude is in stark contrast, for instance, to the French convention according to which a dinner invitation to somebody's house is certainly a higher honor than being taken out to a restaurant.

What exactly is considered a restaurant meal varies significantly according to disposable income and social standing. Besides the obvious differences in price range between restaurants, households with a higher income eat more often in "proper" restaurants, whereas those with lower incomes tend to buy fast food, which can also fulfill the role of marking a special occasion.[1] Although Germany is generally perceived as an almost classless society, the strong opinions and delicate decisions about who eats out where and with whom, as well as anxiety about being at the "wrong" place or not dressed "right" for the occasion, betray the subliminal existence of a distinctive social hierarchy.

Even the packed lunch, which was once as a general rule brought from home for the break at school or work, or while traveling, is becoming passé. It is considered much cooler to buy take-out food. Unwrapping *Stullen* or *Butterbrote* (sandwiches) and bringing along a thermos of tea or coffee is now relegated to those who cannot afford to purchase something on the spot or who have strong opinions about ecological and/or nutritional issues.

Thus, in 2003 German households spent more on food in cafés, fast-food outlets, restaurants, and the like than in 1998 but less on eating in cafeterias, or schools, the latter options regarded as unavoidable necessities when studying or working.[2] The same applies for food in hospitals and nursing homes: its quality obviously varies, but its overall reputation is bad, and a third of the residents in German nursing homes suffer from nutritional deficiencies.[3]

CAFETERIAS

In Germany, there are two classes of workers: *Arbeiter* (worker) and *Angestellte* (employee). *Arbeiter* generally have less freedom in the workplace. From the 1870s on, factories started to install cafeterias for their workers. This was meant to improve working conditions but has also been interpreted as an attempt to bind the workers, who did not have any alternatives during the short breaks. As in restaurants, social distinctions made themselves felt. The new class of employees insisted on separate refreshment rooms. However, the ideal remained either to eat at home or to be affluent enough to choose freely where and when to eat out.

Whereas in West Germany until today schools tend to end around midday with no meals provided, day schools, and with that school cafeterias, used to be the norm in East Germany and are currently on the rise throughout the country. At the end of the 1980s, 85% of East German schoolchildren ate lunch with their classmates, whereas their parents ate with work colleagues. Even today there is a marked difference between western Germany, where only 18% of children eat lunch at school, and the eastern regions of Germany, where much higher numbers eat lunch at school. Free school meals (*Schulspeisung*) have been controversial in Germany since they began at the end of the nineteenth century; historically, they are closely connected with soup kitchens and similar initiatives. School cafeterias were created by official authorities as well as private initiatives to relieve the lot of those children who were not properly fed at home. They were revived by the Allied forces in the immediate postwar years. Just as with factory cafeterias, they ran contrary to the ideal of lunch meals prepared at home by a mother or wife.[4] This possibly explains the negative associations that cafeteria food has for Germans up until today.

However, the *Studentenwerke* (students' administrations) running the *Mensas* (university cafeterias) in contemporary Germany make a big effort to offer a selection of healthy, popular foods at affordable prices (subsidized by tuition fees). There are often vegetarian and organic options, and the menu tends to be a representative mix of home-style cooking and fast food. Of course, the quality varies from one location to another.

RESTAURANTS

The much-traveled Dutch humanist and theologian Erasmus of Rotterdam (1466 or 69–1536) had a very low opinion of German inns in his time, finding them overheated and dirty, and the food and drink served of low, dubious quality.[5] In contrast, he raved about hospitable Lyons in France. Although more favorable accounts were given by other travelers of about the same time, inns were doubtlessly considered a necessity more than an indulgence, including the food, which consisted of a fixed menu served at a common table. Etymologically, *Gast* (guest) first designated any stranger, regardless of the person's peaceful or hostile intentions. It only developed its contemporary meaning—a non–family member who should be looked after with food and lodging—when trade and traveling became more common and far-reaching in the Middle Ages. Once considered a basic Christian gesture at monasteries, the idea spread with the postal stations. Today *Gastfreundschaft* (literally, guest-friendship; hospitality) is the basis of commercial gastronomy.

Gaststätte, Gasthaus, Gaststube, Gasthof, or *Lokal* sound much more down-to-earth than *Restaurant* to German ears, with *Wirtschaft* or *Wirtshaus* more commonly used in the south and sometimes *Krug/Krog* in the north. Any innkeeper must apply for a *Konzession* (license) to run such an establishment, which is linked to his/her own personal reliability (no criminal record) and certain requirements concerning the premises. Sanitary regulations are standard as well as regulations aimed at protecting the neighborhood from too much noise. On paper a distinction is made between *Schankwirtschaften*, bars serving only drinks, and *Speisewirtschaften*, eateries so to speak, but in reality there is not such a clear boundary. Even the most ordinary *Eckkneipe* (corner bar) serving mostly beer or, in the southwest, *Weinbeiz* or *Weinstube* oriented more toward wine also offer some cold fare like *Buletten* (fried meat patties), *Brezeln*, simple sandwiches, or *Soleier*, boiled eggs marinated in vinegar brine, at the very least to support their customers' thirst. However, in most bars and pubs, socializing is as important as alcohol consumption, and inebriation a side effect rather than a desired goal. These bars provide a public space for people to meet outside their home. *Stammtische* (literally, regulars' tables), common among all social classes, consist of groups who meet weekly or monthly to chat, drink, and eat. This socializing can also be traced back to the food stores that sprang up during the nineteenth century in industrial areas. Providing food for workers who had migrated far from their origins, culinary habits, and backgrounds, they also often served schnapps.

Industrialization led not only to new forms of food preparation and consumption but also to stark social distinctions and a parallel diversification of bars and restaurants. Eating out not only became necessary more often and for more people but was also seen as a pastime and status symbol. The new, specifically urban restaurant culture that developed beginning in the last third of the nineteenth century was strongly shaped by the class system of imperial Germany. In Frankfurt am Main, for instance, the number of bars and restaurants doubled between 1890 and 1914.[6] In the 1920s, the people hardest hit by the depression were struggling to be able to afford a bowl of pea soup at one of the famous Aschinger chain's beer taverns (where the soup came with as many rolls as one wanted to eat). At the same time, the huge establishments that had sprung up, above all in Berlin, beginning around 1900 (*Haus Rheingold, Haus Vaterland*) during the so-called Golden Twenties, became ever wilder and more ecstatic—some of them were more like theater than traditional gastronomy. In fact, the term *ausgehen* (to go out) still designates both eating out and entertainment such as concerts or the theater. The various circus-like restaurants of today, run by well-known chefs in the form of *variétés* (the best known of these is probably *Pomp, Duck and Circumstances* by Hans-Peter Wodarz), seem to be a logical next step in that tradition.

Despite the reigning nationalism and the tendency to Germanize culinary terms at the end of the nineteenth century, high restaurant culture as well as the courtly kitchens were above all influenced by French haute cuisine. Meals followed the classic standard recipes, and menus were written in French. The future German Kaiser William I had two of the leading French chefs, Dubois and Bernand, come to Berlin, and his grandson, William II, employed Auguste Escoffier (1846–1935). At that time, almost the only one to break through this French predominance was Alfred Walterspiel (1881–1960). He began his career at the exclusive restaurant Hiller at Berlin's Hotel Adlon, went on to the Hotel Atlantic in Hamburg, and organized the German restaurant at the 1910 World Fair in Brussels. However, he is mostly connected with the restaurant Vier Jahreszeiten in Munich, which he headed from 1925 until 1960. A strong follower of Escoffier and his principles, Walterspiel sought to integrate regional ingredients and dishes.[7]

After the introduction of the Deutschmark currency in 1948, the German culinary scene came to be dominated by the *Fresswelle* (gluttony wave), which also extended to restaurants. Pseudo-exotic creations and quantity were more important than refinement, and the culinary climax more often consisted of the show of flambéing than of precision and careful cooking of quality ingredients. *Gutbürgerliche Küche* (a term still used in Germany that literally translates as "good bourgeois cooking" but in fact stands for German middle-class, home-style cooking) became a hollow expression: the world of aristocratic ways influenced by France that had trickled down into bourgeois kitchens had disappeared, and the earth from which the traditional ingredients had come seemed unreliable.

Following this showy period of German culinary history, the impulse for change again came from France: young German chefs like Eckart Witzigmann (born in 1941 near Salzburg, Austria, but working mostly in Germany) and Franz Keller Junior (born in 1950 in Freiburg in Baden), both of whom trained with Paul Bocuse near Lyons in France, brought a new, lighter, more regionally oriented cooking style with them. This *Nouvelle Cuisine* (new cooking), sometimes called the *Edelfresswelle* (high-end gluttony wave), was promoted by gastro-journalists and embraced by affluent patrons. It quickly became clear that the necessary ingredients for these pared-down dishes were almost impossible to find in top quality on the German market. Karl-Heinz Wolf, an ambitious restaurateur in Bonn, therefore started to drive once a week to the wholesale market in Rungis near Paris to buy fish, poultry, crème fraîche, and so on to supply his kitchen, rather than risk sub-par German ingredients. He soon took orders for colleagues as well and in 1978 founded his hugely successful company Rungis-Express, importing fine French food on a commercial scale. Until the end of the 1980s, the menu at almost all ambitious German restaurants was determined by the twice-a-week delivery of the truck from Rungis-Express. By then, German chefs gradually realized that their restaurants were not actually situated in France. They started to look for and encourage local producers as well as integrate regional recipes into their cooking. The onset of the *Neue deutsche Küche* (*New German Cooking*) was marked by the publication of a recipe book called *Essen wie Gott in Deutschland* (*Eating Like God in Germany*). The book's title played on the German saying *Leben wie Gott in Frankreich* (*Living Like God in France*), which describes a very sumptuous meal or even way of life.[8]

The profession of chef became more attractive, with stereotypes changing from unreliable drunkard to star artist. New technical equipment made kitchen work less physically demanding, and during the 1980s the almost exclusively male profession slowly opened up to include women, although they are still in the minority.[9]

The chef of historic Barthels Hof restaurant in Leipzig shows off the house speciality, *Sächsischer Heubraten*. AP Photo/Eckehard Schulz.

Although today some German chefs are as much influenced by the Spanish chef Ferran Adrià and his futuristic, commonly called "molecular" cuisine, as their colleagues in other Western countries, they are very aware of their origins and surroundings. They use all kinds of ingredients, elements, and styles but tend to integrate them into a regional culinary pattern, striving for clear, straightforward taste. The significantly lower number of Michelin-starred restaurants in Germany as compared to France could thus also be seen as a sign of emancipation from the French model, which in a way is still promoted by that food guide, rather than as a lack of skill and talent.

Beginning as a necessity for travelers that lacked service and variety, as reported by Erasmus, eating out in Germany has developed into a plethora of possibilities. Except for the most informal places, booking a table in advance is advised. It is rare to find a separate bar area in restaurants. Germans usually do not drink hard liquor or cocktails before a meal. They might start the meal with a glass of sparkling wine, sherry, Campari, or a beer as an aperitif, then usually proceed to wine with the meal, and perhaps coffee and a fruit brandy, schnapps, grappa, or more wine afterward. Ice water or tap water is not served automatically as in the United States, but many people order bottled water, with or without carbonation. Although many places offer a *Tagesmenü* (set menu of the day), mostly consisting of a soup or starter, a main course, and dessert, many people prefer to compose their meal themselves, with each person at the table possibly ordering something different. At more down-to-earth venues, however, the *Tagesmenü* or *Tagesgericht* (dish of the day) is very popular and often the freshest and most seasonal choice on offer. In most places bread is served free with the meal, often with butter free as well, although in the south there is sometimes an extra charge for it, as in Austria.

Hot food is served in most places during fixed lunch and dinner hours. It is the exception for German restaurants to do two seatings in the evening as is common in American cities, and guests decide for themselves how long to linger after the meal. The check is brought to the table only when asked for; anything else would be considered very rude, the equivalent of pushing the guests out. Except for self-service restaurants (for instance, in cafeterias, museum cafés, or fast-food outlets or at airports, to name only a few examples where table service is unusual), payment is always expected only at the end of a meal, before leaving. Even in bars, a record is kept of everybody's consumption, most traditionally with marks on the beer coaster, and the complete check is paid at the end. A *Trinkgeld* (tip) of about 10% is usually expected in restaurants and seen as a sign of everything having been satisfactory, but it is not required in any way, as by law all taxes and service fees have to be included in the prices. Until very recently there were few restrictions on smoking in public places, including restaurants, but in 2007 smoking legislation started to change and is gradually being put into practice.

EATING OUTDOORS

Be it in the *Biergärten* (beer gardens) in Bavaria, the traditional *Ausflugsgaststätten* (gastronomic day-trip destinations) around the larger cities, or in their own gardens and on their balconies, Germans love to eat and drink outside. The *Biergärten* came into existence in 1539, when beer brewing was banned during the summer months because of fire risks. The brewers went on to produce a special *Märzenbier* (March beer) that could be kept in improvised "cellars" constructed above ground (the water level being rather high around Munich). They covered these with gravel and planted them with horse chestnut trees for better insulation—hence the beer garden was born. Not only in Bavaria, but everywhere in Germany, sitting in the shade of large trees or an umbrella is associated with summer, fun, and freedom. Even in crowded city centers, cafés and restaurants of all sorts put out tables on the pavement or have a *Terrasse* (patio) at the back. This obsession with *frische Luft* (fresh air), which on principle is considered healthy, in the last few years has led to mushroom-shaped gas heaters being put up throughout the year, in spite of Germany's typically energy-conscious attitude.[10]

CAFÉS AND *KONDITOREIEN* (CAFÉS AND PASTRY SHOPS)

Although the highly popular combination of *Kaffee und Kuchen* is treated more thoroughly in chapter 6, cafés and *Konditoreien* (pastry shops, which are also almost always cafés) also belong in this section: except for fast-food restaurants they offer the most affordable and socially open way to eat out. Since the opening of the first German *Kaffeehaus* in 1679 in Hamburg, coffeehouses have offered public spaces to meet, linger over a cup of coffee or some other drink, or read newspapers and, obviously, treat oneself to cakes and pastry. Berlin's first *Lese-Conditorei* (literally, reading pastry shop) opened in 1818, and in 1833 the Kranzler offered the city's first smoking room.[11] Especially in the summer, many cafés have *Eiskarten* (special ice cream menus) offering an alternative to afternoon cake in the form of ice cream in numerous flavors and often rather large portions, topped with large amounts of whipped cream.

Café culture is not quite as developed as in the Austrian *Kaffeehaus*, but most cafés in Germany open in the morning and offer breakfast and some menu of simple hot and cold food all day long. Some double as a bar and stay open until late, whereas others, mostly the *Konditoreien*, which have their own bakery behind the shop and sell cake and pastries by the piece to take home, tend to close at 6 or 7 P.M.

ETHNIC RESTAURANTS

Affordable, informal restaurants in Germany are often run by immigrants, and in spite of all regional influences, the chances of finding a pizzeria or a Greek or Asian restaurant are probably higher in most of Germany than those of coming across a traditional inn. Even in the southwest with its more indulgent food culture and higher density of restaurants of all categories, people love to go *zum Italiener* or *zum Griechen* (to the Italian or the Greek). This is in large part due to tourism, both contemporary trips and the so-called *Reisewelle*, the wave of holiday travel to the Mediterranean countries that took place in the 1960s. Another reason was the end of the economic boom in the 1970s, when immigrant workers lost their jobs in the factories and looked for alternative business opportunities. These restaurants are typically rather cheap, and the food consequently is rarely of more than average quality. There are, however, also Italian restaurants with very high standards. But in general the perception is that they are not included in the same "ethnic" category but regarded as part of Germany's fascination with Italian high culture and connected with exclusive fashion labels and expensive Piedmontese and Tuscan wines.

Besides Italian and Greek restaurants, French, Austrian, Chinese, Thai, Vietnamese, Lebanese, Japanese (sushi), and many other ethnic restaurants abound. The nationalities represented vary with time and history. For instance, until the war in former Yugoslavia broke out in 1991, Yugoslavian restaurants had a strong foothold in the market, introducing Germans to the gastronomic concept of the wood-fired grill. Some of them renamed or reinvented themselves as *Balkanküche* (Balkan cuisine) or later Croatian.

However, ethnic restaurants sometimes reflect a clever business mind rather than the attempt to create and offer a part of someone's culinary home. There might be a Turkish entrepreneur behind an "Italian" restaurant, and Vietnamese immigrants might offer sushi because they think they stand a better chance of success with pan-Asian offerings. Accordingly, the food and experience on offer is of limited authenticity. The least original probably are Chinese restaurants which, in keeping with the stereotypical plastic-dragon décor, mostly offer a heavily Germanized or completely fake version of this extremely complex and ancient cuisine.

Although the Turks represent the largest ethnic group in Germany, Turkish restaurants are rare, having sprung up only during the last few years, mostly in Berlin and Cologne.[12] This is another example of how former industrial workers (from the countryside with a poor, agricultural background) and their children and grandchildren have established themselves in Germany and now lead a different life. Initially very restricted because of language and religious barriers (most are Muslim), their culinary presence so far had made itself mostly felt in public spaces through Turkish grocery stores and open-air markets offering the familiar wares that could not be found in Germany. Turkish women, traditionally the cooks, were used to entertaining at home, also for larger groups and their extended families on special occasions. The first Turkish impact on the restaurant scene came at the beginning of the 1970s when the first *Dönerbuden* (*Döner Kebab* stands) opened in Kreuzberg, the "Turkish" district of Berlin.[13]

STREET FOOD AND FAST FOOD

Until about a decade ago, with the exception of ice cream and food at fairs, eating while walking in the street was considered unacceptable behavior and was rarely seen. Drinking from a beer bottle in public was just one step further down the social ladder and a sure sign of a homeless person. Respectable people had a home or could afford to sit in a restaurant or bar or, if that was not possible, at least stand at one of the little tables or the counter of an *Imbissbude* (literally, snack shack), a kiosk, or outside a van selling snacks.

But things have changed.[14] A leading food encyclopedia links the abundance or absence of street food to climate, among other factors.[15] It could thus be taken as proof of global warming that today it is quite normal and socially acceptable to walk around German streets eating or with a drink in one's hand—be it a take-out coffee, a soft drink, water, or beer. Certainly the exceptionally hot and dry summer of 2003 saw an explosion of this phenomenon. Sometimes, when watching people eat and drink on the go, one is reminded of young infants clutching their bottle, and it might be a sign of shortening attention spans, which make the postponing of any craving apparently impossible.

Admittedly, most take-out and street food is offered in busy city centers, in open-air markets, around large department stores, near tourist attractions, and in or around train stations (largely replacing the *Bahnhofsrestaurant* [train station restaurant] of old). Small stalls on the platforms sell coffee, cold soft drinks, sandwiches, and pastries. Most bakeries offer the same selection. Freshly squeezed fruit juices and ready-cut fruit, ice cream, salads, pretzels, soup, sushi, wraps, *Chinapfanne* (a stir-fry of "Chinese" vegetables

Imbissbude

in thin strips and soybean sprouts), all kinds of *Bratwurst* (grilled sausages), pizza slices, pickled, smoked, or fried fish in rolls, baked *Leberkäse* (baked meat loaf), or *Schwenkbraten* (pork roast)—the list of goods on offer is almost endless. Most of it is of rather standardized, industrial quality. Furthermore, there are the menu options from the internationally operating fast-food chains with their hamburgers, fried chicken, donuts, and the like.

In Germany, the modern era of fast food—which by now is difficult to distinguish from street food—started after World War II. Until then, eating quickly and in the street had mostly been a necessity for those without hearth and home and for the bourgeois was associated with the lower classes of the industrial era.[16] But hardship and hunger and the lack of city center buildings made it easy to overcome old behavior patterns. The *Trinkhallen* (literally, drink kiosks), or *Wasserhäuschen* (water houses) as they are called in Frankfurt, where they are regarded as special local phenomenon, had sprung up in industrial areas beginning in the second half of the nineteenth century. They represented the cities' attempt to contain the workers' thirst for beer and schnapps by selling the recently invented carbonated mineral water and other nonalcoholic drinks, later including tobacco and—in defiance of all good intentions—beer and schnapps. Only occasionally food was available in form of cookies . In the years immediately after the war these kiosks (as well as improvised shacks on bomb sites) provided a model for a new kind of fast-food outlet, as they were used as sale points for whatever food was available. In Cologne, for instance, some offered fondant, potato fritters, or fried meat patties. Soon after the currency reform, more food was offered in this way, in Cologne again, for example, goulash and hot sausages.[17] Today fast food carries with it notions of fun and social freedom. It is an affordable alternative, especially for allowing young people to escape family restraints and meet with friends over a meal.

The most famous German street and fast-food dish, also found in simpler restaurants and served in cafeterias, is undoubtedly *Currywurst* (curried sausage). It is commonly believed that a certain Herta Heuwer invented it on September 4, 1949, at her food stand on the Kantstrasse in Berlin. She roasted a scalded, very finely grained pork sausage and served it with a sauce made of tomato puree, curry powder, and Worcestershire sauce. However, some claim Hamburg and an earlier date in 1947 as the starting point for this very popular snack that has developed many finely nuanced variations.[18] The simplest preparation for *Currywurst* is to cut the sausage in bite-sized pieces (with a knife or specially developed cutting machine), sprinkle them abundantly with curry powder and sometimes also paprika powder, and then lace them with tomato ketchup. *Currywurst* is usually eaten with a small plastic fork. It can be had *mit* (with skin), in which case the sausage served either is or resembles a bockwurst, or *ohne* (without skin), in which case it is unsmoked and grayish-white. Additional options include *scharf* or *extra scharf* (hot or extra hot with cayenne powder), chopped raw onions with chili, and *Schaschliksauce*, the sauce yielded by the roasted meat skewered with onions and bell peppers that is—like *Buletten*—often sold at the same stands. A roll has to be ordered as an extra, but the most popular combination is with *Pommes*, pronounced pom-miss, also called *Fritten* (French fries). These started to appear on German streets (and menus) in the 1960s, coming from Belgium and the Netherlands. They are also a dish on their own, served with either ketchup or mayonnaise, or both, in which case they are called *Pommes rot-weiss* (red-white). For a few years now the largely standardized industrial offering of fries has been challenged by stands offering hand-cut, freshly fried ware from specific potato varieties, some of them organic.

Bratwurst (grilled sausage) is generally sold at different stands than *Currywurst* and fries. Except for the smaller *Nürnberger Rostbratwürstchen* (Nuremberg sausages), which are served by the half dozen on a plate, *Bratwurst* is typically eaten sticking out of a roll and laced with mustard. Nowadays, *Bratwurst* sellers with round portable grills hanging from their shoulders and an umbrella attached to their back (in case of rain) have replaced the *Würstchenmann* (sausage man) who sold hot frankfurters from a shiny, rectangular, metal hot-water container hung around his neck.

The trend toward grilled and deep-fried fast food—imitating perhaps the higher value that roasted meat has had compared with boiled since the Middle Ages—originated with the first *Wienerwald*, which opened in

Currywurst

Munich in 1955. *Wienerwald* (literally, Viennese Wood), a fast-growing chain of take-out outlets doubling as a family restaurant, almost exclusively sold grilled chicken. Although the smaller British chain Wimpy had already introduced Germans to hamburgers in 1954, they had to wait until 1971 for the first McDonald's experience in their own country (again in Munich), which was soon followed by Burger King. Both apparently took a rather long time to convince people of the value of this new eating experience and thus to become profitable. Although some still see American fast-food chains as symbols of capitalism and industrialization, today they are firmly established on the market.[19]

At the beginning of the 1970s, *Döner Kebab*, or *Döner*, pronounced *doenn*-ner, *Currywurst*'s strongest competitor as Germans' most eaten fast-food began its reign in Berlin. Although it is just as popular in Turkey, and with few exceptions prepared by Turkish immigrants, the German version of *Döner* is different. It does not have much in common neither with the historical Persian dish, where mutton or lamb is roasted on a turning spit, nor with the main course served under that name in contemporary Turkey. In Germany, meat is marinated with salt, spices, onions, milk, or yogurt and layered on a spit with the addition of up to 60% ground meat. Originally mutton, it is now often mixed with beef, and modern variations include chicken or turkey. The meat forms a long oval block of meat, thicker at the upper end and weighing 4.4 to 22 lb. Most of the *Döner* blocks (which legally are considered ground meat) are made by special producers, who produce up to 300 tons daily in Germany. The spit is placed upright in front of a special electric grill that runs along its whole length and about a third of its width. The meat rotates at adjustable speed, slowly roasting. The cooked outer layer is gradually cut off in thin strips, in long strokes with a long knife, falling into a metal scoop placed underneath the *Döner* block. The meat is served in a quarter of a Turkish *Pide* (pita) flatbread cut open to form a pocket or, more recently, as *Dürüm Döner*, that is, wrapped in a very thin bread called *Yufka*. Usually green lettuce, tomatoes, onions, and red cabbage, all cut into thin strips, are added as liberally as the yogurt sauce, with hot chili flakes as an extra. The result is a fat pouch, which requires some practice to eat without leaving traces on one's clothes. *Gyros*, the Greek version of *Döner*, is popular as well. Preparation and presentation are almost identical, except for the condiments and the fact that *Gyros* consists exclusively of recognizable, layered pieces of meat, traditionally pork, but often replaced by chicken.

It is difficult to estimate what the next most important ethnic fast-food category in Germany would be. Pizza is so widely consumed that it could almost be seen as a naturalized dish. As street food, it is often sold under the name of *Minipizza* (comparable to the Italian *pizza al taglio*) and mostly cheap. However, *Minipizza* has recently seen a quality revival with fresh, ingredients rather than plastic cheese, fatty salami, canned mushrooms, and vinegar-brined peppers. Lebanese *falafel* (as well as *Schawarma*, an Arab *Döner* version) started to appear in Germany with the onset of small Arabian fast-food restaurants at the end of the 1980s. The deep-fried balls of pureed chickpeas, served with *tahini* (sesame sauce) in a pita flatbread (although, like *Döner*, they can also be had in a larger portion on a plate), are popular with vegetarians and are now also offered at some *Döner* stands as a nonmeat alternative.

NOTES

1. Deutsche Gesellschaft für Ernährung e.V., ed., *Ernährungsbericht 2004* (Bonn: Deutsche Gesellschaft für Ernährung e.V., 2004), 84. This is obviously not a new development; see, for example, Drummer, who quotes similar statistics from the beginning of the twentieth century. Christian Drummer, "Das sich ausbreitende Restaurant in deutschen Großstädten als Ausdruck bürgerlichen Repräsentationsstrebens 1870–1930," in *Essen und kulturelle Identität: Europäische Perspektiven*, ed. Hans Jürgen Teuteberg, Gerhard Neumann, and Alois Wierlacher (Berlin: Akademie Verlag, 1997), 318.

2. Statistisches Bundesamt, *Wirtschaftsrechnungen. Einkommens- und Verbrauchsstichprobe: Aufwendungen privater Haushalte für Nahrungsmittel, Getränke und Tabakwaren 2003* (Wiesbaden: Statistisches Bundesamt, 2006), 31, www.destatis.de.https://www-ec.destatis.de/csp/shop/sfg/bpm.html.cms.cBroker.cls?cmspath=struktur,vollanzeige.csp&ID=1017148.

3. Source aid infodienst Verbraucherschutz, Ernährung, Landwirtschaft e.V., Bonn, www.aid.de. October 24, 2007.

4. For detailed studies, see Keith R. Allen, "Schul- und Armenspeisungen in Berlin 1880–1914" (190–202) and Ulrike Thoms, "Essen in der Arbeitswelt" (203–218), both in *Die Revolution am Eßtisch: Neue Studien zur Nahrungskultur im 19./20. Jahrhundert*, ed. Hans Jürgen Teuteberg (Stuttgart: Franz Steiner, 2004).

5. *Collected Works of Erasmus*, vol. 39 *Colloquies*, trans. and ann. Craig R. Thompson (Toronto: University of Toronto Press, 1997), 368–80.

6. Drummer, quoted in Gunther Hirschfelder, *Europäische Esskultur: Geschichte der Ernährung von der Steinzeit bis heute* (Frankfurt am Main: Campus, 2001), 204.

7. Walterspiel wrote a highly regarded book about his experiences: *Meine Kunst in Küche und Restaurant* (Munich: Author, 1952).

8. *Essen wie Gott in Deutschland: Die deutsche Küche von 24 Meisterköchen auf neue Art zubereitet* (Munich: Zabert Sandemann, 1987).

9. Waiters still lack the corresponding star models and personalities; their job is mostly held in low esteem. In many cafés, bars, and simpler restaurants, the waiters are students.

10. However, these heaters are no modern invention; in the 1920s some cafés on the Kurfürstendamm in Berlin put out coke-fuelled heaters which closely resembled the gas-heaters of today (pictured in Hans-Christian Täuberich. *Zu Gast im alten Berlin* 2nd ed. (Munich: Hugendubel, 1990), 201.

11. Peter Lummel, *Berlins nimmersatter "Riesenbauch,"* in Hans Jürgen Teuteberg, ed., *Die Revolution am Eßtisch: Neue Studien zur Nahrungskultur im 19./20. Jahrhundert* (Stuttgart: Franz Steiner, 2004), 84–100.

12. According to Susan Stern, the first Muslims came to Prussia in 1732, when the Prussian King Frederick William I was given 20 "Mohammedan" soldiers as a gift. Susan Stern, *These Strange German Ways and the Whys of the Ways* (Berlin: Atlantik-Brücke, 2000), 85.

13. For further reading on ethnic restaurants in postwar Germany, see Maren Möhring, "Transnational Food Migration and the Internalization of Food Consumption: Ethnic Cuisine in West Germany," in *Food and Globalisation: Histories—Politics—Moralities*, ed. Alexander Nützenadel and Frank Trentmann (Oxford: Berg, 2008).

14. They have of course changed before: the renowned German writer Heinrich Böll (1917–85) commented on the postwar trend toward fast food that is eaten while standing. He called the *Frittenbude* the new place of humanity (*Frankfurter Vorlesungen* [Cologne and Berlin: Kiepenheuer & Witsch, 1966], 96). Because of strict regulations the individually run and structured kiosks today are tending to disappear and be replaced by franchise outlets of larger chains.

15. Alan Davidson, ed., *The Oxford Companion to Food* (Oxford: Oxford University Press, 1999), 758.

16. In 1841 the German philosopher Karl Rosenkranz, who followed Immanuel Kant at the East Prussian university of Königsberg (today Russian Kaliningrad), published a detailed account of the street food on sale in the city and those who offered and consumed it.

17. Over time, the kiosks, which were not subject to compulsory closing hours, have developed into public meeting points as well as small grocery stores, often selling newspapers and food and acting as lottery agencies. Ursula Neeb, *Wasserhäuschen: Eine Frankfurter Institution* (Frankfurt am Main: Fachhochschulverlag, 2005).

18. For more information, see Uwe Timm, *The Invention of Curried Sausage*, trans. Leila Vennewitz (New York: New Directions, 1995).

19. The most prominent German anti-McDonald's campaigner is the renowned German journalist Günter Wallraff (b. 1942), who worked in a McDonald's outlet disguised as a Turk and published his experiences as one of a series of reports (*Ganz unten* [Cologne: Kiepenheuer & Witsch], 1986, translated into English as *Lowest of the Low* [London: Methuen, 1988]).

6

Special Occasions

The differentiation between *Alltag* (everyday) and *Festtage* (holidays or special occasions) used to be much more marked in Germany. It was mostly based on Christian religious rules and prohibitions. One used to dress "better," go to church, and eat differently and more sumptuously on those holidays or special occasions. However, with the onset of industrialization and the domination of mechanical production, new time patterns and eating groups emerged. New developments were furthered by general affluence: modern wealthy people moved away from religious holidays spent with the family or a larger social group toward a more globalized and nation-transcending celebratory culture (witness the rise of Halloween in Germany, unknown until a few years ago), accompanied by a loosening of social taboos and peer pressures.

There are relatively few nationwide public holidays in Germany besides those celebrated on weekends: six are religious (Good Friday, Easter Monday, Ascension Day, Whitmonday [the Monday after Pentecost], Christmas Day, and Boxing Day [the day after Christmas]), and three are secular (New Year's Day, May Day, and *Tag der deutschen Einheit,* the German national holiday on October 3). Additional holidays are restricted to certain regions, above all *Fasching, Fastnacht,* or *Karneval* (carnival), originally related to the Lent period and celebrated mostly along the Rhine on *Rosenmontag* (Rose Monday), *Fastnachtsdienstag* (Shrove Tuesday), and *Aschermittwoch* (Ash Wednesday). As religion plays less of a role in most Germans' lives, many originally religious holiday rituals survive as almost secular events, including Christmas. Furthermore, the wide availability of most foodstuffs almost throughout the year makes it difficult for distinctive food traditions related to holidays to survive. But even if the reasons might not be as clear as they once used to be regarding holiday fare, special occasions—which, of course, also include personal festivities such as birthdays or weddings, more official occasions like fairs, and private gatherings, mostly on the weekend—still include special food.

What makes a dish or meal suitable for special occasions? One factor is scarcity, which turns certain ingredients into luxuries suited to mark a special event. Thus, roasts, meatballs, geese, and venison (in different regions) became holiday fare because these meats were expensive and/or hard to come by. Some of these foods have persevered in a folk way, whereas other have disappeared completely. For example, in nineteenth-century Silesia, a water-based soup served with bread rubbed with garlic, salt, and a little butter took the place of fish on Good Friday. Obviously, luxury is interpreted differently with time, as witnessed, for instance, by the changing value of salmon, once so abundant in the Rhine, Elbe, and other German rivers at the end of the nineteenth century that servants refused to eat it more often than three times a week. Pollution relegated it to the status of an expensive luxury good after World War II, but today because of Norwegian aquaculture it is once again quite common and affordable. Other examples are canned asparagus or pineapple, which were suitably festive Christmas fare until the 1960s, whereas today those perishables would more likely be flown in fresh from distant shores. Another factor, surviving more as convention than conscious practice, is the rules linked to fasting, leading to the popularization of fish, egg, and vegetable dishes. Other components strongly linked with certain holiday dishes have a season-related origin, like red cabbage during winter.

As a general rule that remains valid until today, however, holiday meals tend to involve larger gatherings than weekday meals and tend to be richer and longer, for instance, including a more sumptuous dessert like *Schokoladenpudding* (chocolate pudding) or the modern version, chocolate mousse. Sweet baked goods, such as pastries, cakes, and cookies, are the most obvious and continuing markers for special occasions in Germany. They range from a *süßes Stückchen* (sweet pastry), eaten as a private treat on the go, to Sunday afternoon cake, traditional Christmas cookies, and extravagant wedding cakes. Before private households were generally equipped with an oven, all the baking was done at a communal oven or at the bakery. Deep-frying pastries in lard was the housewife's alternative then and represents a category of its own, above all associated with carnival time.

SONNTAG (SUNDAY)

For most Germans the weekend is experienced as a short holiday, as the contrast between *Arbeit* (work) and *Freizeit* (free time) tends to be strongly felt. Friday night, Saturday, and Sunday, when most people do not work, are a highlight to look forward to. Besides household chores, gardening, do-it-yourself car and house projects, and larger shopping trips, these days are spent going out (Friday and Saturday are the busiest nights in German restaurants), meeting friends, or going on day trips to the countryside or other destinations.

Sunday breakfasts tend to be more lavish affairs than on weekdays, frequently including all kinds of yeast breads, which are often plaited like *Hefezopf* (similar to challah) and enriched with raisins. Another reason for their existence is that they can made in advance, as bakers usually do not work on Sunday.

In younger, more modern urban environments, Sunday breakfast, lunch, and afternoon coffee frequently melt into brunch, starting between 10 and 11 A.M. and lasting well into the afternoon. It combines all the usual breakfast offerings with some egg dishes, perhaps a soup, and cake. Beverages typically include fruit juice, hot beverages, possibly sparkling wine, and perhaps later on wine or beer. It is an occasion to meet friends in a café or restaurant or entertain them at home. As it is served buffet-style, it is seen as more relaxed than sitting around a table.

However, for many Germans, Sunday lunch is still an occasion for family gatherings at home or in a restaurant (although, as in other countries, this is sometimes resented by younger generations). In more rural and/or traditional regions, Sunday morning is reserved for church service followed by *Frühschoppen*, when men gather at the local pub or inn for a glass of wine, beer, or schnapps while their wives prepare the midday meal. In southern Germany a whole category of smaller dishes is linked to this custom, such as *saure Kutteln* (sour tripe), *saure Nierle* (sour kidney), *Lüngerl* (lung), *Röschele* (mixed veal offal, such as heart, liver, lung, and spleen), or the Westphalian *Töttchen*, originally resembling *Röschele* but today made from "better" meat. All these dishes come in a brown roux-based sauce that has been soured with wine or vinegar to a greater or lesser degree.

Sunday lunch tends to be meat-heavy. Meat options include pork roast, *Sauerbraten* (sour beef roast), *Rinderrouladen* (beef roulades), *Koteletts* (pork chops), and chicken fricassee; and are accompanied by a vegetable side dish and a starch, ranging from dumplings to egg noodles and all kinds of potato dishes. There might be a clear soup with some dumplings beforehand, and a sweet dessert will certainly follow the meal. Depending on family habits, wine may be drunk with the meal.

KAFFEE UND KUCHEN (AFTERNOON COFFEE AND CAKE)

Kaffee und Kuchen is a German tradition that dates back to the late eighteenth century. Depending on the occasion, a selection of different pieces of cake bought from a pastry shop, or homemade cake, is offered (often with whipped cream on the side), together with coffee (or tea). *Kaffee und Kuchen* is usually served in the living or dining room (as opposed to the informal kitchen table), thus honoring the occasion and the guests. It is an excuse to invite friends or extended family over, and, if weather permits, the coffee table is often set up on the balcony, in the garden, or on the patio. Meeting at a local café for the occasion is popular as well. *Kaffee und Kuchen* is the least formal way to mark a special event with a meal—be it a birthday, confirmation, or just the mere event of a Sunday. A meeting of (mostly female) friends over *Kaffee und Kuchen* is called a *Kaffeekränzchen* (coffee klatsch).

In summer, all kinds of fruit are incorporated into cakes. More fragile varieties, like strawberries, are placed on a round sponge cake and covered with *Tortenguß* (jelly glaze), whereas the more sturdy rhubarb, cherries, or plums are baked on yeast dough, often on a *Blech* (sheet, hence the expression *Blechkuchen*). They can be topped with *Streusel* (butter rubbed with sugar and some flour to form thick crumbs) or *gedeckt*, topped with dough and a sugar glaze. Traditional cakes without fruit include *Butterkuchen*, a yeast dough topped with plenty of butter, sugar, and sometimes slivered almonds, *Streuselkuchen*, topped with streusel, *Mohnkuchen*, which has a thick, blue poppy seed mixture and streusel, and *Bienenstich*, with a topping of chopped almonds, sugar, and butter.

Käsekuchen (cheesecakes) are always made with quark (as opposed to American-style cream cheese; therefore the result is lighter). They range from custard-like cakes that are thickened with egg or gelatin, have a thin shortbread crust, and are not baked to rich, baked versions that can include raisins or other fruit. For *Dresdner Eierschecke*, yeast dough is topped first with a quark-raisin mix, then with egg custard and a thin sugar crust.

Käsekuchen (Cheesecake)

- 2 1/4 c. flour
- 1/2 c. cold butter, diced

- pinch of salt
- 1/3 c. cold water

Rub flour with butter and salt with fingertips to form fine crumbs. Add water, and quickly mix to a dough; do not knead. Wrap and chill for 30 min. Then line a buttered and floured round 10-inch cake pan with it, rolling the dough out to a slightly larger circle, then pressing it into the pan using fingertips and forming a rim.

- 1 3/4 lb. quark
- 2/3 c. granulated sugar
- pinch of vanilla
- zest of 1 lemon
- 6 egg yolks
- 3 heaping tbs. flour
- 6 egg whites
- pinch of sea salt
- 4 tbs. dried currants
- 2 tbs. confectioners' sugar

Combine quark with sugar, vanilla, lemon zest, and egg yolks to form a homogenous mixture. Beat egg whites with salt until they form stiff peaks. Fold egg whites as well as sifted flour and currants into quark mixture. Pour onto crust and bake in moderate oven (180°C/350°F/gas mark 4) for about 50 min. Let cool and sprinkle with sugar.

The simplest but most traditional cake is possibly the *Napfkuchen* (literally, pot cake), baked in a *Gugelhupf* (Bundt cake pan) or *Kastenform* (rectangular cake pan). It may be enriched with nuts and seeds, chocolate, or dried fruit, but often is just a plain mixture of eggs, butter, sugar, and flour. This points back to the time before electric food processors, when the sheer effort to beat the butter, eggs, and sugar made this cake very special. *Frankfurter Kranz* (Frankfurt ring) is a plain round *Napfkuchen* sliced twice horizontally, which is then filled and thinly iced with buttercream, and finally sprinkled with *Krokant* (chopped hazelnut praliné) and decorated with cherries. It forms the link between *Kuchen*, more ordinary cake, and the richer, more elegant *Torte* (gâteau). The latter tend to be the professionals' domain and are reserved for very special occasions like birthdays, weddings, and the like.

Unlike most American cakes, German *Torten* tend to be somewhat lighter, favoring whipped cream and some buttercream over the popular

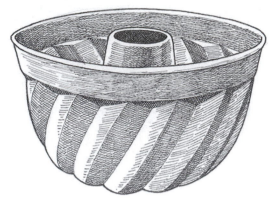

Guglhupfform (bundt cake pan)

American cream icing. Usually, a thin base of shortbread is thinly covered with jam and topped with sponge cake, which is filled with buttercream or whipped cream and possibly fruit in some form. The whole cake is then lightly covered with cream, jam, and marzipan or chocolate, and decorated.

Buchweizentorte mit Preiselbeeren (buckwheat gâteau with cranberries) is a specialty of Lower Saxony in the north. It combines a buckwheat-hazelnut sponge cake with steamed cranberries and whipped cream. In Bavaria, *Prinzregententorte* (Prince Regent's gâteau) is made of several thin layers of butter-enriched sponge cake filled with chocolate buttercream and covered with chocolate icing. The best-known German *Torte*, without doubt, is *Schwarzwälder Kirschtorte* (Black Forest cherry gâteau), at its best a glorious combination of chocolate sponge cake, tart cherries, *Kirschwasser* (cherry brandy), and freshly whipped cream. However, frequently it is only a poor imitation of itself, relying on cheap (and longer-lasting) buttercream and cherries.

Schwarzwälder Kirschtorte (Black Forest Cherry Gâteau)

Note: Make the crust and the sponge cake the day before you want to assemble and serve the *Torte*—the sponge cake will then be much easier to cut into layers.

- 1 1/4 c. flour
- 1 tsp. baking powder
- 1 heaping tbs. cocoa powder
- pinch of salt

- 5 tbs. cold butter, diced
- 1 egg, lightly beaten

Rub the butter into the dry ingredients with your fingertips until fine crumbs result, then add the egg and quickly mix to a dough without kneading. Wrap and chill for 30 min. Roll out evenly on the bottom of a buttered and floured 10-inch round cake pan, and bake in a moderate oven (180°C/350°F/gas mark 4) for about 20 min.

- 4 egg yolks
- 2 tbs. warm water
- 1/2 c. granulated sugar
- pinch of vanilla
- pinch of cinnamon
- 3 egg whites
- pinch of salt
- 1/2 c. plus 1 tbs. flour
- 1 heaping tbs. cocoa powder
- 3 tbs. cornstarch or potato starch
- 1/2 tsp. baking powder

Beat egg yolks and water, gradually adding two-thirds of the sugar and the spices. Beat egg whites with salt to form stiff peaks, adding the rest of the sugar toward the end. Gently fold egg whites into yolks, together with sifted flour, cocoa, cornstarch or potato starch, and baking powder. Immediately pour into a 10-inch round cake pan lined with baking paper, and bake in a moderate oven (180°C/350°F/gas mark 4) for about 35 min.

- 1 3/4 lb. fresh sour cherries (or corresponding amount of canned cherries)
- 1/2 to 3/4 c. granulated sugar
- 4 1/2 tbs. cornstarch or potato starch
- 2 tbs. Kirschwasser (cherry brandy), optionally more for sprinkling sponge cake
- 2 heaping tsp. granulated gelatin
- 3 tbs. cold water
- 2 1/4 c. heavy cream
- pinch of vanilla
- 1 tbs. granulated sugar
- dark chocolate shavings

Pit cherries, mix with 1/2 cup sugar, and let stand a while to draw liquid. Then quickly bring to a boil once. Remove from heat and strain cherries, reserving the liquid. Measure 1 cup of the cold cherry juice (adding water if necessary). Combine one-third of this with the starch, and heat the remaining two-thirds. Stir the starch mixture into the hot juice, and, stirring constantly, bring to a boil, then add the cherries (reserving 12 for garnish). Remove from heat, and let cool. Add the Kirschwasser, and if necessary some more sugar. Let the gelatin soak for 10 min. in the water. Beat the cream until almost stiff. Melt the gelatin over very low heat, stir in a little of the cream, then quickly beat this mixture into the whipped cream, adding vanilla and sugar. Note: If the cake is to be eaten on the same day, the gelatin may be omitted.

Spread half of the cherries on the shortbread crust, and top with one-third of the cream. Cut the sponge cake into two even horizontal layers; put one on top of the cream layer (sprinkle with a little extra Kirschwasser, if desired). Spread the rest of the cherries on it, then half of the remaining cream. Top with sponge cake (again, optionally sprinkle with a little Kirschwasser), then cover the whole cake with the remaining cream. Garnish with reserved cherries (patted dry) and copious amounts of dark chocolate curls. Chill cake for about 2 hours. Serve cold.

Baumkuchen (tree cake) is in a category of its own. It is a specialty of central and northeastern Germany, historically associated with Salzwedel and Berlin, and goes back far into the Middle Ages. It used to be reserved for special occasions like weddings, as its production requires a lot of skill and the best ingredients. *Baumkuchen* is made using a rather liquid dough, rich in butter and eggs, and further enriched with ground almonds. This is gradually dropped on the length of a horizontal spit or cylinder turning in front of a fire, thus forming a multitude of thin layers and ribs on the outside. The finished cake is taken from the spit, glazed or thinly covered with chocolate, and presented upright (it is often up to a yard high). It is cut horizontally into rings for serving.[1]

Butterkuchen (Butter Cake)

For Dough

- 3 3/4 c. flour
- 1 oz. fresh yeast or 1 tbs. active dry yeast
- 1 1/4 c. milk, lukewarm
- 1/3 c. granulated sugar
- 4 1/2 tbs. softened butter
- 1 pinch of sea salt

For Topping

- 5/8 c. butter
- 1/4 c. granulated sugar
- blanched slivered almonds

Sift the flour into a bowl. Make a well into the center, crumble the yeast into it, then add 3 tablespoons of the milk and a pinch of the sugar. Mix with a little of the flour. Cover with a cloth, and let rise in a warm spot for about 10 min. Add the softened butter, sugar, and salt, and knead into a homogenous, soft dough. Cover and let rise again until doubled in volume. Knead dough again, and roll out evenly on a buttered and floured baking sheet. Press little dips into the dough with your finger knuckles. Spread the butter in small knobs on it and sprinkle with the sugar; if you like, add some slivered almonds, too. Let rise again, then bake in a preheated oven (180°C/350°F/gas mark 4) for about 25 min. until golden brown.

GEBURTSTAGE UND NAMENSTAGE (BIRTHDAYS AND NAME DAYS)

Most Germans celebrate their *Geburtstag* (birthday), although in some Catholic areas, the *Namenstag* (name day) is deemed more important. The name day is the day in the church calendar that is dedicated to the saint after whom somebody is named. Children receive presents and invite their friends for the afternoon, to share their *Geburtstagskuchen* or *-torte* (birthday cake). This might be a favorite recipe or a fancy cake decorated with

Baumkuchen

small candles, one for each year, to be blown out in one breath. Among adults, afternoon coffee that leads into an informal dinner of simpler dishes is the traditional way to gather with family and friends on the occasion of a birthday. However, for a fortieth, fiftieth, or other special birthday, a special invitation to lunch or dinner in a fancy restaurant may be issued (with the host picking up the bill), or a big garden party may be organized (and this event moved from the actual birthday to a weekend for convenience). For elderly people, many parishes and charitable institutions organize *Geburtstagskaffee* (birthday afternoon coffee) get-togethers on a regular basis.

HOCHZEITEN (WEDDINGS)

Weddings, highly regulated rituals determined by tradition, used to be organized and financed by the bride's parents. As the ceremony often took place in the morning, the main focus was on the midday meal. It started with a *Hochzeitssuppe* (wedding soup), a strong meat broth containing three different kinds of small bread and meat dumplings that differed according to region. Boiled meat might have been served afterwards, possibly accompanied by pickles or a salad. A roast followed: in the north often a ham served with sauerkraut cooked with white beans, in the south a mix of beef and pork, with various vegetables on platters, noodles, and croquettes, abundance being important. *Milchreis* (rice pudding) was common for dessert in much of central and northern Germany. After this sumptuous meal, afternoon coffee followed, with a large selection of cakes. Dinner was more informal and simple and might have consisted of sausages or schnitzel with potato salad.

Milchreis (Rice Pudding)

- 1 c. white short-grain rice
- 1 qt. whole milk
- pinch of salt
- zest of 1 lemon
- 2 tbs. butter
- granulated sugar and cinnamon to taste, for sprinkling over finished pudding

Rinse rice. Bring to a boil with milk and seasonings, stirring constantly. Cover and bake at very low heat for 45 to 60 min., stirring occasionally, until rice is soft. Stir in butter (add more if you wish). Serve warm, sprinkled liberally with sugar and cinnamon, and possibly with stewed fruit.

However, those standardized wedding meals have all but disappeared. The wedding ceremony (either the obligatory legal one at the registrar's office, or the optional one at church, considered more romantic) frequently takes place in the afternoon (with spring and summer the most popular seasons), and dinner is the festive meal and highlight. With rare exceptions, the modern wedding dinner is held at a restaurant, with everything arranged in advance in long planning sessions. The menu (sometimes a buffet) might reflect the couple's personal preferences, but consideration for everybody invited often is the main priority.

The first slice of the wedding cake is cut by the couple, either at a separate coffee reception in the afternoon or after dinner. Traditionally the cake would be a multitiered affair made from sponge cake and buttercream covered with a thin layer of marzipan, decorated with white piped icing and marzipan roses, and topped by a small figure of a wedding couple. Modern versions, however, explore all sorts of shape and flavors.

LEICHENSCHMAUS (FUNERAL MEALS)

It is an old custom for the family of the deceased to invite everybody present at a funeral to a full meal or just coffee and cake, either at home or in a restaurant, following the service. This *Leichenschmaus* or *Leichenkaffee* (literally, corpse feast; funeral meal or coffee) serves to stress the fact that life goes on in spite of the death of a loved one and revives social contacts among the survivors. After the mournful funeral service, food and drink help to redirect everybody's thoughts toward the present and offer an opportunity to exchange more positive memories. Traditionally, larger families gather mainly at christenings, weddings, and funerals, so they function as a kind of reunion.

GRILLEN (BARBECUING)

When weather permits in the summer months, many German meals on the weekend revolve around the barbecue. Younger Germans and Turkish citizens flock to public parks for this occasion, loaded down with grill, table, and chairs as well as victuals. However, the majority of Germans prefer to retreat to their private yards. The technical equipment tends to be less state of the art than at corresponding events in North America. The fare consists mainly of sausages and marinated pork, lamb, and beef steaks or *Schaschlik* (shish kebab, that is, meat on skewers with onions and bell peppers). The men rule over the fire, be it charcoal or gas, whereas the women do the background work, making salads and sauces to go with the meat. Weekend barbecues are a good occasion to invite neighbors and friends, as they are much less formal than normal dinner invitations.

BOWLE (A KIND OF PUNCH)

Very German, and very much in retro fashion, is *Bowle*. This punch probably has bourgeois origins in the nineteenth century (although it might go back one century further). Some versions are drunk warm, but in its modern form it is a cold concoction. It is offered by bars and restaurants in the summer or made for special occasions at home. The special bulbous glass bowls for *Bowle*, with matching stemless glasses, used to be a standard part of most German households in the 1960s and 1970s but have since become a flea market relic. Generally, some fruit is marinated in white wine overnight, sometimes with the addition of sugar and brandy, and this concentrate is then diluted with more wine, sparkling wine, and/or carbonated mineral water before serving. The fruit is served and consumed with the liquid. Obviously, the flavor and alcohol content can vary enormously with the ingredients, a fact that accounts for the somewhat dubious reputation of *Bowle*. *Erdbeerbowle*, with strawberries, is the most popular version, and *Maibowle* possibly the most traditional: for the latter fresh *Waldmeister* (woodruff) is immersed for a short while in wine but then discarded. Modern *Bowle* versions transform it into a kind of Kir or Kir Royal; as for this traditional aperitif of Burgundy in France, for which a dash of black currant liqueur is added to a glass of dry white wine or sparkling wine, varying liqueurs are added to wine or sparkling wine as well as fresh fruit.

Erdbeerbowle (Cold Strawberry Punch)

2 c. small aromatic strawberries, cleaned and cut in half
1 tbs. granulated sugar
1 bottle fruity, dry white wine, preferably Moselle Riesling
1 bottle dry white or rosé sparkling wine, chilled well

Marinate fruit with the sugar and the wine overnight; chill well. Immediately before serving, add the sparkling wine to the strawberry mixture. Alternatively, replace sugar with a few drops of strawberry or orange liqueur and assemble before serving. Serve with small spoons or forks for the fruit.

WEIHNACHTEN (CHRISTMAS)

For many Germans the religious dimension of Christmas has much retreated to the background. Despite its secular nature, this is undoubtedly the most important holiday of the year, however, connected to special foods of all kinds. Originally it was linked to the fasting period that began on *Martinstag* (Martinmas), November 11, a day still celebrated with singing children parading with lanterns through the streets after dark. *Martinsgans* (roasted Martin's goose) is typically eaten for dinner on this day, served with stuffing and trimmings that differ depending on the region.

Although November is regarded as a dark and quiet month with a number of religious and secular holidays around the theme of death, Christmas jingling starts at this time (sometimes earlier) in the shops and in the advertising world. The real festive spirit, however, builds up during *Advent* with its four Sundays leading up to Christmas, as a new candle is lit each week on the Advent wreath. Children have Advent calendars filled with chocolate or little gifts, and in many towns an open-air *Weihnachtsmarkt* (Christmas market or fair) opens on the weekends or, in larger cities, during the whole of December. The largest and most renowned are the *Nürnberger Christkindlmarkt* and the *Dresdner Striezelmarkt*. Although more regular fare can be found as well, many stalls offer *Glühwein* (mulled wine), all kinds of *Lebkuchen* (gingerbread), Christmas decorations, and arts and crafts.

On the evening of December 5, children put out their polished shoes before going to bed, for *Nikolaus* (St. Nicholas), a close cousin of the American Santa Claus, to fill them with goodies during the night. Traditionally, the treats consist of oranges, mandarin oranges, nuts, gingerbread, marzipan, and chocolates, but today include small presents.

At its core, German Christmas in its present form goes back to the bourgeois families of the nineteenth century. It is still very much a rather quiet family affair, *eine besinnliche Zeit* (a time of contemplation), but also the occasion for a *Weihnachtsfeier* (Christmas party) at businesses and offices during the Advent weeks. This once-a-year get-together generally takes the form of a festive dinner at a restaurant, which is paid for by the employer.

During the whole Advent period, besides shopping for presents for family and friends, *Weihnachtsbäckerei* (Christmas baking) plays an important role. In cafés, at the baker's, and in pastry shops and food stores, all kind of specialties are offered, but baking at home is regarded as almost essential. It is often an occasion for friends to gather, with children joining in the mixing and stirring and especially the cutting and decorating of cookies.

The most traditional German Christmas cake is the *Stollen* (with the *Bremer Klaben* a close relative). Looking at today's recipe heavy with butter, almonds, and dried fruit, it is hard to believe that *Stollen* originally started as a cake for the Advent fasting period before Christmas. The

Stollen symbolizes the infant Jesus wrapped in diapers, and the first recorded mention of this cake dates back to 1329 in Naumburg an der Saale near Leipzig. Back then, strict Catholic rules apparently only allowed it to be made from water, oats, and rape seed (canola) oil. Only in 1491 did the pope allow the use of butter by sending a so-called *Butterbrief* (butter letter). Subsequently, the lean cake for fasting time developed into the familiar treat rich in fruit and almonds. In some industrial modern versions, it is almost absurdly overloaded with marzipan.

The most famous recipe for this cake undoubtedly is the yeast *Stollen* from Dresden in Saxony, which since 1996 has been recognized as a European Union Protected Geographical Indication. However, in Berlin a version with quark and baking powder is favored. This might go back to the fact that baking powder, the alternative to sourdough and yeast, was invented by a former student of the German chemist Justus von Liebig during the famines in East Prussia in the second half of the nineteenth century (when many East Prussians found their way to Berlin)—or perhaps Berlin housewives were particularly open to modern developments. Regardless, *Stollen* is traditionally made several weeks before Christmas in order to mature.

Quarkstollen (Christmas Cake with Quark)

For Cake

- 5 c. plain flour, sifted
- 1 tbs. baking powder
- 1 c. granulated sugar
- 2 eggs
- pinch of vanilla
- 1/2 tsp. cardamom
- pinch of grated nutmeg
- 4 bitter almonds, finely ground, or equivalent amount in liquid extract
- pinch of salt
- zest of 1 lemon
- 3 tbs. rum
- 5/8 c. cold butter
- 1 c. plus 2 tbs. quark, squeezed dry
- 4 tbs. beef suet, finely chopped (alternatively, try using the fat you find in a goose or duck)
- 1 c. dried currants
- 2 c. raisins

- 1 1/2 c. blanched almonds, chopped
- 1 c. candied lemon peel, chopped

For Glaze

- 4 tbs. melted butter
- 1/2 c. confectioners' sugar

Mix flour and baking powder in a large bowl. Make a well in the center, and add sugar, eggs, spices, and rum. Combine with some of the flour. Cut the butter in small pieces, and add together with the suet, quark, fruit, and almonds, and knead quickly to form a homogeneous dough. Shape into a 1 1/2-inch-thick rectangle; then fold lengthwise, folding about one-third (or slightly more) of the dough lengthwise onto the other two-thirds; the top should not cover the base completely. Set on a sheet covered with baking parchment and bake in a preheated oven (180°C/350°F/gas mark 4) for about 1 hour. Test for doneness with a toothpick. Immediately after taking the *Stollen* out of the oven, brush liberally with the melted butter and coat with confectioners' sugar. Let cool completely, wrap carefully in wax paper and foil, and let sit in a cool, dry place for at least 15 days.

Cakes with a poppy seed filling rolled up in a yeast dough are another Christmas tradition that has Silesian roots.

Mohnrolle (Round Poppy Seed Yeast Cake)

For Dough

- 3 c. flour
- 4 tsp. active dry yeast (or 1 oz. fresh yeast, if available)
- 1/2 c. lukewarm milk
- 6 tbs. butter, melted
- 2 1/2 tbs. granulated sugar
- pinch of salt
- zest of 1/2 lemon

Sift flour into a bowl, and make a well in the center for the yeast. Pour milk over yeast, and mix, adding a little of the flour. Cover and let rise for about 20 min. Add butter, sugar, salt, and lemon zest, then knead to form an elastic, smooth dough. Cover and let rise again for 20 min.

For Filling

- 2/3 c. raisins
- 2 tbs. rum

- 1 c. milk
- 4 tbs. butter
- 1/3 c. semolina
- 0.6 lb. freshly ground blue poppy seeds
- 2 eggs, lightly beaten
- 3/4 c. granulated sugar
- pinch of vanilla
- 1/3 c. blanched almonds, chopped

Soak raisins in rum. Heat milk with butter, stir in semolina, and cook, stirring constantly, until it thickens to form a stiff mixture. Add poppy seeds, eggs, spices, almonds, and the soaked raisins with the rum. Roll out dough to form a rectangle of about 12 × 16 inches, and spread the filling on it. Roll the dough up lengthwise and place in a buttered and floured Bundt cake pan, joining the ends. Cover and let rise once more for about 30 min. Bake in a moderate oven (180°C/350°F/gas mark 4) for about 30 min., brushing it with some egg yolk toward the end. Let cool, wrap well, and store for several days.

Lebkuchen (gingerbread) is rarely made at home. Its tradition goes back to when the crusaders brought exotic spices home with them, like cloves and cinnamon, and it remained popular above all in the southern regions. Instead of baking powder or yeast, *Hirschhornsalz* (ammonium carbonate) and *Pottasche* (potash) are used as leaveners. There are two historically distinct styles. *Nürnberger Lebkuchen* are rich in almonds and eggs, reminiscent of wealthy patrician times and only available before Christmas (although the industrial manufacturers inundate the shelves with their wares from September on). *Pulsnitzer Pfefferkuchen* from Saxony are a much more modest, eggless, honey-based version, produced all year round. *Aachener Printen* (hard gingerbread made with honey and syrup), *Spekulatius* (dark brown, flat, syrup-flavored), and various other Christmas cookies, like cream-colored aniseed-flavored *Springerle*, which are shaped using carved wooden moulds, and *Zimtsterne* (cinnamon stars), belong to the same family. A simple gingerbread dough is used for the construction of a *Knusperhäuschen* (literally, nibbling house) or *Hexenhäusle* (literally, little witch's house), a small house decorated with piped white icing, cookies, and sweets, and possibly illuminated from within. The name refers to the Brothers' Grimm fairy tale of Hänsel and Gretel, specifically the witch's house, which was covered with gingerbread. Sometimes three small dolls representing these characters complete the arrangement.

Zimtsterne (Cinnamon Stars)

- 3 egg whites
- 2 1/4 c. confectioners' sugar, sifted
- 1 tbs. cinnamon
- 1 tbs. Kirschwasser
- 2 1/2 c. blanched almonds, ground
- about 1 c. fine granulated sugar

Beat the egg whites until they form stiff peaks, adding the confectioners' sugar gradually toward the end. Reserve 2/3 cup of this mixture for the glaze. Add the cinnamon, Kirschwasser, and the almonds, and knead lightly until homogenous. Roll the dough out on a surface sprinkled with granulated sugar, to a thickness of 1/4 inch, then cut into stars with a cookie cutter and glaze. Let the stars rest for about 1 hour in a cool room, then bake in a preheated oven (230°C/455°F/gas mark 8) for about 3 to 5 min.

In contrast to Anglo-Saxon custom, in Germany Christmas proper starts on the afternoon of December 24, *Heiligabend* (Christmas Eve). As on December 31, shops close at 1 or 2 P.M., and the working day turns into a holiday with the streets almost deserted. In most families, lunch on this day is very simple and not regarded as important. Behind closed doors the tree is decorated, and wrapped presents are placed underneath. In many families, the *Stollen* is cut for the first time during the afternoon coffee time. After church—for once in the year uncharacteristically crowded, as the Christmas service is deemed by many an essential part of the ritual—the candles are lit, a bell is rung, and children might have to recite Christmas poems and sing carols before they are allowed to open their presents. Dinner on this day tends to be much less important than the more festive lunch on the following day but is just as strongly shaped by family traditions. Lengthy activities in the kitchen are generally avoided on Christmas Eve. Potato salad with frankfurter sausages and *Heringssalat*, a salad of potatoes, salted herring, mayonnaise, apple, and pickled beet, are two classics of old. Since the end of the 1970s, fondue has been popular in different versions. A very old custom also going back to Silesian influence is *Mohnpielen*, an uncooked bread dish made of white rolls, poppy seeds, and raisins, all soaked in milk; it is eaten later in the evening. In some families, however, this dish belongs to New Year's Eve.

Bunte Teller (mixed plates) with Christmas sweets, chocolates, and cookies are often assembled for each family member, the consumption of which is not regulated; contrary to normal rules, children may thus eat chocolate whenever they want, as long their stock lasts. *Marzipan* (almond paste) is generally regarded as special. For Christmas it mostly takes the shape of *Marzipankartoffeln* (literally, marzipan potatoes), small balls coated in cocoa powder, or other imitations of fruits and vegetables. Marzipan, long a staple in Arab countries, along with other sugar confections, has been an absolute necessity on German noble tables from the sixteenth century on. Similar to gingerbread, marzipan has two distinct schools in Germany, one originating in Lübeck, the other in Königsberg (which today is Russian Kaliningrad). Both cities are situated on the northern coast, where almonds and sugar (which are combined in a ratio of two to one) and other aromatic ingredients like rosewater (kept secret by most producers) were readily available due to imports. *Lübecker Marzipan* is generally covered in dark chocolate, whereas *Königsberger Marzipan* is traditionally browned, and some say that the latter tastes somewhat fruitier and less sweet. *Frankfurter Bethmännchen* and *Brenten* as well as *Mannheimer Dreck* are local marzipan specialties.

Christmas lunch on December 25 is for most Germans quite a grand affair, depending on personal means. Restaurant dining is more of an option than on Christmas Eve, but, for the most part, geese, ducks, or venison legs or rack are roasted in private ovens, to be served with Brussels sprouts or red cabbage. A good bottle of wine is opened, and a dessert such as a wine jelly with whipped cream is sure to follow, as well as afternoon coffee and *Stollen* later in the day and perhaps smoked salmon at night. Because the day after Christmas (in Germany called the second day of Christmas) is also a holiday, people stock up on food beforehand as if starvation might be a possibility, and upset stomachs are a common complaint.

SILVESTER (NEW YEAR'S EVE)

As on Christmas Eve, shops close in the early afternoon on *Silvester* (New Year's Eve), but Silvester is a much merrier affair, spent by most Germans at parties with friends or at a ball. Traditionally *Karpfen blau*, carp boiled with wine and vinegar so that its skin turns blue, is eaten for dinner. The saying goes that the scale of a carp carried in the purse will bring money. Piglets are another symbol of good luck, often formed from marzipan and with a shiny *Glückspfennig* in their mouth (literally lucky penny, *Pfennig* was the smallest coin before the introduction of the euro, now replaced by one cent). But food rarely takes center stage on New Year's Eve, as everything is focused on midnight. To greet the new year, sparkling wine corks are popped, *Berliner* (doughnuts filled with jam, called *Pfannkuchen* in Berlin) are eaten, and, above all, enormous amounts of fireworks and firecrackers are set off by everybody, everywhere, as the partying continues. Subsequently, *Neujahr* (New Year's Day) tends to be quiet.

DREIKÖNIGSTAG (EPIPHANY)

Epiphany is a public holiday in southern Germany and is seen as the end of the Christmas season. Children go from door to door on January 6, dressed as the magi. They sing and bless the houses, marking door frames with "C+M+B" and the year, receiving small gifts of food or cash in return. The letters stand for the magi's names Caspar, Melchior, and Balthasar. The names derive from the Christian blessing *Christus Mansionem Benedicat* (Christ blesses the house).

FASTNACHT, FASCHING, KARNEVAL (CARNIVAL)

Carnival season officially starts at 11:11 A.M. on November 11, but festivities culminate on *Rosenmontag* and *Fastnachtsdienstag* (Rose Monday and Shrove Tuesday). Carnival celebrations are not uniform throughout Germany. They are most popular in Mainz and Cologne. In the southwest of Germany, with Alemannic traditions, carnival starts later and customs are different, whereas in the north, the population is almost unaffected, work continues as usual, and celebrations are often restricted to the consumption of *Berliner* or *Pfannkuchen*. In the areas where it is celebrated most heavily, carnival is a very public holiday with merrymaking in the streets, speeches, and parades. Costumes are essential, as are *Kamellen* (candies) thrown into the crowd from the floats. A wealth of small pastries deep-fried in lard are made on that occasion, and alcohol is consumed rather liberally. Historically, carnival was meant to celebrate the good life one last time before the *Fastenzeit* (literally, fasting time; Lent) began on *Aschermittwoch* (Ash Wednesday). Although fasting is rarely observed nowadays, some people might abstain from smoking, alcohol, or some other personal indulgence during the 40 days of Lent following carnival.

MUTTERTAG (MOTHER'S DAY)

Whereas Valentine's Day is mostly advertised by florists and otherwise has much less importance than in Anglo-Saxon countries, *Muttertag* (Mother's Day) on the second Sunday of May is a bigger deal. Huge amounts of flowers are sold and restaurant tables are filled, as mothers are taken out for the customary lunch. In East Germany, Mother's Day was seen as an antifeminist legacy of Nazi propaganda and replaced by the International Women's Day on March 8.

OSTERN (EASTER)

The final days of Lent are *Gründonnerstag* (Maundy Thursday) and *Karfreitag* (Good Friday), the latter a public holiday. With Easter Sunday and Monday following, this period is like a miniholiday used by many people as an excuse for a vacation. Although the *Grün* of *Gründonnerstag* does not derive from the color green, dishes with green herbs and vegetables are traditionally served on this day, such as *Frankfurter Grüne Sauce* (Frankfurt green sauce), *Sauerampfersuppe* (sorrel soup), and spinach. On Good Friday, fish or vegetarian dishes mostly replace meat, even for non-religious people. For Easter, birch twigs or whole trees are decorated with colored eggs (mostly empty shells that have been painted, or plastic). Eggs were originally forbidden during Lent and were a symbol for Jesus rising from the dead. Easter Sunday breakfast often includes plaited yeast buns and cakes, sometimes holding colored hard-boiled eggs. Sponge cakes are baked in lamb-shaped metal moulds for *Oster-Biskuitlämmer*, which are dusted with confectioners' sugar and provided with a small flag as a Christian symbol. They are popular as presents. According to legend, the *Osterhase* (Easter bunny) hides eggs for children to search for, nowadays mostly chocolate eggs with various fillings, which are wrapped in colorful foil, along with small presents. Lunch on Easter Sunday (Monday is less significant food-wise) is sumptuous, be it at home or in a restaurant. It might include lamb, and nowadays asparagus and the first strawberries are associated with Easter as well. However, this is a sign of globalization, as both are usually still imported at that point in the year.

Frankfurter Grüne Sauce, or Grie Soss in Frankfurt Dialect (Frankfurt Green Sauce)

- 3 hard-boiled eggs
- sea salt
- white pepper
- 2 tbs. vinegar
- 6 tbs. salad oil
- 2 tbs. chives
- 2 tbs. parsley

- 2 tbs. chervil
- 2 tbs. watercress
- 2 tbs. sorrel
- 2 tbs. borage
- 2 tbs. scallions (optional)
- 1 tbs. tarragon (optional, similarly to dill and savory by some not considered traditional ingredients)
- 1 tbs. dill (s.a.)
- 1 tbs. savory (s.a.)
- about 3 tbs. sour cream (optional)

Mash the egg yolks with a fork, season with salt and pepper, and mix thoroughly with oil and vinegar. Add the finely chopped herbs, as well as the chopped egg white and sour cream, if desired. The sauce should have the consistency of mayonnaise. Serve with crudités, boiled potatoes, boiled meat, or poached fish.

HIMMELFAHRT (ASCENSION DAY)

This public holiday on a Thursday (usually in May) is also called Father's Day. It is above all marked by so-called *Herrenpartien* (men-only outings) involving more beer and schnapps than food.

PFINGSTEN (PENTECOST)

As *Pfingstsonntag* (Pentecost Sunday, or Whitsunday) and *Pfingstmontag* (the Monday after Pentecost, or Whitmonday) are both public holidays, this is another long weekend that is frequently used for a short vacation. At the same time, christenings, Catholic first communions, and Protestant confirmations often take place on this day (another popular day for these events is Palm Sunday before Easter). They can be the occasion for quite large family gatherings, with corresponding laborious meals mostly at restaurants, as restaurants are believed to exceed what would be possible at home.

ERNTEDANK (HARVEST FESTIVAL)

In contrast to American Thanksgiving, the day when *Erntedank* is celebrated in Germany varies from region to region (the church calendar, however, has one fixed Sunday reserved for it). The festival mostly takes the form of a special church service. Fruit, vegetables, and wreaths, as well as crowns made from grain, are used to decorate the area around the church altar. In some Alpine areas, cattle are driven down from the higher pastures on this day and included in the festivities. In wine regions the end of the harvest is often celebrated as well. On the Moselle River this is called *Hahne* and involves a sumptuous meal for all vineyard and cellar workers. It used to culminate with a (then-precious) *Hahn* (rooster) being let free in the vineyard, offered as a gift to whomever could catch it.

SCHLACHTFEST (CELEBRATING THE FRESHLY SLAUGHTERED PIG AND ITS GIFTS)

When a pig was slaughtered on somebody's estate, or in the backyard behind the kitchen, usually at the end of November, the day used to be a major event. It was very laborious work to make good use of all bits and parts of the animal but also an occasion to celebrate. Whereas the best parts were made into more durable ham and smoked or air-dried sausages, other parts, for instance, blood and liver sausages, had to be eaten fresh. A large kettle was set up to scald these as well as other parts of the animal. The water from scalding yielded the *Metzelsuppe* (slaughtering broth), which was traditionally shared with neighbors and friends on the spot. Today, as slaughtering with very rare exceptions has to take place in huge central slaughterhouses, *Schlachtfest* has mostly become a themed event in restaurants with a special menu for a day or for a limited time.

VOLKSFESTE (FAIRS)

A multitude of *Volksfeste* (fairs) all over Germany offer a mix of fun rides, amusements, and food and drink. The custom goes back to medieval church festivals that attracted traveling performers and traders who offered their wares around the church. In rural areas this often represented a rare chance for shopping and distraction. The largest and most famous fairs in Germany are the *Cannstatter Wasen* near Stuttgart, the *Wurstmarkt* in Bad Dürkheim (in the Palatinate), the *Freimarkt* in Bremen (literally, free market, referring to the historical fact that outsiders, that is, nonresidents of the city, were allowed to offer their wares), the *Frühlingsdom* in Hamburg, and of course the *Oktoberfest* or *Wiesn* in Munich. The latter takes place during 16 to 18 days starting at the end of September. It dates back to when the Bavarian crown prince married Princess Therese in 1810. The event was celebrated with a horse race on the *Theresienwiese*. This ground was then situated on the outskirts of Munich, but as the city has grown, it has become quite central. Over the years it has developed into an event of huge economic and logistic dimensions that draws more than 6 million visitors. A lot of them sport the Bavarian *Tracht* (supposedly traditional attire that was actually an invention of the nineteenth century), including *Dirndl* (dresses) for women and *Lederhosen* (leather knee breeches) for men. The 103-acre *Wiesn* is open from 9 or 10 A.M. until 11 P.M. It attracts many foreign visitors, especially from northern Italy and the United States and is as much a family destination as an occasion for companies to treat their customers to a night out. Everything from breakfast to coffee and cake, to all kinds of Bavarian *Schmankerl* (small savoury dishes usually served as starter or in between meals), is on offer. In recent years, *Brathendl* (grilled chicken) alone reached consumption rates of about half a million. Grilled *Haxn* (pork shanks) and grilled sausages are also popular. As in Munich's beer gardens, people can bring along their own food as well. The main action takes place in more than 30 tents, some of them gigantic halls seating up to almost 10,000 people. They are run by the larger breweries or independent restaurateurs. All have live music, mostly by traditional brass bands. Although there is also a wine tent, the *Oktoberfest* is all about beer.

Oktoberfest participants, Munich, 2006. AP Photo/Christof Stache.

Oktoberfest beer is served in a *Maß* (beer mug containing a liter, or 2.11 pints), of which about 60 million are consumed each year. The *Wiesnbier* is brewed especially for the occasion and is somewhat stronger in alcohol than regular beer. Mugs traditionally used to be of glazed earthenware, but because of frequent complaints about not being filled up to the correct level are now all (transparent) glass. Each year the price for a *Maß* is almost a political issue; in 2007 it was between 7.30 and 7.90 euro.

KOHL- UND PINKELFAHRTEN (KALE PARTIES)

Kale parties are but one example of numerous local customs found all over Germany that involve special food, dishes, or meals. Robust and undemanding, curly kale is indigenous to the north of Germany. Commonly thought to taste sweeter after the first frost, it is continually harvested until spring. In East Friesland, Maundy Thursday traditionally is the last time kale is harvested. Kale has always been popular with all social classes, and as a winter vegetable it symbolizes regional cultural identity and provides a festive dish for many occasions. Many local customs are linked to kale; for instance, some leaves are left outdoors with bread crusts to feed St. Nicholas's and Father Christmas's horses. Kale parties take place all over northwestern Germany around Oldenburg and Bremen. Departing from some point outside the town or city (reached by public transport), they are always undertaken in a group, consisting of colleagues from work or a club (choral societies, gymnastic clubs, bowling clubs, card-playing clubs, etc.), and involve all social classes, today including women and even children. The atmosphere is relaxed, casual, and very jolly, making this almost the northern equivalent of carnival.

First on the kale party agenda is the hike to the chosen restaurant. Equipment is deemed essential for this ritual and is previously agreed upon among the group. Everybody carries a drinking vessel. In its most minimalistic form, this is a colored plastic eggcup or a small schnapps glass with a handle, attached to a colored ribbon and hung around the neck. The cup identifies the bearer as a participant of a kale party. Beverages, above all *Korn* (clear grain schnapps), but also all kinds of other spirits as well as beer and mineral water, coffee, or tea, are carried in an old pram or handcart, decorated with balloons, kale stalks, garlands, and so on, and equipped with bells and horns. Sometimes a portable radio or musical instrument provides entertainment. Costumes—consisting of hats, scarves, or bibs and sometimes open umbrellas decorated with balloons, garlands, small sausages, schnapps bottles, and the like—to a certain degree serve to distinguish the group.

The first round of drinks is usually poured at the meeting point, followed by more drinks at numerous stops along the way. Large, colored dice made of foam or wood are brought along to determine the drinking order. A *Meß-* or *Sauflatte* consists of several eggcups attached to a wooden slat, all filled at once and ideally emptied by a group of people of the same height. This drinking ritual is sometimes imposed on an innocent passerby. Sandwiches, cheese, and salted pretzels provide sustenance.

At the destination, chosen according to location and the reputation of its food and service, a meal of kale is served, garnished with *Pinkel* (a pork sausage containing oats), bacon, *Kasseler Rippenspeer* (cured pork spare rib), *Kochwurst* (scalded, finely ground pork sausage), as well as boiled or fried potatoes, all in unlimited quantities. There might be a clear soup to start with and a simple dessert afterward. Speeches, songs, and the appointment of a kale king or queen, decorated with a *Freßorden* (a medal for gluttony), provide entertainment. The day may finish with dancing or bowling.

NOTE

1. The German novelist Theodor Fontane (1819–98) gives a detailed description of this procedure in *Meine Kinderjahre* (My childhood years), the chronicle of his youth, first published in 1894 (Berlin and Weimar: Aufbau, 1984).

7

Diet and Health

For most Germans, diet and health are closely linked. In a representative study of Germans, when asked about the most important factor for general well-being, more than 98% of respondents mentioned health, followed by inner harmony (more than 92%). The right composition of food ranked in the middle, judged "very important" by 75% of the interviewees. Asked about the most important aspects when preparing food at home or eating out in a workplace cafeteria, taste ranked highest, followed by healthiness and digestibility.[1]

This apparently strong awareness of the connection between diet and health could be traced back to the holistic approaches to medicine that were practiced in medieval times (and thus to its roots in India where it is still alive in the ayurvedic school). Preventing illness and poor health through the right food at the right time, prepared in the right way, was part of the cook's task. This "medicine" from the kitchen was judged better than the one from the pharmacy. As late as 1865, articles appeared in German magazines about the right preventive cooking in the case of a cholera epidemic.[2]

An eminent contemporary sociologist also sees the link between diet and health as a question of morality. With collective morality loosening, moral obligations have become more individualized and today include the obligation to eat "right," that is, healthily.[3]

LAWS AND REGULATIONS

It should not be surprising then, that food production, preparation, and trade are strongly regulated in contemporary Germany. The *Lebensmittelrecht* (food law) goes back to 1879. Through industrialization, food production gradually became more centralized and standardized, thus providing the base for general laws and controls. Today it is a federal law falling under the jurisdiction of both the Ministry for Consumer Protection and the Ministry for Health. Its main purpose is to guarantee food safety as well as a certain level of quality. At the same time, trade regulations deal with labeling, additives, health claims, and the like to prevent fraud. Foods of animal origin have to be traceable back to their place of origin.

In the course of the standardization of the European Single Market and the European Law for Consumer Protection, Germany, like the other members of the European Union, had to cede certain powers to the central European Food Safety Authority. However, the *Länder* (states) are responsible for the *Lebensmittelkontrolle* (inspection of food) on site. They have to report any observed risk or anomaly. Risk assessment and crisis management lie with the Federal Office for Consumer Protection and Food Safety, which then provides the information to Brussels, in order to be able to react all over Europe.

Whereas in the United Kingdom, for instance, "Brussels" is generally perceived as the annoying source of laws and regulations that oppose national traditions, German consumers' perception of this centralization is somewhat less negative. Most of them are aware of the vast movements of produce needed to ensure the uninterrupted supply and affordability they are used to in the supermarket and the control organs necessitated by that. The discussion about European law endangering national and regional cultural identity is limited to very select circles, perhaps because Germans have only very recently started to feel at ease again with their own cultural roots on a national level. A European directive ruling that henceforth only jam made from citrus fruit was to be called marmalade barely caused a shrug in 1982, although the German word *Marmelade* has never been associated with English-style marmalade. It was and still is informally used for all types of jam, which since 1982 have to be labeled with the fancy-sounding word *Konfitüre*.

However, some matters are more hotly disputed than others: when the European Court ruled against the German regulation that allowed only beer brewed according to the German *Reinheitsgebot* (literally, purity law, see chapter 2) into the German market, this caused an uproar. Beer containing anything other than malted barley or wheat, hops, yeast, and water was (and by some still is) seen as adulterated. But European law overruled national law, and free trade had to be guaranteed in 1987. However, German beer still has to be produced according to the *Reinheitsgebot*, sometimes dubbed the world's oldest consumer protection law, and several regional German beers have been granted the status of a Protected Geographical Indication by the European Union.

Clearly German consumers expect state authorities to guarantee food safety as well as a healthy environment that is free of harmful emissions, radiation, and the like. At the same time, they are protective about their own personal freedoms. Unlike in the United States, it has so far proved impossible to introduce a general speed limit in Germany. Likewise, the temperance league never succeeded in imposing a general prohibition of alcohol, although the movement was quite strong at the end of the nineteenth and beginning of the twentieth centuries in the form of the Independent Order of Good Templars, the Blue Cross, and political parties. Alcohol consumption in Germany, at 22.2 pints pure alcohol per person per year (in 2001), is among the highest in Europe, and costs for alcohol-related illnesses are estimated at about 20 billion euros per year.[4] The only restrictions on alcohol consumption are in connection with the *Jugendschutzgesetz* (law for the protection of children and young people) and the *Straßenverkehrsordnung* (road traffic act), which sets the maximum blood alcohol level for drivers, at present 0.5 parts per thousand.

It is generally accepted that smoking is related to severe health risks, but this as well is regarded as a personal freedom by 28% of German women and 37% of German men. The ban on smoking in public, unlike in France, Italy, Spain, Norway, the United Kingdom, or Ireland, was to be introduced in 2005 as a voluntary step on the part of hotels, restaurants, and pubs. Within three years 90% of these establishments should have transformed at least half of their space into nonsmoking areas. As it became clear that this strategy would not succeed, the German parliament passed a law for protection against the dangers of secondhand smoke, which became effective on September 1, 2007. Smoking is now generally banned in all public spaces, including on public transportation and in taxis. However, the law concerning restaurants and the catering trade is subject to the jurisdiction of the individual *Länder* (states). Many restaurant and pub owners are lobbying against a total ban, for fear of losing customers, so that a patchwork of different regulations is to be expected, similar to the differing alcohol laws in the United States.

FOOD SCARES AND SCANDALS

The perception and assessment of food safety and quality are similarly subject to personal interpretations. For instance, in a survey published in 2004 concerning the influence of television on food habits in Germany, 28.8% of the interviewees thought that food quality had deteriorated during the last decade, whereas almost 42% were of the opposite opinion.[5] In another survey in 2003, 78%, especially women and households with children under the age of 14 years, considered it important to check very carefully what kind of food they were buying. In general, the information about food scandals seems widely known. However, in spite of being informed through television, the daily newspaper, or the radio, it appears that about half of the population continues to eat whatever they like, regardless of any warnings.[6]

In fact, food often makes it into the German mass media in the form of scares and scandals, especially in tabloid newspapers, TV news shows, and weekly magazines with a large circulation. The general attitude seems to be one of resignation: that in the end it cannot possibly matter much what one buys and eat, because so many food items at one point or another are said to be contaminated, poisonous, or carcinogenic. It appears that buying and eating patterns change for only a brief period following a scandal, or until the next problem flares up.

Looking back over the last decades, a long list of food scares and scandals becomes apparent. Although no one issue caused as many casualties as the deadly Spanish cooking oil scandal in 1981 or the Italian red wine poisoned with methyl alcohol in 1986, they spread an atmosphere of fear and disgust in consumers. Pesticides and/or heavy metals were discovered in milk, butter, vegetables, and animal feed; salmonella is found in poultry from intensive livestock farming; and growth hormones have been discovered in meat although they have been banned in Germany since 1988. Unclean liquid egg was used in noodle production; pesticides and heavy metals are found in sea fish, salmonella in salami, and listeria in soft French cheese and German pâté. Fraudulent labeling of fruit and vegetables regarding origin and age was discovered, as were pesticides in baby food and tea leaves, and antibiotics in honey. Fresh fish was found to be heavily contaminated with bacteria including E. coli; illegal beef imports came from the United Kingdom, which was stricken with bovine spongiform encephalopathy (BSE); dioxin was found in Belgian eggs, butter, and meat; conventionally grown grain was sold as organic. Fungicides and pesticides were found in Spanish bell peppers; antibiotics in farmed shrimp from Asia; listeria in vacuum-packed smoked salmon; salmonella in chocolate; acrylamide in potato chips, French fries, and crispbread among other foods; antibiotics in chicken from Thailand. Dutch deep-frozen chicken had been injected with beef protein; antibiotics were found in Italian turkey products; prepackaged chicken was often unhygienic; and Italian bottled water contained poison. Dioxin was discovered in European farmed salmon and carcinogenic substances in various kinds of imported spices; ground meat with expired sell-by dates was relabeled in supermarkets. There were pesticide residues in strawberries imported from Spain and Morocco, and genetically engineered soy was detected in baby food. Additional scares came in the form of outbreaks of Severe Acute Respiratory Syndrome (SARS or avian flu), causing a ban on outdoor rearing of poultry, and swine fever (always latent among wild boar, it is not infectious for humans but an existential threat to pig farmers, as outbreaks lead to the destruction of whole herds).

The first report about BSE in the United Kingdom reached Germany in November 1987. In 1990, a German health inspector came across the first indications of the disease in Germany but lost her job when she reported her findings to the public. In 1997 preemptive cullings took place, with government officials insisting that Germany was BSE-free and at no risk. In November 2000, however, Germany had to admit its first official BSE case. A total ban of meat and bone meal for animal feed followed, as well as nationwide tests of all animals slaughtered at under 24 months of age. In January 2001, the responsible ministers had to leave and Renate Künast from the Green Party became the new Minister for Consumer Protection, Nutrition, and Agriculture. As at the European Union level, new structures were formed, separating risk assessment from crisis management. Although discrepancies were later found in the testing of cattle, Künast managed to make the crisis a turning point in German food politics, as she from that point on heavily promoted transparency and organic agriculture. In 2007, the official statistics declared 4 BSE cases, a significant drop from the 125 cases reported in 2001. So far it seems there have not been any BSE-related human casualties in Germany.

Perhaps, physiologically as well as psychologically, the most disgusting recent food scandal in Germany concerns *Gammelfleisch* (literally, rotten meat). This is meat not fit for human consumption either because it has been kept too long or because it was originally from the so-called *K3*, the third meat category at slaughtering, which is not considered a health hazard but should only be used for pet food and the like. The first *Gammelfleisch* consisted of beef and turkey that was too old and was discovered at a German wholesaler at the end of 2005. Since then the problem has spread nationwide. It quickly became clear to what extent the meat trade had become international, and how the price wars in discount stores lead to criminal activity. The scandal has since extended to poultry, venison, and the production of *Döner Kebab*. In 2007, meat was even being resold and used for *Döner* after having been confiscated. As a preventive method, K3 material will eventually be marked with special coloring at the time of slaughter. In the meantime, *Döner Kebab* consumption in Berlin has gone down, according to surveys.

Genetically engineered food is another much discussed and very controversial topic in Germany, where the first experimental plantings have only recently been allowed. However, additives from genetically engineered soybeans, mostly imported from the United States, are being used in all kinds of food, and they do not always have to be declared on the label.

The unknown, spectacular, and outrageous clearly make for better headlines and are remembered longer than cases of food poisoning through salmonella, campylobacter, E. coli, or listeria (which all have to be reported to the relevant authorities). However, the contamination potential in large-scale production units, along with ever more miles for foods to travel and ever longer shelf lives, certainly presents risks at a scale hitherto unknown.

Looked at rationally and put into a larger perspective, most of these scares and scandals seem somewhat overblown when set against the actual casualties. Undoubtedly, objective food safety in Germany has never been as high as today.

A HEALTHY DIET

Life expectancy in Germany is increasing; currently, it is at more than 75 years for men (of which more than 68 years are spent in good health) and more than 81 for women (of which 72 in good health).[7] But it is still thought that nutritional knowledge is insufficient. Overall alcohol consumption is decreasing, and there is a trend toward eating poultry and fish instead of red meat, but fat consumption remains too high and not enough vegetables and fruit are eaten. Varying levels of education, financial means, and gender make for different patterns. The higher social classes and women have significantly better nutritional knowledge than the lower classes and men, respectively. On television, watched on average 3.5 hours daily and thought to influence nutritional behavior strongly, the foods that tend to be presented are sweets, snacks rich in fat, and alcoholic beverages.[8]

What is considered a healthy diet in Germany? The 10 dietary guidelines of the German Nutrition Society (DGE) mention the following:

- Choose among a variety of foods, preferably high-nutrient and low-energy foods.
- Eat plenty of cereal products and potatoes, combined with low-fat food items.
- Fruit and vegetables—eat five servings a day, preferably fresh, in the form of juice, or quickly cooked, in total 1.43 lb. (considerably more than the 0.88 lb. recommended by the World Health Organization).
- Consume milk and dairy products daily, fish once or twice a week, and meat, sausages, and eggs only in moderation, maximum 0.66 to 1.32 lb. per week; generally low-fat products are to be preferred.
- Moderate fat intake, preferably of vegetable origin, in total 0.13 to 0.15 lb. per day, is advised.
- Sugar and salt should be consumed in moderation, preferably avoiding drinks sweetened with glucose syrup, and using only iodized salt.
- Plenty of liquid should be consumed, about 3.17 pints of water per day, but alcohol only occasionally and only in small amounts.
- Make sure your dishes are prepared carefully and taste good; cook at low temperatures, using water and fat sparingly.
- Take your time and enjoy eating.
- Watch your weight and stay active; 30 to 60 minutes of physical activities and sports per day is advised.

Cardiovascular diseases and malignant tumors are the most frequent
causes of death in Germany. In spite of research, direct connections with
single food items and patterns are thought difficult to establish. The most
important current official recommendation concerning cancer prevention
is not to smoke, not to be overweight, and to eat more fruits and vegetables.
An official campaign called *Fünf am Tag* (five a day), that is, five portions
of fruit and vegetables, was started in 1999 to change nutritional behavior.

OVERWEIGHT AND OBESE GERMANS

According to a survey conducted in 2003, 66.9% of all German men
are overweight, with a body mass index (BMI) of 25 or above, including
17.1% who are obese, with a BMI of 30 or above. For women the percentages are 55.7 and 19.0, respectively. For all groups, weight peaks between
60 and 69 years, except for obese men, where the peak is a decade earlier.
Especially for women, overweight and obesity are clearly linked to lower
education levels.

Of German children between the ages of 3 and 17 years, 15% are overweight and 6.3% are obese. These numbers seem to be rising, especially for obesity, and lower social status and overweight mothers increase the risk. Children and young people eat too few vegetables and fruit and far too much saturated fat and sugar.[9]

These numbers add up to about 37 million overweight adults and 2 million overweight children who risk health-related problems, above all type 2 diabetes. Already in the 1970s, the West German government had started an official *Trimm-dich* (keep fit) campaign. *Trimm-dich-Pfade* (fitness trails) were set up in parks and woodlands to encourage physical activity. The situation seems to have been the same in East Germany, where 20% of the men and 40% of the women were said to be overweight, and efforts—to no great avail—were made with diet food products and special menus for workplace cafeterias.[10] In 2007, the Ministry of Health started another campaign, called *Gesunde Ernährung und Bewegung* (healthy nutrition and physical activity).

Special "light" food products with reduced fat content and sugar replaced by artificial sweeteners have been widely available since the 1980s, but today are seen as controversial among nutrition experts. The food industry's newest trend is called "wellfood." Natural foods like fruit and vegetables are the most obvious to fall under this heading, but it extends from functional foods enriched with vitamins, lactic acid bacteria, and the like to diet foods for allergy sufferers, as well as organic food.

EATING DISORDERS, ALLERGIES, AND INTOLERANCES

As in most Western countries, slimness is seen as an ideal and is projected as such in the media. In its most excessive forms, for instance in fashion advertising, it is also publicly criticized, however. The link to eating disorders, which are seen as psychological in origin, is widely accepted. It is difficult to give exact figures for anorexia, bulimia, and binge eating, as eating disorders are not easy to categorize with official World Health Organization coding for medical diagnoses used in Germany. An estimated 100,000 Germans seem to suffer from anorexia, of whom 90% would be women between the age of 15 and 35, and about 600,000 from bulimia. It is thought that about 2% of the population, about 1.64 million people, are subject to attacks of binge eating. In a health study of children and young people conducted between 2003 and 2006, 28.9% of the girls between 11 and 17 years old and 15.2% of the boys of the same age group were diagnosed with some eating disorder.[11] 70% of girls between 14 and

15 years are thought to have a diet history.[12] Indeed, diets are an ever-present subject in newspapers, magazines, and books, ranging from the old *FdH* (*Friß die Hälfte*, eat half the amount) to the *Kohlsuppendiät*, in which only cabbage soup is allowed, the French *Montignac* diet and *Trennkost* (which both separate the intake of carbohydrates from that of protein and fat), to the newest diet fad from the United States. Some German food experts criticize the whole discussion pertaining to weight for blaming the individual. They think the blame should lie with designed industrial foods and the financial interests of that industry.[13]

Anorexia is difficult to cure and leads to severe health risks including kidney failure, brittle bones, cardiac arrhythmia, and pneumonia. The chances of recovery are seen as higher with bulimia, where outing often is the first step in the healing process. Although these eating disorders are mostly seen as contemporary phenomena, some experts trace their origin back to the war food policy of World War I. Back then the constraints of the sea blockade popularized the new scientific approach to food, reducing it to numbers of calories and nutrients. Today the labeling of prepackaged food with exact indications of calories, nutrients, and the like is mandatory but also the subject of constant discussion, as the government tries to issue guidelines that would make this information more easily understandable for consumers.

Another discussion concerns ingredients seen as potential allergens or for those who are subject to lactose, gluten, and other food intolerances. Forty percent of the German population suffers from allergies (although this number includes all kinds of allergies, not just food allergies). Their occurrence seems clearly linked to social rank: 13.6% of children from lower social classes, 17.8% from the middle class, and 18.9% from the upper strata of German society have allergies. Since November 2005 the 12 most important allergens have to be indicated on food labels, although disclaimers like "can contain traces of nuts" are seen as too general and therefore unhelpful to allergy sufferers.

ALTERNATIVES

Not only calorie-counting goes back over a century in Germany; the idealization of preindustrial "natural" food also first appeared at that time in the *Lebensreform* (life reform) movement. As back then, in recent decades, this has led to a rise in vegetarianism—these days about 8% of all Germans are vegetarians—as well as growing environmental awareness, apparent in a multitude of ecological groups, notable among them the Green Party. Both streams today combine in the general demand of the German Vegetarians' Association that people eat less meat for environmental reasons, as meat production requires much more energy. A rejection of what some perceive as too much technology—although historians argue that contemporary affluence is based on technological rationality and efficiency—culminates in the public discussion about genetically engineered food.[14] Insecurity and angst resulting from the inability to understand the often-complex interrelations between diet and health combine with a romanticization of supposedly "pure" natural food versus "artificial" human-made food.[15]

But many today apply *gesunder Menschenverstand* (literally, healthy common sense) to seek a balance between human-scale artisanal and industrial perfection in food. Doubts regarding scientists' claims to omniscience are supported by findings, for instance, about phytochemicals. Whereas one chapter in the nutrition report of the German Nutrition society—based on the latest scientific research and the official line—protests that against all doubts conventionally produced food today does of course have as many nutrients as it used to 50 years ago, a subsequent chapter entitled "Influence of Phytochemicals on Health" makes clear how little is known about their concentrations in food but clearly indicates their importance.

Healthy alternatives take different forms for different people. Abstention from smoking, alcohol, and/or sweets during Lent (the weeks leading up to Easter) is not necessarily linked to religious practice. Homeopathic treatment is gradually being recognized by health insurers. Pharmacies expand to become health centers. Ayurvedic treatment is in, and yoga schools are booming. But most important, going back to origins of over a century ago, is the growing market for organic and biodynamic food. It goes beyond the *Reformhäuser* (health food stores) that originated during the *Lebensreform* movement and the *Ökoläden* (organic stores) of today; even regular discount stores offer organic food. However, the market is led by small chains of organic supermarkets. Customers are mainly families with young children from the middle to upper classes, but generally (in spite of discussions about what is acceptable as such) the organic alternative, though not affordable for all, is seen as the better option for reasons beyond personal health.

NOTES

1. Bundesministerium für Forschung und Technologie, ed., *Die Nationale Verzehrsstudie: Ergebnisse der Basisauswertung* (Bonn: Bundesministerium für Forschung und Technologie, 1991), 52–53 and 58–59.

2. Hans Wiswe, *Kulturgeschichte der Kochkunst: Kochbücher und Rezepte aus zwei Jahrtausenden mit einem lexikalischen Anhang zur Fachsprache von Eva Hepp* (Munich: Moos, 1970), 66.

3. Eva Barlösius, "Von der kollektiven zur individualisierten Eßmoral?" in Hans Jürgen Teuteberg, ed., *Die Revolution am Eßtisch: Neue Studien zur Nahrungskultur im 19./20. Jahrhundert* (Stuttgart: Franz Steiner, 2004), 39–50.

4. Robert-Koch-Institut, http://www.rki.de/cln_049/nn_196910/sid_0CB 00921060DEC51C73FC264B9F44F8E/nsc_true/DE/Content/GBE/Auswertung sergebnisse/VersorgungsrelevanteAspekte/AlkoholKosten/alkohol__inhalt.html ?__nnn=true.

5. Deutsche Gesellschaft für Ernährung e.V., ed., *Ernährungsbericht 2004* (Bonn: Deutsche Gesellschaft für Ernährung e.V., 2004), 386. The former group spends more hours in front of the television than the latter.

6. Survey conducted by TNS Emnid, Bielefeld and published by mediaedge: in October 2003, http://www.presseportal.de/pm/50784/494098/mediaedge_cia.

7. Deutsche Gesellschaft für Ernährung, *Ernährungsreport 2004,* 100, WHO data from 2001.

8. Deutsche Gesellschaft für Ernährung, *Ernährungsreport 2004,* 360.

9. Surveys conducted by Robert-Koch-Institut, http://www.rki.de/cln_049/ nn_205760/DE/Content/GBE/Erhebungen/Gesundheitsurveys/Eskimo/es kimo__node.html?__nnn=true.

10. Jutta Voigt, *Der Geschmack des Ostens: Vom Essen, Trinken und Leben in der DDR* (Berlin: Kiepenheuer, 2005), 162.

11. Survey conducted by Robert-Koch-Institut, http://www.rki.de/cln_049/ nn_222956/SharedDocs/Publikationen/DE/2007/H/Hoelling__H__03,templateI d=render,layoutVariant=StandardMitAbstract.html.

12. Utz Thimm and Karl-Heinz Wellmann, eds., *In aller Munde: Ernährung heute* (Frankfurt am Main: Suhrkamp, 2004), 170.

13. Udo Pollmer, interview given to the *Frankfurter Allgemeine Sonntagszeitung,* May 6, 2007.

14. For a more detailed historical discussion, see Jörn Sieglerschmidt, "Die Mechanisierung der organischen Substanz," in *Essen und kulturelle Identität: Europäische Perspektiven,* ed. Hans Jürgen Teuteberg, Gerhard Neumann, and Alois Wierlacher (Berlin: Akademie Verlag, 1997), 336–55.

15. Hans Jürgen Teuteberg and Günter Wiegelmann, eds., *Unsere tägliche Kost: Studien zur Geschichte des Alltags* (Münster: Coppenrath, 1986), 9.

Glossary

Abendbrot   Warm or cold evening meal; also called *Abendessen*.

Abendessen   Warm or cold evening meal; also called *Abendbrot*.

ablöschen   Adding water or wine to turn roasting into braising.

Auflauf   Sweet or savory pie, casserole or soufflé.

Ausflugsgaststätte   A restaurant that is a gastronomic day-trip destination because of its location (*Ausflug* = day trip).

ausgehen   To go out, used for eating out as well as going to the theater or dancing.

Buletten (Berlin, sometimes also spelled Bouletten)   Small fried meat patties, usually a mix of pork and beef with egg and bread added, eaten cold and warm; also called *Frikadellen* (throughout Germany) or *Fleischpflanzerl* (in Bavaria).

Backshop   Baking chain outlet.

Bärlauch   Wild garlic leaves (*allium ursinum*).

Baumkuchen   Literally, tree cake; a traditional specialty made from a dough rich with ground almonds and baked in many thin layers on a spit.

Beiz   Word for pub in the south (*Kneipe* is used in the north).

Berliner   Doughnut-like, deep-fried pastry in the shape of a flattened ball, filled with jam (*Pfannkuchen* is the term used in Berlin).

Bioladen   Organic store; also called *Ökoladen*.

Biomarkt   All-organic open-air (farmer's) market; also called *Ökomarkt*.

Blechkuchen   Cake baked on a baking sheet, cut into rectangular pieces for serving.

Bratapfel   Baked apple, usually cored and filled with raisins, marzipan, and so on, and served with vanilla custard, mainly in winter.

Brathendl   Grilled chicken.

Brezel   Pretzel; the Bavarian *Bierbrezel* is larger and softer whereas the *Laugenbrezel* is crunchy around the knot and darker brown because of more liberal use of the *Lauge* (lye).

Brötchen   Plain white bread roll; also called *Semmel* (in the south) or *Schrippe* (in Berlin).

Brotzeit   Savory midmorning or afternoon snack, cold or warm; also called *Vesper* or *Jause*.

Buabespitzle   Small gnocchi-like dumplings, made from boiled potato and a little egg, shaped into small, pointed, finger-sized rolls, which are first boiled, then often fried; also called *Schupfnudeln*.

Buchweizen   Buckwheat.

Bückling   Whole smoked herring.

Bückware   Literally, bending ware; East German term for merchandise that never made it onto the shelves and was instead kept under the counter for favored customers.

bunter Teller   A plate of chocolate and cookies put out for every family member during Christmas time.

bürgerliche/gutbürgerliche Küche   Literally, (good) bourgeois cooking; German middle-class, home-style cooking.

Butterbrot   Sandwich from a bread loaf; also called *Stulle* (in Berlin).

Capitulare de Villis   King Charlemagne's inventory of his estates around 800 A.D., which included precise rules on all aspects of agriculture for the running of the royal estates and hunting.

CARE paket   Packages sent to West Germany from 1946 on by the Cooperative for American Remittances to Europe (CARE, mainly a privately funded aid organization seeking to relieve suffering and hunger in Europe), containing preserved meat and fat, canned and dried fruit, honey, chocolate, sugar, powdered egg and milk, as well as coffee.

Chinapfanne   Pseudo-Chinese fast-food dish; a mix of vegetables, bean sprouts, glass noodles, and sometimes chicken.

Christstollen or Stollen   Traditional Christmas cake, usually made with yeast and containing dried fruit.

Currywurst   Literally, curried sausage; a fast-food dish originally from Berlin.

Dampfnudeln   Steamed yeast dumplings.

Delikatladen   Special East German shops that sold rare delicacies in exchange for Western currency.

didschen   Saxon dialect word for dunking cake in coffee or dumplings or potatoes in sauce.

Ebbelwoi   Hessian dialect word for *Apfelwein* (hard apple cider).

Eierkuchen   Crêpe-like pancakes; called *Flädle* in the south.

Einbauküche   Fitted kitchen.

Eintopf-Sonntag   Literally, stew-Sunday; during the Nazi period, a collective effort to save meat and lift general morale.

Erbswurst   Dried pea flour that has been formed in shape of a sausage; used for making soup (by adding hot water), one of the first convenience foods.

Eßzimmer   Dining room; term is often also used for living room.

falscher Hase   Literally, mock hare; meat loaf.

Fanta   Orange-flavored soft drink introduced in Nazi Germany by the Coca-Cola company; the name was derived from *fantasia* to avoid anti-American feeling.

Fdh   Abbreviation for *Friß die Hälfte* (eat half the amount), a diet scheme.

Feinschmecker   Gourmet.

Flädle   Term for crêpe-like pancakes in the south; also called *Eierkuchen*.

Fleischkäse   A somewhat confusing term, literally, meat cheese; baked loaf made from very finely ground meat; also called *Leberkäse* (liver cheese).

Fleischpflanzerl (Bavaria)   Small fried meat patties, usually a mix of pork and beef with egg and bread added, eaten cold and warm; also called *Frikadellen* (throughout Germany) or *B(o)uletten* (in Berlin).

Frankfurter   Small, lightly smoked, scalded sausages, made from pork or veal, recently also from poultry; also called *Würstchen* or *Wiener*. In Germany they are almost exclusively offered under these two terms, occasionally also as *Halberstädter* (Thuringia) or *Schübling* (Swabia); in Frankfurt am Main also known as *Rindswürstchen*, made from beef.

Frankfurter Küche   First fitted kitchen design, developed in the 1920s for Frankfurt am Main council flats.

Freizeit   Free time (vs. working time).

Fresswelle   Gluttony wave following World War II.

Frikadellen   Small fried meat patties, usually a mix of pork and beef with egg and bread added, eaten cold and warm; also called *B(o)uletten* (in Berlin) or *Fleischpflanzerl* (in Bavaria).

Fritten   Informal word for French fries; also called *Pommes*.

Früchtebrot   Fruit bread, sometimes made from rye and sourdough, mainly using dried pears; also called *Hutzelbrot* or *Kletzenbrot*.

Frühschoppen   Gathering for a midmorning drink, usually on Sunday between church and lunch; a predominantly male custom.

Gammelfleisch   Literally, rotten meat; stems from a food scandal in 2005–6.

Gasthaus   Restaurant or inn; also called *Gaststätte*, *Gaststube*, or *Gasthof*.

GDR   German Democratic Republic (in German, the *DDR*, or *Deutsche Demokratische Republik*); official name of former East Germany.

geschmaltzt or geschmälzt   Literally, larded; a flour-based dish (sometimes vegetables) enriched with fat, originally to make up for little or no meat.

Glühwein   Mulled wine.

Goldbroiler   East German for grilled chicken, term coined by former eponymous East German chain serving them.

grillen   Literally, broiling; barbecue.

Gründerjahre   Literally, founder years; the economic boom following the founding of the German state in 1871.

Grütze   Gruel; an ancient dish, usually made from coarsely ground grain.

Gug(e)lhupf   fluted round cake pan with a hole in the center, somewhat similar to Bundt cake pan; also the name of the cake baked in it. Also called *Napfkuchen*.

Gummibärchen   Gummy bears.

guten Appetit   Bon appétit/enjoy your meal; traditionally the signal to start eating when in a group around a table.

Hackepeter (Berlin)   Coarsely ground pork with a certain fat content, eaten raw on buttered bread; also called *Mett*.

Handkäse   Traditional small cheese made from low-fat, curdled sour milk; also called *Harzer*.

Harzer   Traditional small cheese made from curdled sour milk; also called *Handkäse*.

Haxe   Shank; also called *Haxn* in Bavaria, and, for beef, the word *Hesse* is used as well.

Hefezopf   Challah-like soft white plaited yeast bread, sometimes containing raisins; also called *Stuten*.

Heidschnucke   Moorland sheep with black heads and feet and long shaggy gray coats, roaming the heath around Lüneburg; yield highly valued aromatic, venison-like meat.

Herd   Stove.

HO-Laden   former East German state-run grocery store chain; also called *Konsum* (although the two were structured slightly differently).

Hutzelbrot   Fruit bread, sometimes made from rye and sourdough, mainly using dried pears; also called *Kletzenbrot* or *Früchtebrot*.

Jause   Savory midmorning or afternoon snack, cold or warm; also called *Brotzeit* or *Vesper*.

Kaffee und Kuchen   Afternoon coffee and cake.

Kaffeekränzchen   Coffee klatsch.

Kaffeepause   Coffee break.

Kaffeesahne   Condensed, sterilized milk added to traditional filter coffee.

Kamellen   Candies thrown from carnival floats; also used in *olle* (old) *Kamellen*, which means "old hat."

Kantine   Canteen, university cafeteria; also called *Mensa*.

Kartoffelpuffer   Latke-style potato pancakes made from grated raw potatoes with egg and sometimes a little flour added; also called *Reiberdatschi* or *Reibekuchen*.

Kass(e)ler   Cured pork, originating not in the town of Kassel but supposedly invented by a Berlin butcher named Kassel.

Kletzenbrot   Fruit bread, sometimes made from rye and sourdough, mainly using dried pears; also called *Hutzelbrot* or *Früchtebrot*.

Kloß (pl. Klöße)   Word for dumplings in the north; called *Knödel* in the south.

Kneipe   Word for pub in the north; called *Beiz* in the south.

Kneippkaffee   Coffee surrogate from malted barley developed by Sebastian Kneipp, a pastor.

Knödel   Word for dumplings in the south; called *Klöße* in the north.

Kohl   Cabbage (in the north; also called *Kraut* in the south); in the compound *Apfelkraut* or *Rübenkraut*, a treacle-like syrup made from apples or sugar beets.

Kohl- or Steckrüben   Rutabagas or swedes.

Kompott   Fruit compote; stewed fruit eaten cold as dessert.

Konditorei   Pastry shop, most often doubling as a café.

Konfitüre   Jam; informally also called *Marmelade* (Germans do not use a specific term for citrus marmalade).

Königsberger Klopse   Meatballs in a roux-based white sauce flavored with lemon, capers, and herring or anchovies.

Konsum   East German state-run grocery store chain; also called *HO-Laden* (although the two were structured slightly differently).

Konzession   License to run a pub or restaurant.

Korn   Literally, grain, but most often refers to clear liquor/schnapps.

Kotelett   A chop, traditionally pork, often *paniert* (coated in egg and bread crumbs).

Krabben   Small, brown North Sea shrimp.

Kraut   Cabbage (in the south; also called *Kohl* in the north); in the compound *Apfelkraut* or *Rübenkraut*, a treacle-like syrup made from apples or sugar beets.

Kuchen   A fairly simple kind of cake, but also used as general term.

Kürbis   Pumpkin or squash.

Kutteln   Tripe.

Labskaus   Traditional Hamburg skillet dish that developed as ship fare; a somewhat coarse mix of potatoes, beets, pickled cucumber, and corned beef, often served with a fried egg on top.

Land (pl. Länder)   Country, state, or land; within Germany *Länder* refers to the states that make up Germany.

Lebensmittelskandal   Food scandal.

Lebensreform   Movement that began at the end of the nineteenth century as a counterreaction to industrialization and its consequences, which were perceived as antinatural and antihuman; its main slogan was "back to nature."

Leberkäse   A somewhat confusing term, literally, liver cheese; baked loaf made from very finely ground meat and only exceptionally containing liver; also called *Fleischkäse* (meat cheese).

Leberknödel   Liver dumpling; also called *Lewwerknepp* in the Palatine dialect.

Lebkuchen   Gingerbread; also called *Pfefferkuchen*.

Leichenschmaus   Postfuneral meal.

Letscho   Popular dish in East German times; of vague Hungarian provenance, it resembles a kind of spicy ratatouille made exclusively from tomatoes, onions, and bell peppers.

Lokal   Restaurant.

Maggi(würze)   Liquid seasoning with a strong flavor of lovage.

Maibowle   Cold white wine punch infused with woodruff.

Marmelade   Informal term for jam; Germans do not use a specific term for citrus marmalade. Jam is officially called *Konfitüre*.

Martinsgans   Stuffed, roasted Martinmas goose.

Maß   Bavarian beer mug containing one liter (2.11 pints).

Matjes   (Dutch) salted herring, almost exclusively sold in fillets.

Maultasche   Swabian specialty resembling ravioli.

Mehlspeisen   Family of flour-based (sweet and savory) dishes in southern Germany and Austria.

Mensa   University cafeteria, canteen; also called *Kantine*.

Mett   Coarsely ground pork with a certain fat content, eaten raw on buttered bread; also called *Hackepeter* in Berlin.

Mittagessen   Midday meal.

Mostrich   East German term for mustard.

Napfkuchen   Fluted round cake pan with a hole in the center, similar to Bundt cake pan; also the name of the cake baked in it. Also called *Gug(e)lhupf*.

neue deutsche Küche   Refined regional German cuisine, a trend starting in the 1990s, and based on French Nouvelle Cuisine.

Ökoladen   Organic store, also called *Bioladen*.

Ökomarkt   All-organic open-air (farmer's) market, also called *Biomarkt*.

Paprika   Refers to paprika powder as well as to bell peppers.

Pellkartoffeln   Potatoes boiled in their skins, which are then sometimes peeled off, sometimes eaten (especially when the potatoes are new and small).

Pfannkuchen   Term used in Berlin for doughnut-like, deep-fried pastry in the shape of a flattened ball, filled with jam (called *Berliner* outside of Berlin).

Pfefferkuchen   Gingerbread; also called *Lebkuchen*.

Pinkel   Smallish, coarse, smoked sausages with oats, served with curly kale.

Pommes   French fries; also called *Fritten* in informal usage.

Pudding   Commonly used for custard, mainly vanilla or chocolate; a somewhat old-fashioned dessert.

Quark   Curdled milk; this is the *lac concretum* (solid/curdled milk) mentioned in Tacitus' *Germania*; in the United States, bakers' or fresh soft farmers' cheese, resembling a smooth, homogenous cottage cheese.

Reformhaus   Store selling natural food and health food and cosmetics; originated with the *Lebensreform* movement at the end of the nineteenth century.

Reibekuchen   Latke-style potato pancakes made from grated raw potatoes with egg and sometimes a little flour added; also called *Reiberdatschi* or *Kartoffelpuffer*.

Reinheitsgebot   Purity law for beer brewing in Germany that originated in Bavaria in the sixteenth century.

Rohkost   Literally, raw food; more exactly salads made from raw vegetables.

Rohrnudeln   Baked yeast dumplings (southern Germany).

Rollmops   Vinegar-brined herring fillet, rolled up around a pickle.

Rosinenbomber   Literally, raisin bomber; Allied planes flying vital provisions to West Berlin during the airlift necessitated by the Soviet blockade (June 1948–May 1949).

rote Grütze   Literally, red gruel; a popular semiliquid dessert made from all kinds of red berries, cherries, rhubarb, and the like, originally from northern Germany.

Rouladen   Rolls made from thinly sliced beef wrapped around onions, mustard, and pickles, then braised; *Kohlrouladen* are cabbage rolls with a ground meat stuffing.

Rüben   Family of root vegetables including carrots, beets, turnips, rutabagas (swedes), most exclusive among them *Teltower Rübchen*.

Rübenwinter   Winter of 1916–17, when provisions were very scarce during World War I, due to insufficient planning and the failure of the potato crop, so that *Kohlrüben* (rutabagas or swedes), normally considered cattle feed, were eaten as a last resource.

Rübstiel   Vegetable side dish made from chopped turnip greens, popular in the Rhineland; also called *Stielmus*.

Salat   Salad or lettuce.

Salzwiesenlamm   Literally, salt-meadow lamb; lamb from marshes along the coast, equivalent of French *pré-salé*.

sauer   Literally, sour; traditional southern German way of preparing offal, lentils, or spätzle in a roux-based brown sauce soured with vinegar.

Saumagen   Literally, pig's stomach; a popular dish in the Palatinate in which a cleaned pig's stomach is filled with finely ground sausage, ham, and potato, then poached, fried, sliced, and served with sauerkraut.

Schabefleisch   Very lean, finely ground beef, mixed with raw egg yolk, capers, onions, pepper, and salt and served raw; also called *Tartar*.

Schaschlik   Fast-food dish akin to shish kebab; pork on a skewer with bell pepper and onion.

Schillerlocken   Literally, Schiller locks; smoked belly of *Dornhai*, a shark variety.

Schlacht(e)platte   German version of Alsatian *choucroûte garni*, sauerkraut garnished with all kinds of cured pork meat and sausages, served with boiled potatoes.

Schlagsahne   Whipped cream, but also used for liquid cream.

Schmalz   Lard, rendered fat, mostly from pork and goose, used as a spread and for (deep-)frying.

Schmankerl (Bavaria)   Literally, delicacy; a small dish for a midmorning or afternoon snack, also served as starter.

Schmorbraten   (Braised) roast.

Schnaps   Liquor, spirits.

Schorle   Wine or juice mixed with sparkling mineral water.

Schrebergarten   Allotment, community garden plot.

Schrippe (Berlin)   Plain white bread roll; also called *Brötchen* and *Semmel* (in the south).

Schupfnudeln   Small gnocchi-like dumplings, made from boiled potato and a little egg, shaped into small, pointed, finger-sized rolls, which are first boiled, then often fried; also called *Buabespitzle*.

Schwammerl   Bavarian term for wild mushrooms.

Seele   Literally, soul; in Swabia, refers to a medium-sized white breadstick.

Sektsteuer   Sparkling wine tax introduced in 1909 to finance the German fleet; still in effect today at a rate of one euro per regular-size bottle.

Semmel (south)   Plain white bread roll; also called *Brötchen* and *Schrippe* (in Berlin).

Semmelknödel   Bread dumpling.

Sinalco   Citrus-flavored soft drink introduced in 1908 during the antialcohol campaign related to the *Lebensreform* movement; name is derived from Latin *sine* or Spanish *sin* (without).

Sitzecke   Corner seat with table, often found in kitchens.

Soljanka   Very popular soup during East German times, of varying quality; originally Russian and Ukrainian dish based on pickled vegetables, cucumbers or mushrooms but most often modified and prepared from whatever was available, including leftover cooked meat and sausage, in a stew flavored with tomato paste and paprika, invariably garnished with lemon slices, sour cream, and dill.

Spanferkel   Suckling pig.

Sparschäler   Peeler with swivel blade used for potatoes, carrots, and asparagus.

Spätzle   A type of noodle originally from Swabia, made from a semiliquid egg-flour mixture and traditionally scraped by hand with a palette knife from a wooden board (*Spätzlebrett*) into boiling water, although a press (*Spätzleschwob*) is also used.

Speck   Bacon, can be *fett* (all white) or *durchwachsen* (streaky).

Speisekammer   Larder or pantry.

Spreewaldgurken   Pickled cucumbers from the Spreewald area southeast of Berlin.

Sprotte   Sprat, almost exclusively eaten smoked as *Kieler Sprotte*.

Stammtisch   Literally, regulars' table; regular meetings of a group of friends or colleagues at a pub or restaurant, usually around a large, round table.

Steck- or Kohlrüben   Rutabagas (swedes).

Steinmetzbrot   Special whole-grain bread introduced during the *Lebensreform* movement; can still be found today.

Stielmus   Vegetable side dish made from chopped turnip greens, popular in the Rhineland; also called *Rübstiel*.

Stollen or Christstollen   Traditional Christmas cake, usually made with yeast and containing dried fruit.

Streuselkuchen   Cake with a yeast dough base topped with streusel, always baked in sheets, sometimes filled with vanilla custard, possibly with eastern European roots.

Stubenküken   Very young chick (*poussin*).

Stulle (Berlin)   Sandwich from a bread loaf; also called a *Butterbrot*.

Stuten   Challah-like soft white yeast bread, often plaited. sometimes containing raisins; also called *Hefezopf*.

Sülze   Meat in aspic.

Suppengrün   Literally, soup green; carrot, celeriac, leek, parsley root, and fresh parsley sold in a bundle for soups.

süßes Stückchen or Teilchen Literally, sweet little piece; Danish pastry.

Tagesgericht or Tagesmenü Dish or menu of the day.

Tartar Very lean, finely ground beef, mixed with raw egg yolk, capers, onions, pepper, and salt and served raw; also called *Schabefleisch*.

Terrasse Patio.

Torte Gâteau, traditionally round, more extravagant and rich than *Kuchen*.

Trennkost Diet scheme where carbohydrates and protein are consumed strictly separately.

Trinkgeld Tip.

Trinkhalle Kiosk selling newspapers, bottled beer, and small bottles of spirits, traditionally catering to commuting workers.

Tunke Germanized word for sauce or gravy, old-fashioned.

Vanillinzucker Sugar infused with artificial vanilla flavor.

Vater Staat Father state; refers to German social security system.

Vesper Savory midmorning or afternoon snack, cold or warm; also called *Brotzeit* and *Jause*.

Waldmeister Woodruff.

Weihnachtsbäckerei Christmas baking of traditional cakes and cookies.

Weihnachtsmarkt Christmas fair, mostly outdoors.

Weinstube Wine bar or small restaurant.

Weißwurst Literally, white sausage; Bavarian specialty made from uncured veal, traditionally eaten as a midmorning snack with a special sweet mustard.

Wiener Schnitzel Very thin, large veal schnitzel coated in egg and bread crumbs (if pork is used instead of veal, it legally must be called *nach Wiener Art*).

Wiener Small, lightly smoked, scalded sausages, made from pork or veal, re-cently also from poultry; also called *Würstchen* or *Frankfurter*. In Germany they are almost exclusively offered as *Wiener* or *Wiener Würstchen*, occasion-ally also as *Halberstädter* (Thuringia) or *Schübling* (Swabia); in Frankfurt am Main also known as *Rindswürstchen*, made from beef.

Wild Game, designating living animals as well as the meat thereof.

Wilhelminismus Period during the reign (1888–1918) of Kaiser Bill, William II; an economic boom combined with saber-rattling nationalism. German world politics gradually became more aggressive, leading to political isolation. Inner fragmentation through social, religious, and old territorial divides was hidden under a pompous, neobaroque façade.

Wirtschaftswunder Literally, economic miracle; economic boom under Ludwig Ehrhardt, minister for trade and commerce (1949–63, then chancellor until 1966).

Wurst Sausage; this term is mostly used for larger-size sausages that are sliced and eaten as *Aufschnitt* (cold cuts), in contrast to *Würstchen*.

Würstchen Small, lightly smoked, scalded sausages, made from pork or veal, recently also from poultry; also called *Wiener* or *Würstchen*. In Germany they are almost exclusively offered under these two terms, occasionally also as *Halberstädter* (Thuringia) or *Schübling* (Swabia); in Frankfurt am Main also known as *Rindswürstchen*, made from beef.

Zander Pike perch; popular regional river and lake fish.

Zichorienkaffee Coffee surrogate made from roasted chicory root.

Zwetschgen or Zwetschken A medium-sized, oblong, dark purple plum variety with yellow meat (called *Quetsche* in Alsace and the Palatinate), mostly used for baking a cake called *Zwetschgenkuchen*, *Quetschekuche* (Palatinate), or *Zwetschkendatschi* (Bavaria), which is a flat cake made of yeast dough baked on a sheet, and for jam (*Zwetschgenmus*).

Resource Guide

GENERAL

Arndt, Alice, ed. *Culinary Biographies*. Houston: YesPress, 2006.

Davidson, Alan, ed. *The Oxford Companion to Food*. Oxford: Oxford University Press, 1999.

Melcer, Michael, and Patricia Schon. *Milch und Hering: Jewish Foodshops in New York*. Bonn: Weidle, 2002.

Mennell, Stephen, Anne Murcott, and Anneke H. van Otterloo. *The Sociology of Food: Eating, Diet and Culture*. London: Sage Publications, 1992.

Metzger, Christine, ed. *Culinaria Germany*. Köln: Konemann, 1999.

Schulze, Hagen. *Germany: A New History*. Translated by Deborah L. Schneider. Cambridge, MA: Harvard University Press, 1998.

STATISTICS

Deutsche Gesellschaft für Ernährung e.V., ed. *Ernährungsbericht 2004*. Bonn: Deutsche Gesellschaft für Ernährung, 2004.

Federal Statistical Office of Germany. *Key Data on Germany*. Wiesbaden: Federal Statistical Office of Germany, 2007. www.destatis.de.

COOKBOOKS

Anderson, Jean, and Hedy Würz. *The New German Cookbook*. New York: Harper-Collins, 1993.

German Cooking Today. Bielefeld: Dr. Oetker, 2006.

Ott-Dörfer, Sonja, ed. *Deutsche Küche*. Munich: Teubner, 2007.

Scharfenberg, Horst. *The Cuisines of Germany*. New York: Poseidon, 1989 (translation of a 1980 German publication).

Walterspiel, Alfred. *Meine Kunst in Küche und Restaurant*. Munich: Author, 1952.

HISTORY AND SOCIAL STUDIES

Albala, Ken. *Eating Right in the Renaissance*. Berkeley: University of California Press, 2002.

Burmeister, Irmgard, ed. *These Strange German Ways*. Hamburg: Atlantik-Brücke, 1980.

Cummings Johnson, Anna. *Peasant Life in Germany*. New York: Scribner, 1858. Electronic version can be found by a search at http://books.google.com.

Davidis, Henriette. *Pickled Herring and Pumpkin Pie: A Nineteenth-Century Cookbook for German Immigrants to America*. Reprint of a 1904 original going back to 1879. Madison, WI: Max Kade Institute, 2003.

Hazelton, Nika Standen. *The Cooking of Germany: Time Life Foods of the World*. New York: Time Life Books, 1969.

Heinzelmann, Ursula. "Children's Cookery Books: Nurturing Adults' Ideas about Society." In *Proceedings of the Oxford Symposium on Food and Cookery*. edited by Richard Hosking. Bristol: Footwork, 2004, 112–123.

———. "Goodbye Lenin." *Slow: The Magazine of the Slowfood Movement*, Engl. ed., no. 56 (2007): 100–105.

———. "Rumohr's Falscher Rehschlegel: The Significance of Venison in German Cuisine." *Gastronomica: The Journal of Food and Culture* 6, no. 4 (2006): 53–58.

———. "Spreewälder Gurken: Pickled Cucumbers from the Spreewald." *Gastronomica: The Journal of Food and Culture* 4, no. 3 (2004): 13–17.

———. "The Teltow Turnip." *Slow: The Magazine of the Slowfood Movement*, Engl. ed., no. 55 (2006): 98–109.

Möhring, Maren. "Transnational Food Migration and the Internalization of Food Consumption: Ethnic Cuisine in West Germany." In *Food and Globalisation: Histories—Politics—Moralities*, edited by Alexander Nützenadel and Frank Trentmann. Oxford: Berg, 2008.

Montaigne, Michel de. *Tagebuch einer Reise durch Italien, die Schweiz und Deutschland in den Jahren 1580 und 1581*. edited and translated by Otto Flake. Frankfurt am Main and Leipzig: Insel Verlag, 1988.

Poutrus, Patrice G. *Die Erfindung des Goldbroilers: Über den Zusammenhang zwischen Herrschaftssicherung und Konsumentwicklung in der DDR*. Cologne: Böhlau, 2002.

Roden, Claudia. *The Book of Jewish Food: An Odyssey from Samarkand and Vilna to the Present Day*. London: Penguin, 1999.

Rumohr, Karl Friedrich von. *The Essence of Cookery*. Translated by Barbara Yeomans. Totnes (Devon/UK): Prospect Books, 1993.

Stern, Susan. *These Strange German Ways and the Whys of the Ways*. Berlin: Atlantik-Brücke, 2000.

Timm, Uwe. *The Invention of Curried Sausage*. Translated by Leila Vennewitz. New York: New Directions, 1995.

Voigt, Jutta. *Der Geschmack des Ostens: Vom Essen, Trinken und Leben in der DDR*. Berlin: Kiepenheuer, 2005.

Wallraff, Günter. *Lowest of the Low*. London: Methuen, 1988.

Weiss Adamson, Melitta. *Daz buch von guter spise (The Book of Good Food). A Study, Edition, and English Translation of the Oldest German Cookbook*. Krems, 2000.

Wiegelmann, Günter. *Alltags- und Festspeisen in Mitteleuropa: Innovationen, Strukturen und Regionen vom späten Mittelalter bis zum 20. Jahrhundert*. 2nd ed., with Barbara Krug-Richter. Münster: Waxmann, 2006.

Wildt, Michael. "Promise of More: The Rhetoric of (Food) Consumption in a Society Searching for Itself: West Germany in the 1950s." In *Food, Drink and Identity*, edited by Peter Scholliers. Oxford: Berg, 2001, 63–80.

Wiswe, Hans. *Kulturgeschichte der Kochkunst: Kochbücher und Rezepte aus zwei Jahrtausenden mit einem lexikalischen Anhang zur Fachsprache von Eva Hepp*. Munich: Moos, 1970.

WEB SITES

www.bmelv.de. Official site of the Federal Ministry for Food, Agriculture, and Consumer Protection with a lot of data.

www.germanfoods.org. Official site of the Centrale Marketing-Gesellschaft der deutschen Agrarwirtschaft mbH (CMA), a government-related agency marketing German agricultural products.

www.goethe.de. The Goethe Institut represents German culture abroad, and its site contains information on all aspects of Germany and many useful links.

www.rki.de. The Robert-Koch-Institut is part of the Federal Ministry for Health and has a wealth of data on its site, such as surveys on children's health, smoking-related diseases, and so on.

www.young-germany.de. A site supported by German Federal Foreign Office with up-to-date, unbiased information on all aspects of life in Germany.

FILMS

Angst essen Seele auf (Fear eat soul). Directed by Rainer Werner Fassbinder, Munich: Filmverlag der Autoren, 1974.

Bella Martha. Directed by Sandra Nettelbeck, Munich: Bavaria Film, 2002.

Das Leben der Anderen (The life of others). Directed by Florian Henckel von Donnersmarck, Munich: Bayerischer Rundfunk, 2006.

Die Blechtrommel (The tin drum). Directed by Volker Schlöndorff, Berlin: Argos
    Film, 1980.
Good Bye Lenin. Directed by Wolfgang Becker, Berlin: X-Filme Creative Pool,
    2003.

MAGAZINES

Der Feinschmecker. Monthly. Hamburg: Jahreszeiten-Verlag. www.der-feinsch
    mecker-club.de.
Essen & trinken. Monthly. Hamburg: Gruner und Jahr. www.essen-und-trinken.de.

Selected Bibliography

Albala, Ken. *Eating Right in the Renaissance*. Berkeley: University of California Press, 2002.

Anderson, Jean, and Hedy Würz. *The New German Cookbook*. New York: Harper-Collins, 1993.

Arndt, Alice, ed. *Culinary Biographies*. Houston: YesPress, 2006.

Ausonius, D. Magnus. *Mosella*. Edited and translated by Paul Dräger. Düsseldorf: Artemis & Winkler, 2004.

Barlösius, Eva. *Naturgemäße Lebensführung: Zur Geschichte der Lebensreform um die Jahrhundertwende*. Frankfurt am Main: Campus, 1997.

———. "Soziale und historische Aspekte der deutschen Küche." In *Die Kultivierung des Appetits: Die Geschichte des Essens vom Mittelalter bis heute*, edited by Stephen Mennell. Translated by Rainer von Savigny. Frankfurt am Main: Athenäum, 1988.

Bergenthal, Josef. *Schinken, Korn und Pumpernickel*. Münster: Regensberg, 1972.

Bober, Phyllis Pray. *Art, Culture, and Cuisine: Ancient and Medieval Gastronomy*. Chicago: University of Chicago Press, 1999.

Bringemeier, Martha, ed. *Vom Brotbacken in früherer Zeit*. Münster/Westfalen: Selbstverlag der Volkskundlichen Kommission der Landschaftsverbände, 1961.

Bundesministerium für Ernährung, Landwirtschaft und Forsten, ed. *Der Gartenbau in der Bundesrepublik Deutschland*. Bonn: Köllen, 1997.

Bundesministerium für Forschung und Technologie, ed. *Die Nationale Verzehrsstudie: Ergebnisse der Basisauswertung*. Bonn: Bundesministerium für Forschung und Technologie, 1991.

Burmeister, Irmgard, ed. *These Strange German Ways*. Hamburg: Atlantik-Brücke, 1980.

Cummings Johnson, Anna. *Peasant Life in Germany*. New York: Scribner, 1858.

Curschmann, Fritz. *Hungersnöte im Mittelalter*. Leipzig: Teubner, 1900.

Davidis, Henriette. *Pickled Herring and Pumpkin Pie: A Nineteenth-Century Cookbook for German Immigrants to America*. Reprint of a 1904 original going back to 1897. Madison, WI: Max Kade Institute, 2003.

Davidson, Alan, ed. *The Oxford Companion to Food*. Oxford: Oxford University Press, 1999.

Deutsche Gesellschaft für Ernährung e.V., ed. *Ernährungsbericht 2004*. Bonn: Deutsche Gesellschaft für Ernährung, 2004.

Dittmer, Hans. *Deutschland erweitert seinen Nahrungsraum durch Landeskulturmaßnahmen*. Berlin: Deutsche Informationsstelle, 1941.

Drummer, Christian. "Das sich ausbreitende Restaurant in deutschen Großstädten als Ausdruck bürgerlichen Repräsentationsstrebens 1870–1930." In *Essen und kulturelle Identität: Europäische Perspektiven*, edited by Hans Jürgen Teuteberg, Gerhard Neumann, Alois Wierlacher. Berlin: Akademie Verlag, 1997.

Elias, Norbert. *Gesammelte Schriften*. *Über das Verhalten beim Essen* in Vol. 3.1 Wandlungen des Verhaltens in den weltlichen Oberschichten des Abendlandes, edited by Heike Hammer. Frankfurt am Main: Suhrkamp, 1997. 202–65.

Ellerbrock, Karl-Peter. *Geschichte der deutschen Nahrungs- und Genußmittelindustrie 1750–1914*. Stuttgart: Franz Steiner, 1993.

Federal Statistical Office of Germany. *Key Data on Germany*. Wiesbaden: Federal Statistical Office of Germany, 2007. www.destatis.de.

Frenzel, Ralf, ed. *Das Parlament kocht: Was Politiker so anrichten*. Wiesbaden: Tre Torri, 2007.

Hahn, Mary. *Praktisches Kochbuch für die bürgerliche Küche*. 16th ed. Berlin, Mary Hahn's Kochbuch-Verlag, n.d. [1930].

Hartmeyer, Hans. *Der Weinhandel im Gebiete der Hanse im Mittelalter*. Jena: Fischer, 1904.

Heinzelmann, Ursula. "Children's Cookery Books: Nurturing Adults' Ideas about Society." In *Proceedings of the Oxford Symposium on Food and Cookery*. Ed. Richard Hosking Bristol: Footwork, 2004. 112–23.

———. "Goodbye Lenin." *Slow: The Magazine of the Slowfood Movement* Engl. ed., no. 56 (2007). 100–105.

———. "Rumohr's Falscher Rehschlegel: The Significance of Venison in German Cuisine." *Gastronomica: The Journal of Food and Culture* 6, no. 4 (2006): 53–58.

———. "Spreewälder Gurken: Pickled Cucumbers from the Spreewald." *Gastronomica: The Journal of Food and Culture* 4, no. 3 (2004): 13–17.

———. "The Teltow Turnip." *Slow: The Magazine of the Slowfood Movement*, Engl. ed., no. 55 (2006). 98–109.

Hirschfelder, Gunther. *Europäische Esskultur: Geschichte der Ernährung von der Steinzeit bis heute*. Frankfurt am Main: Campus, 2001.

Kochen. 6th ed. Leipzig: Verlag für die Frau, DDR, 1983.

Lößnitzer, Ernst. *Verdeutschungs-Wörterbuch der Fachsprache der Kochkunst und Küche*. Dresden: Verlag von Wolf Reinecke, 1889.

Mennell, Stephen, Anne Murcott, and Anneke H. van Otterloo. *The Sociology of Food: Eating, Diet and Culture*. London: Sage Publications, 1992.

Metzger, Christine, ed. *Culinaria Germany*. Köln: Konemann, 1999.

Mintz, Sidney. "Eating Communities: The Mixed Appeals of Sodality." In *Eating Culture: The Poetics and Politics of Food*, edited by Tobias Döring, Markus Heide, and Susanne Mühleisen. Heidelberg: Winter, 2003.

Möhring, Maren. "Transnational Food Migration and the Internalization of Food Consumption: Ethnic Cuisine in West Germany." In *Food and Globalisation: Histories—Politics—Moralities*, edited by Alexander Nützenadel and Frank Trentmann. Oxford: Berg, 2008.

Neeb, Ursula. *Wasserhäuschen: Eine Frankfurter Institution*. Frankfurt am Main: Fachhochschulverlag, 2005.

Ott-Dörfer, Sonja, ed. *Deutsche Küche*. Munich: Teubner, 2007.

Poutrus, Patrice G. *Die Erfindung des Goldbroilers: Über den Zusammenhang zwischen Herrschaftssicherung und Konsumentwicklung in der DDR*. Cologne: Böhlau, 2002.

Roeb, Frank. *Käsebereitung und Käsespeisen in Deutschland seit 1800*. PhD diss., Mainz, 1976.

Scharfenberg, Horst. *The Cuisines of Germany*. New York: Poseidon, 1989 (translation of a 1980 German publication).

Schmitz, Maria. *Wir kochen praktisch: Neuzeitliches Tabellen-Kochbuch*. 36th to 38th ed. Cologne-Braunsfeld: Müller, 1965.

Schulze, Hagen. *Germany: A New History*. Translated by Deborah L. Schneider. Cambridge, MA: Harvard University Press, 1998.

Silbermann, Alphons. *Die Küche im Wohnerlebnis der Deutschen*. Opladen: Leske + Budrich, 1995.

Staël, Germaine de. *De l'Allemagne*. 1813. Reprint, Paris: Garnier-Flammarion, 1968.

Statistisches Bundesamt. *Statistisches Jahrbuch 2006 für die Bundesrepublik Deutschland*. Wiesbaden: Statistisches Bundesamt, 2006. www.destatis.de.

———. *Wirtschaftsrechnungen. Einkommens- und Verbrauchsstichprobe: Aufwendungen privater Haushalte für Nahrungsmittel, Getränke und Tabakwaren 2003*. Wiesbaden, 2006. www.destatis.de.

Stein, Werner. *Der große Kultur Fahrplan: Die wichtigsten Daten der Weltgeschichte*. Munich: Herbig, 1946. Exp. ed., 1987.

Stern, Susan. *These Strange German Ways and the Whys of the Ways*. Berlin: Atlantik-Brücke, 2000.

Tacitus, Cornelius. *Germania*. Edited and translated by Alfons Städele. Munich: Artemis & Winkler, 1991. Original from between 98 and 111 A.D.

Teuteberg, Hans Jürgen, ed. *Durchbruch zum modernen Massenkonsum: Lebensmittelmärkte und Lebensmittelqualität im Städtewachstum des Industriezeitalters*. Münster: Coppenrath, 1987.

Teuteberg, Hans Jürgen, ed. *Die Revolution am Eßtisch: Neue Studien zur Nahrungskultur im 19./20. Jahrhundert.* Stuttgart: Franz Steiner, 2004.

———. "Studien zur Volksernährung unter sozial- und wirtschaftsgeschichtlichen Aspekten." In *Nahrungsgewohnheiten in der Industrialisierung des 19. Jahrhunderts,* edited by Hans Jürgen Teuteberg and Günter Wiegelmann. Münster: Lit Verlag, 2005, 13–210.

Teuteberg, Hans Jürgen, Gerhard Neumann, and Alois Wierlacher, eds. *Essen und kulturelle Identität: Europäische Perspektiven.* Berlin: Akademie Verlag, 1997.

Teuteberg, Hans Jürgen, and Günter Wiegelmann, eds. *Unsere tägliche Kost: Studien zur Geschichte des Alltags.* Münster: Coppenrath, 1986.

Thimm, Utz, and Karl-Heinz Wellmann, eds. *In aller Munde: Ernährung heute.* Frankfurt am Main: Suhrkamp, 2004.

Timm, Uwe. *The Invention of Curried Sausage.* Translated by Leila Vennewitz. New York: New Directions, 1995.

Tolksdorf, Ulrich. "Der Schnellimbiss und the World of Ronald McDonald's." In *Kieler Blätter zur Volkskunde,* edited by Konrad Köstlin, Karl-S. Kramer, and Kai Detlev Sievers. Kiel: Mühlau, 1981, 117–162.

Treskow, Maria von. *Berliner Kochbuch: Aus alten Familienrezepten.* Weingarten: Weingarten, 1987.

Treue, Wilhelm. *Kleine Kulturgeschichte des deutschen Alltags.* Potsdam: Rütten & Loening, 1942.

Voigt, Jutta. *Der Geschmack des Ostens: Vom Essen, Trinken und Leben in der DDR.* Berlin: Kiepenheuer, 2005.

Wallraff, Günter. *Lowest of the Low.* London: Methuen, 1988.

Walterspiel, Alfred. *Meine Kunst in Küche und Restaurant.* Munich: Author, 1952.

Weiss Adamson, Melitta. *Daz buch von guter spise (The Book of Good Food): A Study, Edition, and English Translation of the Oldest German Cookbook.* Krems, 2000.

Westphal, Martin. *Kohl- und Pinkelfahrten.* Münster: Coppenrath, 1988.

Wiegelmann, Günter. *Alltags- und Festspeisen in Mitteleuropa: Innovationen, Strukturen und Regionen vom späten Mittelalter bis zum 20. Jahrhundert.* 2nd ed., with Barbara Krug-Richter. Münster: Waxmann, 2006.

Wildt, Michael. "Promise of More: The Rhetoric of (Food) Consumption in a Society Searching for Itself: West Germany in the 1950s." In *Food, Drink and Identity,* edited by Peter Scholliers. Oxford: Berg, 2001. 63–80.

Wiswe, Hans. *Kulturgeschichte der Kochkunst: Kochbücher und Rezepte aus zwei Jahrtausenden mit einem lexikalischen Anhang zur Fachsprache von Eva Hepp.* Munich: Moos, 1970.

Index

About the Author

URSULA HEINZELMANN is a Berlin-based journalist and author specializing in food and wine. She trained as a professional chef, ran her own Michelin-starred restaurant on Lake Constance, trained as a sommelier, and built up a wine and cheese business in Berlin. She is the author of *Erlebnis Essen* (2006) as well as numerous essays on German food topics.

Recent Titles in
Food Culture around the World

Food Culture in Japan
Michael Ashkenazi and Jeanne Jacob

Food Culture in India
Colleen Taylor Sen

Food Culture in China
Jacqueline M. Newman

Food Culture in Great Britain
Laura Mason

Food Culture in Italy
Fabio Parasecoli

Food Culture in Spain
Xavier F. Medina

Food Culture in the Near East, Middle East, and North Africa
Peter Heine

Food Culture in Mexico
Janet Long-Solís and Luis Alberto Vargas

Food Culture in South America
José Raphael Lovera

Food Culture in the Caribbean
Lynn Marie Houston

Food Culture in Russia and Central Asia
Glenn R. Mack and Asele Surina

Food Culture in Sub-Saharan Africa
Fran Osseo-Asare

Food Culture in France
Julia Abramson